Java For Dummies, 4th Edition

W9-CCH-718

Java Keywords

Keyword	What It Does
abstract	Indicates that the details of a class, a method, or an interface are given elsewhere in the code.
assert	Tests the truth of a condition that the programmer believes is true.
boolean	Indicates that a value is either `true` or `false`.
break	Jumps out of a loop or switch.
byte	Indicates that a value is an 8-bit whole number.
case	Introduces one of several possible paths of execution in a `switch` statement.
catch	Introduces statements that are executed when something interrupts the flow of execution in a `try` clause.
char	Indicates that a value is a character (a single letter, digit, punctuation symbol, and so on) stored in 16 bits of memory.
class	Introduces a class — a blueprint for an object.
const	You can't use this word in a Java program. The word has no meaning. Because it's a keyword, you can't create a `const` variable.
continue	Forces the abrupt end of the current loop iteration and begins another iteration.
default	Introduces a path of execution to take when no case is a match in a `switch` statement.
do	Causes the computer to repeat some statements over and over again (for instance, as long as the computer keeps getting unacceptable results).
double	Indicates that a value is a 64-bit number with one or more digits after the decimal point.
else	Introduces statements that are executed when the condition in an `if` statement isn't true.
enum	Creates a newly defined *type* — a group of values that a variable can have.
extends	Creates a *subclass* — a class that reuses functionality from a previously defined class.
final	Indicates that a variable's value cannot be changed, that a class's functionality cannot be extended, or that a method cannot be overridden.
finally	Introduces the last will and testament of the statements in a `try` clause.
float	Indicates that a value is a 32-bit number with one or more digits after the decimal point.
for	Gets the computer to repeat some statements over and over again (for instance, a certain number of times).
goto	You can't use this word in a Java program. The word has no meaning. Because it's a keyword, you can't create a `goto` variable.
if	Tests to see whether a condition is true. If it's true, the computer executes certain statements; otherwise, the computer executes other statements.
implements	Reuses the functionality from a previously defined interface.
import	Enables the programmer to abbreviate the names of classes defined in a package.

For Dummies: Bestselling Book Series for Beginners

Java For Dummies, 4th Edition

Cheat Sheet

Keyword	What It Does
instanceof	Tests to see whether a certain object comes from a certain class.
int	Indicates that a value is a 32-bit whole number.
interface	Introduces an interface, which is like a class, but less specific. (Interfaces are used in place of the confusing multiple-inheritance feature that's in C++.)
long	Indicates that a value is a 64-bit whole number.
native	Enables the programmer to use code that was written in another language (one of those awful languages other than Java).
new	Creates an object from an existing class.
package	Puts the code into a *package* — a collection of logically related definitions.
private	Indicates that a variable or method can be used only within a certain class.
protected	Indicates that a variable or method can be used in subclasses from another package.
public	Indicates that a variable, class, or method can be used by any other Java code.
return	Ends execution of a method and possibly returns a value to the calling code.
short	Indicates that a value is a 16-bit whole number.
static	Indicates that a variable or method belongs to a class, rather than to any object created from the class.
strictfp	Limits the computer's ability to represent extra large or extra small numbers when the computer does intermediate calculations on float and double values.
super	Refers to the superclass of the code in which the word *super* appears.
switch	Tells the computer to follow one of many possible paths of execution (one of many possible cases), depending on the value of an expression.
synchronized	Keeps two threads from interfering with one another.
this	A self-reference — refers to the object in which the word *this* appears.
throw	Creates a new exception object and indicates that an exceptional situation (usually something unwanted) has occurred.
throws	Indicates that a method or constructor may pass the buck when an exception is thrown.
transient	Indicates that, if and when an object is serialized, a variable's value doesn't need to be stored.
try	Introduces statements that are watched (during runtime) for things that can go wrong.
void	Indicates that a method doesn't return a value.
volatile	Imposes strict rules on the use of a variable by more than one thread at a time.
while	Repeats some statements over and over again (as long as a condition is still true).

*You can't make up new meanings for the words false, null, and true. But for technical reasons, these words aren't called keywords. Whatever!

For Dummies: Bestselling Book Series for Beginners

Java™

FOR

DUMMIES®

4TH EDITION

by Barry Burd

BICENTENNIAL
1807
WILEY
2007
BICENTENNIAL

Wiley Publishing, Inc.

Java™ For Dummies®, 4th Edition

Published by
Wiley Publishing, Inc.
111 River Street
Hoboken, NJ 07030-5774
www.wiley.com

For general information on our other products and services, please contact our Customer Care Department within the U.S. at 800-762-2974, outside the U.S. at 317-572-3993, or fax 317-572-4002.

For technical support, please visit www.wiley.com/techsupport.

Wiley also publishes its books in a variety of electronic formats. Some content that appears in print may not be available in electronic books.

Library of Congress Control Number: 2006934836

ISBN-13: 978-0-470-08716-9

ISBN-10: 0-470-08716-1

Manufactured in the United States of America

10 9 8 7 6 5 4 3 2

4O/RV/QU/QXP/IN

WILEY

About the Author

Dr. Barry Burd received an M.S. degree in Computer Science at Rutgers University and a Ph.D. in Mathematics at the University of Illinois. As a teaching assistant in Champaign-Urbana, Illinois, he was elected five times to the university-wide List of Teachers Ranked as Excellent by their Students.

Since 1980, Dr. Burd has been a professor in the Department of Mathematics and Computer Science at Drew University in Madison, New Jersey. When he's not lecturing at Drew University, Dr. Burd leads training courses for professional programmers in business and industry. He has lectured at conferences in the United States, Europe, Australia, and Asia. He is the author of several articles and books, including *Eclipse For Dummies* and *Beginning Programming with Java For Dummies,* both from Wiley Publishing, Inc.

Dr. Burd lives in Madison, New Jersey, with his wife and two children. In his spare time, he enjoys being a workaholic.

Dedication

for

Jennie, Sam, and Harriet,

Ruth and Sam,

Jennie and Benjamin, Katie and Abram,

and Basheva

Author's Acknowledgments

Thank you again. (You know who you are.)

—Barry Burd

Publisher's Acknowledgments

We're proud of this book; please send us your comments through our online registration form located at www.dummies.com/register/.

Some of the people who helped bring this book to market include the following:

Acquisitions, Editorial, and Media Development

Project Editor: Paul Levesque

Acquisitions Editor: Katie Feltman

Copy Editor: Mary Lagu and Heidi Unger

Technical Editor: John Purdum

Editorial Manager: Leah Cameron

Media Development Specialists: Angela Denny, Kate Jenkins, Steven Kudirka, Kit Malone

Media Development Coordinator: Laura Atkinson

Media Project Supervisor: Laura Moss

Media Development Manager: Laura VanWinkle

Editorial Assistant: Amanda Foxworth

Sr. Editorial Assistant: Cherie Case

Cartoons: Rich Tennant (www.the5thwave.com)

Composition Services

Project Coordinator: Erin Smith

Layout and Graphics: Carl Byers, Lavonne Cook, Denny Hager, Clint Lahnen, Barbara Moore, Barry Offringa, Rashell Smith, Alicia B. South, Ronald Terry

Proofreaders: Jessica Kramer, Ethel M. Winslow

Indexer: Techbooks

Anniversary Logo Design: Richard Pacifico

Special Help: Mary Lagu

Publishing and Editorial for Technology Dummies

    Richard Swadley, Vice President and Executive Group Publisher

    Andy Cummings, Vice President and Publisher

    Mary Bednarek, Executive Acquisitions Director

    Mary C. Corder, Editorial Director

Publishing for Consumer Dummies

    Diane Graves Steele, Vice President and Publisher

    Joyce Pepple, Acquisitions Director

Composition Services

    Gerry Fahey, Vice President of Production Services

    Debbie Stailey, Director of Composition Services

Contents at a Glance

Table of Contents

Introduction

Java is good stuff. I've been using it for years. I like Java because it's very orderly. Almost everything follows simple rules. The rules can seem intimidating at times, but this book is here to help you figure them out. So, if you want to use Java and want an alternative to the traditional techie, soft-cover book, sit down, relax, and start reading *Java For Dummies,* 4th Edition.

How to Use This Book

I wish I could say, "Open to a random page of this book and start writing Java code. Just fill in the blanks and don't look back." In a sense, this is true. You can't break anything by writing Java code, so you're always free to experiment.

But let me be honest. If you don't understand the bigger picture, writing a program is difficult. That's true with any computer programming language — not just Java. If you're typing code without knowing what it's about, and the code doesn't do exactly what you want it to do, you're just plain stuck.

So, in this book, I divide Java programming into manageable chunks. Each chunk is (more or less) a chapter. You can jump in anywhere you want — Chapter 5, Chapter 10, or wherever. You can even start by poking around in the middle of a chapter. I've tried to make the examples interesting without making one chapter depend on another. When I use an important idea from another chapter, I include a note to help you find your way around.

In general, my advice is as follows:

- ✔ If you already know something, don't bother reading about it.

- ✔ If you're curious, don't be afraid to skip ahead. You can always sneak a peek at an earlier chapter if you really need to do so.

Conventions Used in This Book

Almost every technical book starts with a little typeface legend, and *Java For Dummies,* 4th Edition, is no exception. What follows is a brief explanation of the typefaces used in this book:

- ✔ New terms are set in *italics.*
- ✔ If you need to type something that's mixed in with the regular text, the characters you type appear in bold. For example: "Type **MyNewProject** in the text field."
- ✔ You also see this `computerese` font. I use computerese for Java code, filenames, Web page addresses (URLs), on-screen messages, and other such things. Also, if something you need to type is really long, it appears in computerese font on its own line (or lines).
- ✔ You need to change certain things when you type them on your own computer keyboard. For instance, I may ask you to type

```
public class Anyname
```

which means that you type **public class** and then some name that you make up on your own. Words that you need to replace with your own words are set in *`italicized computerese`.*

What You Don't Have to Read

Pick the first chapter or section that has material you don't already know and start reading there. Of course, you may hate making decisions as much as I do. If so, here are some guidelines that you can follow:

- ✔ If you already know what kind of an animal Java is and know that you want to use Java, skip Chapter 1 and go straight to Chapter 2. Believe me, I won't mind.
- ✔ If you already know how to get a Java program running, skip Chapter 2 and start with Chapter 3.
- ✔ If you write programs for a living but use any language other than C or C++, start with Chapter 2 or 3. When you reach Chapters 5 and 6, you'll probably find them to be easy reading. When you get to Chapter 7, it'll be time to dive in.
- ✔ If you write C (not C++) programs for a living, start with Chapters 3 and 4 but just skim Chapters 5 and 6.

✔ If you write C++ programs for a living, glance at Chapter 3, skim Chapters 4 through 6, and start reading seriously in Chapter 7. (Java is a bit different from C++ in the way it handles classes and objects.)

✔ If you write Java programs for a living, come to my house and help me write *Java For Dummies,* 5th Edition.

If you want to skip the sidebars and the Technical Stuff icons, please do. In fact, if you want to skip anything at all, feel free.

Foolish Assumptions

In this book, I make a few assumptions about you, the reader. If one of these assumptions is incorrect, you're probably okay. If all these assumptions are incorrect . . . well, buy the book anyway.

✔ **I assume that you have access to a computer.** Here's the good news: You can run the code in this book on almost any computer. The only computers that you can't use to run this code are ancient things that are more than six years old (give or take a few years).

✔ **I assume that you can navigate through your computer's common menus and dialog boxes.** You don't have to be a Windows, Unix, or Macintosh power user, but you should be able to start a program, find a file, put a file into a certain directory . . . that sort of thing. Most of the time, when you practice the stuff in this book, you're typing code on your keyboard, not pointing and clicking your mouse.

On those rare occasions when you need to drag and drop, cut and paste, or plug and play, I guide you carefully through the steps. But your computer may be configured in any of several billion ways, and my instructions may not quite fit your special situation. So, when you reach one of these platform-specific tasks, try following the steps in this book. If the steps don't quite fit, consult a book with instructions tailored to your system.

✔ **I assume that you can think logically.** That's all there is to programming in Java — thinking logically. If you can think logically, you've got it made. If you don't believe that you can think logically, read on. You may be pleasantly surprised.

✔ **I make very few assumptions about your computer programming experience (or your lack of such experience).** In writing this book, I've tried to do the impossible. I've tried to make the book interesting for experienced programmers, yet accessible to people with little or no programming experience. This means that I don't assume any particular programming background on your part. If you've never created a loop or indexed an array, that's okay.

On the other hand, if you've done these things (maybe in Visual Basic, COBOL, or C++), you'll discover some interesting plot twists in Java. The developers of Java took the best ideas in object-oriented programming, streamlined them, reworked them, and reorganized them into a sleek, powerful way of thinking about problems. You'll find many new, thought-provoking features in Java. As you find out about these features, many of them will seem very natural to you. One way or another, you'll feel good about using Java.

How This Book Is Organized

This book is divided into subsections, which are grouped into sections, which come together to make chapters, which are lumped finally into six parts. (When you write a book, you get to know your book's structure pretty well. After months of writing, you find yourself dreaming in sections and chapters when you go to bed at night.) The parts of the book are listed here.

Part 1: Getting Started

This part is your complete, executive briefing on Java. It includes a "What is Java?" chapter and a complete set of instructions on installing and running Java. It also has a jump-start chapter — Chapter 3. In this chapter, you visit the major technical ideas and dissect a simple program.

Part II: Writing Your Own Java Programs

Chapters 4 through 6 cover the basic building blocks. These chapters describe the things that you need to know so you can get your computer humming along.

If you've written programs in Visual Basic, C++, or any another language, some of the material in Part II may be familiar to you. If so, you can skip some sections or read this stuff quickly. But don't read too quickly. Java is a little different from some other programming languages, especially in the things that I describe in Chapter 4.

Part III: Working with the Big Picture: Object-Oriented Programming

Part III has some of my favorite chapters. This part covers the all-important topic of object-oriented programming. In these chapters, you find out how to map solutions to big problems. (Sure, the examples in these chapters aren't big, but the examples involve big ideas.) In bite-worthy increments, you discover how to design classes, reuse existing classes, and construct objects.

Have you read any of those books that explain object-oriented programming in vague, general terms? I'm very proud to say that *Java For Dummies,* 4th Edition, isn't like that. In this book, I illustrate each concept with a simple-yet-concrete program example.

Part IV: Savvy Java Techniques

If you've tasted some Java and want more, you can find what you need in this part of the book. This part's chapters are devoted to details — the things that you don't see when you first glance at the material. So, after you read the earlier parts and write some programs on your own, you can dive in a little deeper by reading Part IV.

Part V: The Part of Tens

The Part of Tens is a little Java candy store. In the Part of Tens, you can find lists — lists of tips for avoiding mistakes, resources, and all kinds of interesting goodies.

Appendices

The book has two appendices. One appendix tells you all about this book's CD-ROM (what's on the CD, how to use the CD, how to make the CD look like a UFO at night, and so on). The other appendix (housed on the CD, as a matter of fact) summarizes some important rules for writing Java programs. To find out which parts of your code spill over automatically into other peoples' code, read the second appendix.

Additional Bonus Chapters on the CD-ROM!

You've read the *Java For Dummies* book, seen the *Java For Dummies* movie, worn the *Java For Dummies* T-shirt, and eaten the *Java For Dummies* candy. What more is there to do?

That's easy. Just pop in the book's CD-ROM and you can find four additional chapters:

✔ **In Chapter 15,** you combine several smaller programs to create a bigger program. As part of that process, you find out which parts of one program are of use to any other program. You get an expanded description of the material in Appendix B.

✔ **In Chapter 16,** you handle button clicks, keystrokes, and other such things. You find out about one additional Java language feature (something like a Java class) called an *interface.*

✔ **In Chapter 17,** you deal with Java applets. You put applets on Web pages, draw things, and make things move. You create a small game that visitors to your site can play.

✔ **In Chapter 18,** you see an example of Java database handling. The example takes you from start to finish — from establishing a connection and creating a table to adding rows and making queries.

Note: For you Web fanatics out there, you can also read the bonus chapters on the Web at www.dummies.com/go/javafordummies4e.

Icons Used in This Book

If you could watch me write this book, you'd see me sitting at my computer, talking to myself. I say each sentence in my head. Most of the sentences I mutter several times. When I have an extra thought, a side comment, or something that doesn't belong in the regular stream, I twist my head a little bit. That way, whoever's listening to me (usually nobody) knows that I'm off on a momentary tangent.

Of course, in print, you can't see me twisting my head. I need some other way of setting a side thought in a corner by itself. I do it with icons. When you see a Tip icon or a Remember icon, you know that I'm taking a quick detour.

Here's a list of icons that I use in this book.

A tip is an extra piece of information — something helpful that the other books may forget to tell you.

Everyone makes mistakes. Heaven knows that I've made a few in my time. Anyway, when I think people are especially prone to make a mistake, I mark it with a Warning icon.

Question: What's stronger than a Tip, but not as strong as a Warning?
Answer: A Remember icon.

"If you don't remember what such-and-such means, see blah-blah-blah," or "For more information, read blahbity-blah-blah."

This icon calls attention to useful material that you can find online. (You don't have to wait long to see one of these icons. I use one at the end of this introduction!)

I use this icon to point out useful stuff that's on the CD (obviously).

Occasionally, I run across a technical tidbit. The tidbit may help you understand what the people behind the scenes (the people who developed Java) were thinking. You don't have to read it, but you may find it useful. You may also find the tidbit helpful if you plan to read other (more geeky) books about Java.

Where to Go from Here

If you've gotten this far, you're ready to start reading about Java. Think of me (the author) as your guide, your host, your personal assistant. I do everything I can to keep things interesting and, most importantly, help you understand.

If you like what you read, send me a note. My e-mail address, which I created just for comments and questions about this book, is JavaForDummies@ BurdBrain.com. And don't forget — for the latest updates, visit one of this book's support Web sites. The support sites' addresses are www.dummies. com/go/javafordummies4e and www.BurdBrain.com.

Part I
Getting Started

The 5th Wave   By Rich Tennant

"Before I go on to explain more advanced procedures like the 'Zap—Rowdy—Students—Who—Don't—Pay—Attention' function, we'll begin with some basics."

In this part . . .

*B*ecome acquainted with Java. Find out what Java is all about and whether you do (or don't) want to use Java. If you've heard things about Java and aren't sure what they mean, the material in this part can help you. If you're staring at your computer, wondering how you're going to get a Java program running, this part has the information that you need. Maybe you've told people that you're a Java expert, and now you need to do some serious bluffing. If so, this part of the book is your crash course in Java. (Of course, if the word *bluffing* describes you accurately, you may also want to pick up a copy of *Ethics For Dummies*.)

Chapter 1

All about Java

· ·

· ·

Say what you want about computers. As far as I'm concerned, computers are good for just two simple reasons:

▶ **When computers do work, they feel no resistance, no stress, no boredom, and no fatigue.** Computers are our electronic slaves. I have my computer working 24/7 doing calculations for SETI@home — the search for extraterrestrial intelligence. Do I feel sorry for my computer because it's working so hard? Does the computer complain? Will the computer report me to the National Labor Relations Board? No.

I can make demands, give the computer its orders, and crack the whip. Do I (or should I) feel the least bit guilty? Not at all.

▶ **Computers move ideas, not paper.** Not long ago, when you wanted to send a message to someone, you hired a messenger. The messenger got on his or her horse and delivered your message personally. The message was on paper, parchment, a clay tablet, or whatever physical medium was available at the time.

This whole process seems wasteful now, but that's only because you and I are sitting comfortably at the dawn of the electronic age. The thing is that messages are ideas. Physical things like ink, paper, and horses have little or nothing to do with real ideas. These physical things are just temporary carriers for ideas (temporary because people used them to carry ideas for several centuries). But, in truth, the ideas themselves are paperless, horseless, and messengerless.

So the neat thing about computers is that they carry ideas efficiently. They carry nothing but the ideas, a couple of photons, and a little electrical power. They do this with no muss, no fuss, and no extra physical baggage.

When you start dealing efficiently with ideas, something very nice happens. Suddenly, all the overhead is gone. Instead of pushing paper and trees, you're pushing numbers and concepts. Without the overhead, you can do things much faster, and do things that are far more complex than ever before.

What You Can Do with Java

It would be so nice if all this complexity was free, but unfortunately, it isn't. Someone has to think hard and decide exactly what the computer will be asked to do. After that thinking is done, someone has to write a set of instructions for the computer to follow.

Given the current state of affairs, you can't write these instructions in English or any other language that people speak. Science fiction is filled with stories about people who say simple things to robots and get back disastrous, unexpected results. English and other such languages are unsuitable for communication with computers for several reasons:

- **An English sentence can be misinterpreted.** "Chew one tablet three times a day until finished."

- **It's difficult to weave a very complicated command in English.** "Join flange A to protuberance B, making sure to connect only the outermost lip of flange A to the larger end of the protuberance B, while joining the middle and inner lips of flange A to grommet C."

- **An English sentence has lots of extra baggage.** "Sentence has unneeded words."

- **English is difficult to interpret.** "As part of this Publishing Agreement between John Wiley & Sons, Inc. ('Wiley') and the Author ('Barry Burd'), Wiley shall pay the sum of one-thousand-two-hundred-fifty-seven dollars and sixty-three cents ($1,257.63) to the Author for partial submittal of *Java For Dummies,* 4th Edition ('the Work')."

To tell a computer what to do, you have to speak a special language and write terse, unambiguous instructions in that language. A special language of this kind is called a *computer programming language.* A set of instructions written in such a language is called a *program.* When they're looked at as a big blob, these instructions are called *software* or *code.* Here's what code looks like when it's written in Java:

```
import static java.lang.System.out;

class PayBarry {
```

```
public static void main(String args[]) {

    double checkAmount = 1257.63;
    out.print("Pay to the order of ");
    out.print("Dr. Barry Burd ");
    out.print("$");
    out.println(checkAmount);
}
}
```

Why You Should Use Java

It's time to celebrate! You've just picked up a copy of *Java For Dummies,* 4th Edition, and you're reading Chapter 1. At this rate, you'll be an expert Java programmer in no time at all, so rejoice in your eventual success by throwing a big party.

To prepare for the party, I'll bake a cake. I'm lazy, so I'll use a ready-to-bake cake mix. Let me see . . . add water to the mix, and then add butter and eggs . . . Hey, wait! I just looked at the list of ingredients. What's MSG? And what about propylene glycol? That's used in antifreeze, isn't it?

I'll change plans and make the cake from scratch. Sure, it's a little harder. But that way, I get exactly what I want.

Computer programs work the same way. You can use somebody else's program or write your own. If you use somebody else's program, you use whatever you get. When you write your own program, you can tailor the program especially for your needs.

Writing computer code is a big, worldwide industry. Companies do it, freelance professionals do it, hobbyists do it, all kinds of people do it. A typical big company has teams, departments, and divisions that write programs for the company. But you can write programs for yourself or someone else, for a living or for fun. In a recent estimate, the number of lines of code written each day by programmers in the United States alone exceeds the number of methane molecules on the planet Jupiter.* Take almost anything that can be done with a computer. With the right amount of time, you can write your own program to do it. (Of course, the "right amount of time" may be very long, but that's not the point. Many interesting and useful programs can be written in hours or even minutes.)

* I made up this fact all by myself.

Getting Perspective: Where Java Fits In

Here's a brief history of modern computer programming:

- **1954–1957: FORTRAN is developed.**

  FORTRAN was the first modern computer programming language. For scientific programming, FORTRAN is a real racehorse. Year after year, FORTRAN is a leading language among computer programmers throughout the world.

- **1959: COBOL is created.**

  The letter *B* in COBOL stands for *Business,* and business is just what COBOL is all about. The language's primary feature is the processing of one record after another, one customer after another, or one employee after another.

  Within a few years after its initial development, COBOL became the most widely used language for business data processing. Even today, COBOL represents a large part of the computer programming industry.

- **1972: Dennis Ritchie at AT&T Bell Labs develops the C programming language.**

  The look and feel that you see in this book's examples come from the C programming language. Code written in C uses curly braces, if statements, for statements, and so on.

  In terms of power, you can use C to solve the same problems that you can solve by using FORTRAN, Java, or any other modern programming language. (You can write a scientific calculator program in COBOL, but doing that sort of thing would feel really strange.) The difference between one programming language and another isn't power. The difference is ease and appropriateness of use. That's where the Java language excels.

- **1986: Bjarne Stroustrup (again at AT&T Bell Labs) develops C++.**

  Unlike its C language ancestor, the language C++ supports object-oriented programming. This represents a huge step forward. (See the next section in this chapter.)

- **May 23, 1995: Sun Microsystems releases its first official version of the Java programming language.**

  Java improves upon the concepts in C++. Java's "Write Once, Run Anywhere" philosophy makes the language ideal for distributing code across the Internet.

  In addition, Java is a great general-purpose programming language. With Java, you can write windowed applications, build and explore databases, control handheld devices, and more. Within five short years, the Java programming language had 2.5 million developers worldwide. (I know. I have a commemorative T-shirt to prove it.)

✔ **November 2000: The College Board announces that, starting in the year 2003, the Computer Science Advanced Placement exams will be based on Java.**

Wanna know what that snot-nosed kid living down the street is learning in high school? You guessed it — Java.

✔ **2002: Microsoft introduces a new language named C#.**

Many of the C# language features come directly from features in Java.

✔ **March 2003: SkillMarket (`mshiltonj.com/sm`) reports that the demand for Java programmers tops the demand for C++ programmers by 42 percent.**

And there's more! The demand for Java programmers beats the combined demand for C++ and C# programmers by 10 percent. Java programmers are more employable than VB (Visual Basic) programmers by a whopping 111 percent.

✔ **2005: Over 90 percent of the Fortune 500 depend on Java technology for some aspect of their business transactions.**

Well, I'm impressed.

Object-Oriented Programming (OOP)

It's three in the morning. I'm dreaming about the history course that I failed in high school. The teacher is yelling at me, "You have two days to study for the final exam, but you won't remember to study. You'll forget and feel guilty, guilty, guilty."

Suddenly, the phone rings. I'm awakened abruptly from my deep sleep. (Sure, I disliked dreaming about the history course, but I like being awakened even less.) At first, I drop the telephone on the floor. After fumbling to pick it up, I issue a grumpy, "Hello, who's this?" A voice answers, "I'm a reporter from *The New York Times*. I'm writing an article about Java and I need to know all about the programming language in five words or less. Can you explain it?"

My mind is too hazy. I can't think. So I say anything that comes to my mind and then go back to sleep.

Come morning, I hardly remember the conversation with the reporter. In fact, I don't remember how I answered the question. Did I tell the reporter where he could put his article about Java?

I put on my robe and rush to the front of my house's driveway. As I pick up the morning paper, I glance at the front page and see the two-inch headline:

Burd calls Java "A Great Object-Oriented Language"

Object-oriented languages

Java is object-oriented. What does that mean? Unlike languages, such as FORTRAN, which focus on giving the computer imperative "Do this/Do that" commands, object-oriented languages focus on data. Of course, object-oriented programs still tell the computer what to do. They start, however, by organizing the data, and the commands come later.

Object-oriented languages are better than "Do this/Do that" languages because they organize data in a way that lets people do all kinds of things with it. To modify the data, you can build on what you already have, rather than scrap everything you've done and start over each time you need to do something new. Although computer programmers are generally smart people, they took awhile to figure this out. For the full history lesson, see the sidebar "The winding road from FORTRAN to Java" (but I won't make you feel guilty if you don't read it).

Objects and their classes

In an object-oriented language, you use objects *and* classes to organize your data.

Imagine that you're writing a computer program to keep track of the houses in a new condominium development (still under construction). The houses differ only slightly from one another. Each house has a distinctive siding color, an indoor paint color, a kitchen cabinet style, and so on. In your object-oriented computer program, each house is an object.

But objects aren't the whole story. Although the houses differ slightly from one another, all the houses share the same list of characteristics. For instance, each house has a characteristic known as *siding color*. Each house has another characteristic known as *kitchen cabinet style*. In your object-oriented program, you need a master list containing all the characteristics that a house object can possess. This master list of characteristics is called a *class*.

So there you have it. Object-oriented programming is misnamed. It should really be called "programming with classes and objects."

The winding road from FORTRAN to Java

Back in the mid-1950s, a team of people created a programming language named FORTRAN. It was a good language, but it was based on the idea that you should issue direct, imperative commands to the computer. "Do this, computer. Then do that, computer." (Of course, the commands in a real FORTRAN program were much more precise than "Do this" or "Do that.")

In the years that followed, teams developed many new computer languages, and many of the languages copied the FORTRAN "Do this/Do that" model. One of the more popular "Do this/Do that" languages went by the one-letter name *C.* Of course, the "Do this/Do that" camp had some renegades. In languages named SIMULA and Smalltalk, programmers moved the imperative "Do this" commands into the background and concentrated on descriptions of data. In these languages, you didn't come right out and say, "Print a list of delinquent accounts." Instead, you began by saying, "This is what it means to be an account. An account has a name and a balance." Then you said, "This is how you ask an account whether it's delinquent." Suddenly, the data became king. An account was a thing that had a name, a balance, and a way of telling you whether it was delinquent.

Languages that focus first on the data are called *object-oriented* programming languages. These object-oriented languages make excellent programming tools. Here's why:

✔ Thinking first about the data makes you a good computer programmer.

✔ You can extend and reuse the descriptions of data over and over again. When you try to teach old FORTRAN programs new tricks, however, the old programs show how brittle they are. They break.

In the 1970s, object-oriented languages like SIMULA and Smalltalk became buried in the computer hobbyist magazine articles. In the meantime, languages based on the old FORTRAN model were multiplying like rabbits.

So in 1986, a fellow named Bjarne Stroustrup created a language named C++. The C++ language became very popular because it mixed the old C language terminology with the improved object-oriented structure. Many companies turned their backs on the old FORTRAN/C programming style and adopted C++ as their standard.

But C++ had a flaw. Using C++, you could bypass all the object-oriented features and write a program by using the old FORTRAN/C programming style. When you started writing a C++ accounting program, you could take either fork in the road:

✔ You could start by issuing direct "Do this" commands to the computer, saying the mathematical equivalent of "Print a list of delinquent accounts, and make it snappy."

✔ You could take the object-oriented approach and begin by describing what it means to be an account.

Some people said that C++ offered the best of both worlds, but others argued that the first world (the world of FORTRAN and C) shouldn't be part of modern programming. If you gave a programmer an opportunity to write code either way, the programmer would too often choose to write code the wrong way.

So in 1995, James Gosling of Sun Microsystems created the language named *Java.* In creating Java, Gosling borrowed the look and feel of C++. But Gosling took most of the old "Do this/Do

(continued)

(continued)

that" features of C++ and threw them in the trash. Then he added features that made the development of objects smoother and easier. All in all, Gosling created a language whose object-oriented philosophy is pure and clean. When you program in Java, you have no choice but to work with objects. That's the way it should be.

Now notice that I put the word *classes* first. How dare I do this! Well, maybe I'm not so crazy. Think again about a housing development that's under construction. Somewhere on the lot, in a rickety trailer parked on bare dirt, is a master list of characteristics known as a blueprint. An architect's blueprint is like an object-oriented programmer's class. A blueprint is a list of characteristics that each house will have. The blueprint says, "siding." The actual house object has gray siding. The blueprint says, "kitchen cabinet." The actual house object has Louis XIV kitchen cabinets.

The analogy doesn't end with lists of characteristics. Another important parallel exists between blueprints and classes. A year after you create the blueprint, you use it to build ten houses. It's the same with classes and objects. First, the programmer writes code to describe a class. Then when the program runs, the computer creates objects from the (blueprint) class.

So that's the real relationship between classes and objects. The programmer defines a class, and from the class definition, the computer makes individual objects.

What's so good about an object-oriented language?

Based on the previous section's story about home building, imagine that you have already written a computer program to keep track of the building instructions for houses in a new development. Then, the big boss decides on a modified plan — a plan in which half the houses have three bedrooms, and the other half have four.

If you use the old FORTRAN/C style of computer programming, your instructions look like this:

```
Dig a ditch for the basement.
Lay concrete around the sides of the ditch.
Put two-by-fours along the sides for the basement's frame.
...
```

This would be like an architect creating a long list of instructions instead of a blueprint. To modify the plan, you have to sort through the list to find the instructions for building bedrooms. To make things worse, the instructions could be scattered among pages 234, 394–410, 739, 10, and 2. If the builder had to decipher other peoples' complicated instructions, the task would be ten times harder.

Starting with a class, however, is like starting with a blueprint. If you decide to have both three- and four-bedroom houses, you can start with a blueprint called the *house* blueprint that has a ground floor and a second floor, but has no indoor walls drawn on the second floor. Then, you make two more second-floor blueprints — one for the three-bedroom house and another for the four-bedroom house. (You name these new blueprints the *three-bedroom house* blueprint and the *four-bedroom house* blueprint.)

Your builder colleagues are amazed with your sense of logic and organization, but they have concerns. They pose a question. "You called one of the blueprints the 'three-bedroom house' blueprint. How can you do this if it's a blueprint for a second floor and not for a whole house?"

You smile knowingly and answer, "The three-bedroom house blueprint can say, 'For info about the lower floors, see the original house blueprint.' That way, the three-bedroom house blueprint describes a whole house. The four-bedroom house blueprint can say the same thing. With this setup, we can take advantage of all the work we already did to create the original house blueprint and save lots of money."

In the language of object-oriented programming, the three- and four-bedroom house classes are *inheriting* the features of the original house class. You can also say that the three- and four-bedroom house classes are *extending* the original house class. (See Figure 1-1.)

The original house class is called the *superclass* of the three- and four-bedroom house classes. In that vein, the three- and four-bedroom house classes are *subclasses* of the original house class. Put another way, the original house class is called the *parent class* of three- and four-bedroom house classes. The three- and four-bedroom house classes are *child classes* of the original house class. (See Figure 1-1.)

Needless to say, your home-builder colleagues are jealous. A crowd of home-builders is mobbing around you to hear about your great ideas. So, at that moment, you drop one more bombshell: "By creating a class with subclasses, we can reuse the blueprint in the future. If someone comes along and wants a five-bedroom house, we can extend our original house blueprint by making a five-bedroom house blueprint. We'll never have to spend money for an original house blueprint again."

"But," says a colleague in the back row, "what happens if someone wants a different first-floor design? Do we trash the original house blueprint or start scribbling all over the original blueprint? That'll cost big bucks, won't it?"

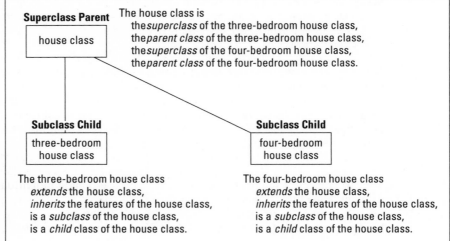

Superclass Parent

house class

The house class is
the *superclass* of the three-bedroom house class,
the *parent class* of the three-bedroom house class,
the *superclass* of the four-bedroom house class,
the *parent class* of the four-bedroom house class.

Subclass Child

three-bedroom
house class

Subclass Child

four-bedroom
house class

The three-bedroom house class
  extends the house class,
  inherits the features of the house class,
  is a *subclass* of the house class,
  is a *child* class of the house class.

The four-bedroom house class
  extends the house class,
  inherits the features of the house class,
  is a *subclass* of the house class,
  is a *child* class of the house class.

Figure 1-1:
Terminology
in object-
oriented pro-
gramming.

In a confident tone, you reply, "We don't have to mess with the original house blueprint. If someone wants a Jacuzzi in his living room, we can make a new, small blueprint describing only the new living room and call this the *Jacuzzi-in-living-room house* blueprint. Then, this new blueprint can refer to the original house blueprint for info on the rest of the house (the part that's not in the living room)." In the language of object-oriented programming, the Jacuzzi-in-living-room house blueprint still *extends* the original house blueprint. The Jacuzzi blueprint is still a subclass of the original house blueprint. In fact, all the terminology about superclass, parent class, and child class still applies. The only thing that's new is that the Jacuzzi blueprint *overrides* the living room features in the original house blueprint.

In the days before object-oriented languages, the programming world experienced a crisis in software development. Programmers wrote code, then discovered new needs, and then had to trash their code and start from scratch. This happened over and over again because the code that the programmers were writing couldn't be reused. Object-oriented programming changed all this for the better (and, as Burd said, Java is "A Great Object-Oriented Language").

Refining your understanding of classes and objects

When you program in Java, you work constantly with classes and objects. These two ideas are really important. That's why, in this chapter, I hit you over the head with one analogy after another about classes and objects.

Close your eyes for a minute and think about what it means for something to be a chair. . . .

A chair has a seat, a back, and legs. Each seat has a shape, a color, a degree of softness, and so on. These are the properties that a chair possesses. What I describe is *chairness* — the notion of something being a chair. In object-oriented terminology, I'm describing the chair class.

Now peek over the edge of this book's margin and take a minute to look around your room. (If you're not sitting in a room right now, fake it.)

Several chairs are in the room, and each chair is an object. Each of these objects is an example of that ethereal thing called the Chair class. So that's how it works — the class is the idea of *chairness,* and each individual chair is an object.

A class isn't quite a collection of things. Instead, a class is the idea behind a certain kind of thing. When I talk about the class of chairs in your room, I'm talking about the fact that each chair has legs, a seat, a color, and so on. The colors may be different for different chairs in the room, but that doesn't matter. When you talk about a class of things, you're focusing on the properties that each of the things possesses.

It makes sense to think of an object as being a concrete instance of a class. In fact, the official terminology is consistent with this thinking. If you write a Java program in which you define a Chair class, each actual chair (the chair that you're sitting on, the empty chair right next to you, and so on) is called an *instance* of the Chair class.

Here's another way to think about a class. Imagine a table displaying all three of your bank accounts. (See Table 1-1.)

Table 1-1	A Table of Accounts	
Account Number	*Type*	*Balance*
16-13154-22864-7	Checking	174.87
1011 1234 2122 0000	Credit	−471.03
16-17238-13344-7	Savings	247.38

Think of the table's column headings as a class, and think of each row of the table as an object. The table's column headings describe the Account class.

According to the table's column headings, each account has an account number, a type, and a balance. Rephrased in the terminology of object-oriented programming, each object in the Account class (that is, each instance of the `Account` class) has an account number, a type, and a balance. So, the bottom row of the table is an object with account number *16-17238-13344-7*. This same object has type *Savings* and a balance of *247.38*. If you opened a new account, you would have another object, and the table would grow an additional row. The new object would be an instance of the same `Account` class.

What's Next?

This chapter is filled with general descriptions of things. A general description is good when you're just getting started, but you don't really understand things until you get to know some specifics. That's why the next several chapters deal with specifics.

So please, turn the page. The next chapter can't wait for you to read it.

Chapter 2

Running Canned Java Programs

. . . .

In This Chapter

▶ Setting up your computer to run Java

▶ Running text-based programs

▶ Running window-based programs

▶ Running Java applets

. . . .

*T*he best way to get to know Java is to do Java. When you're doing Java, you're writing, testing, and running your own Java programs. This chapter gets you ready to do Java by having you run and test programs. Instead of writing your own programs, however, you get to run programs I've already written for you — nice guy that I am.

Downloading and Installing the Java Development Kit (JDK)

First you need some Java development software. You can choose from several products. In fact, you may already have one of these products on your own computer. If you don't, you can download the basic software by visiting a Sun Microsystems Web site. The product that you want to download is known by a few different names. It's called the Java Development Kit (JDK), the Java Software Development Kit (SDK), and the Java Standard Edition (Java SE). You may even see an extra 2 in a name like Java 2 Standard Edition (J2SE), but the 2 doesn't mean anything. (Sun Microsystems added the 2 several years ago and then dropped the 2 in 2006.)

This section tells you how to download and install the Java SDK. First, I give a condensed, quick-start set of instructions. Then, I present a detailed, read-every-step-carefully version.

So what follows is the condensed, quick-start version of instructions for use with Microsoft Windows systems. If these instructions are too condensed for you, follow the detailed instructions that come immediately after these quick instructions.

If you're using Linux, Unix, Macintosh, or some other non-Windows system, visit this book's Web site for further instructions.

1. **Visit java.sun.com.**

2. **Find a link to download the Java SE 6 (the Java Standard Edition, version 6).**

   If you find some other version, like 6_02 or 6.02, that's fine. Just make sure that you have a version numbered 6 or higher.

3. **Download the JDK, not the JRE.**

   The JRE (Java Runtime Environment) isn't harmful to your computer, but the JRE isn't enough. To create your own Java programs, you need more than the JRE. You need the entire JDK. (Besides, when you run the install program for the JDK, the install program offers to put both the JDK and the JRE on your computer.)

4. **Double-click the icon of the downloaded file and follow the wizard's instructions for installing the JDK.**

   As the installation begins, the wizard asks you to choose from among several components that can possibly by installed. You can choose to have some or all of the components installed. Just make sure that your choice includes the development tools and the JRE.

   You also see the name of the directory in which the JDK is to be installed. Jot down the exact name of the directory. It's something like jdk1.6.0 or C:\Program Files\Java\jdk1.6.0. Whatever the directory's name is, I call this your *Java home* directory.

   At some point, the wizard asks whether you want to register your Web browser with the latest Java plug-in. If you plan to create Java applets, accept this option and register your browser. (Even if you won't be writing applets, it's a good idea to register your browser.)

5. **Return to the page where you found the JDK download. Get another download — the Java SE Documentation (also known as the Java SE API Documentation).**

6. **Extract the zipped Java SE Documentation to your Java home directory.**

   Your Java home directory comes with several subdirectories — bin, jre, lib, and a few others. After the extraction, your Java home directory has a new directory named docs. I call this new directory your *Javadoc* directory.

Downloading Java

If the previous instructions are too quick for you, you can follow this section's detailed instructions.

 The Sun Microsystems Web site changes from week to week. By the time you read this book, my detailed instructions may be obsolete. So as you read these instructions, be ready for some surprises. Be prepared to do some hunting on Sun's Java Web site. Expect to find a few options that were added to the site after I wrote this chapter. If you get lost, check this book's Web site for more up-to-date instructions.

Here are the detailed instructions for downloading the Java JDK:

1. **Visit `java.sun.com`.**

2. **On the `java.sun.com` home page's right margin, look for something called Popular Downloads.**

3. **Under Popular Downloads, look for a Java SE 6 link.**

    By the time you read this book, it may be a Java SE 6 Update 2 link, or a plain old Java SE link (with no number). In any case, click this link. The next thing you see is a page full of download links.

What's in a name?

The numbering of Java's SDK versions is really confusing. Instead of "Java 1," "Java 2," and "Java 3," the numbering of Java versions winds through an obstacle course. Here's how it works:

✔ Java JDK 1.0 (1996)

✔ Java JDK 1.1 (1997)

✔ Java 2 SDK, 1.2 (1998): Sun Microsystems added an additional "2" and changed "JDK" (Java Development Kit) to "SDK" (Software Development Kit)

✔ Java 2 SDK, 1.3 (2000)

✔ Java 2 SDK, 1.4 (2002)

✔ Java 2 JDK, 5.0 (2004): Sun reverts to "JDK" and gives up on the silly 1.x numbering scheme.

✔ Java 6 JDK (2006): Sun drops the unnecessary 2 and gets rid of the .0 too.

To make things worse, the file-numbering scheme isn't consistent with the product numbering scheme. So when you install Java 6 JDK, you get a directory named `jdk1.6.0`. The *1.x* numbering returns to haunt you, and so does the *.0* decimal point business.

You can find the old versions of Java, along with all the intermediate releases not listed here, at `java.sun.com/products/archive`.

Most of the programs in this book run *only* under Java 5.0, or later. They do *not* run under any version earlier than Java 5.0. In particular, they do not run under Java 1.4 or under Java 1.4.2.

4. Take a few minutes to examine the download links.

Depending on what Sun Microsystems has cooking when you visit the Web site, you may find variations on the simple Java SE link. You may see the word *Platform* and the abbreviations JDK and JRE. You may also see version numbers, such as 6 or "6 Update 2." You want the highest version number that's available at the Web site.

Avoid links that are labeled JRE because they lead to the software for running existing Java programs, not the software for writing new Java programs. It's not bad to have the JRE on your computer, but in order to write new Java programs, you need something more powerful than the JRE. You need the JDK. (In fact, when you download the JDK, you get the JRE along with the JDK. So don't download the JRE separately.)

5. Click the link to download the latest version of the JDK.

At `java.sun.com`, you can find downloads for Windows, Linux, and Solaris. If your favorite operating environment isn't Windows, Linux, or Solaris, don't despair. Many third-party vendors have converted Java to other environments. If the Mac is your thing, visit `developer.apple.com/java`.

Clicking the JDK download link brings you to the Sun Microsystems License Agreement page.

6. Do whatever you normally do with license agreements.

I won't be the one to tell you not to bother reading it. If you accept the agreement, you're taken to yet another Web page.

7. On this final Web page, click the link or button to start the download.

For Windows, the Web page offers two kinds of installation downloads — the regular (online) installation and the offline installation. I prefer the offline installation, but you may prefer the online installation.

- **The online installation is good if you want to save space on your hard drive.**

  Clicking the online installation link puts a tiny file on your hard drive. Eventually, your hard drive has one tiny file plus the installed Java JDK.

- **The offline installation is good if you ever want to reinstall the Java JDK.**

  Clicking the offline installation link downloads a huge setup file on your hard drive. Eventually, your hard drive has a huge setup file plus the installed Java JDK.

The huge setup file takes an extra 50MB on your hard drive, but if you ever want to reinstall Java, you have the setup file right where you need it.

As you begin downloading the tiny online file or the huge offline setup file, note the directory on your hard drive where the file is being deposited.

8. **Return to the Web page that you were visiting in Step 4. On that page, find a link to the Java SE Documentation (also known as the Java SE API Documentation).**

The Java language has a built-in feature for creating consistent, nicely formatted documentation in Web page format. As a Java programmer, you won't survive without a copy of the Application Programming Interface (API) documentation by your side. You can bookmark the documentation at the `java.sun.com` site and revisit the site whenever you need to look up something. But in the long run (and in the not-so-long run), you can save time by downloading your own copy of the API docs.

See Chapter 3 for more about the API.

9. **Download the API documentation.**

The documentation comes inside a big Zip file. Just leave this file on your hard drive for now. You don't unzip the file until you read the next section's instructions.

Installing Java on your computer

After you download the Java JDK, you're ready to install the software on your computer. Of course, you can do this 900 different ways, depending on your operating system, the names of directories on your hard drive, the wind velocity, and other factors. The following steps offer some guidelines:

1. **Open My Computer and find the JDK file that you downloaded.**

The file has a name like `jdk-6-blah-blah.exe`. The exact name depends on the operating system you're using, the version number that Sun has reached with Java, and whatever naming conventions the people at Sun have changed since this book was written.

2. **Double-click the JDK file's icon.**

What happens next depends on which option you chose in Step 7 of the previous set of instructions.

- If you downloaded the tiny online installation file, your computer downloads more files from the Internet and installs Java while it downloads.

• If you downloaded the huge offline installation file, your computer extracts the contents of the huge setup file and installs Java from these contents.

3. **Among the features that you select to install, make sure you select Development Tools and Public Java Runtime Environment. (See Figure 2-1.)**

You can choose to have some or all of the components installed. Just make sure that your choice includes these two items. To select or unselect an item, click the icon to the left of the item's name.

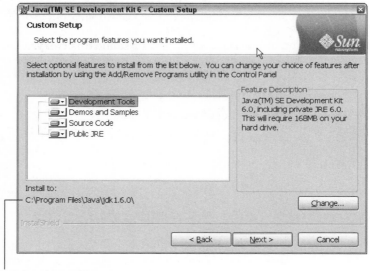

Figure 2-1:
A page of the Java JDK installation wizard.

Your Java home directory

4. **Jot down the name of the directory in which the Java SDK is being installed and then click Next.**

From one version to the next, the installation package puts Java in different directories on the computer's hard drive. Lately the package has installed Java in a directory named `C:\Program Files\Java\jdk1.6.0`. During the installation on your computer, you may see a different directory name. (One way or another, the name probably has `jdk` in it.)

Take note of this directory name when the installation package displays it. (Refer to Figure 2-1.) This directory is called your *Java home* directory. You need the name of this directory in other sections of this chapter and in other chapters of this book.

If you're a Windows user, Program Files is probably part of your Java home directory's name. Whenever I tell you to type the directory's name, it's a good idea to type an abbreviated version that doesn't include the blank space. The official Windows abbreviation for Program Files is progra~1 (with a squiggly little tilde character and 1 at the end). So if my Java home directory is C:\Program Files\Java\jdk1.6.0, when I need to type the directory's name, I usually type **C:\progra~1\Java\ jdk1.6.0**.

5. **Enjoy the splash screens that you see while the software is being installed.**

   At the end of the installation, you click the proverbial Finish button. But you're still not done with the whole kit 'n caboodle. The next step is installing the Java documentation.

6. **Copy the documentation to your Java home directory.**

   In Step 9 of the previous section, you downloaded a file named jdk-6-doc.zip (or something like that). Unzip (extract) this file so that its contents are in your Java home directory.

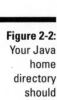

   Your Java home directory has a name like jdk1.6.0. That's not the same as another directory that you may find on your hard drive — a directory with a name like jre1.6.0.

7. **Check to make sure that you unzipped the documentation correctly.**

   After unzipping the documentation's Zip file, you should have a subdirectory named docs in your Java home directory. So open My Computer and navigate to your new jdkwhatever folder. Directly inside that folder, you should see a new folder named docs. This directory is called your *Javadoc* directory. (See Figure 2-2.)

Figure 2-2:
Your Java home directory should contain a docs directory.

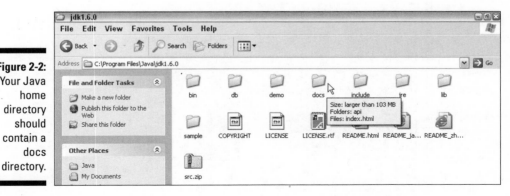

When your docs are all lined up in a row, you can proceed to the next step — installing a Java development environment.

Preparing to Use an Integrated Development Environment

If you followed the instructions up to this point, you have all the software that you need for writing and running your own Java programs. But there's one more thing you may want. It's called an *Integrated Development Environment* (IDE). If you don't have an IDE, writing and running a program involves opening several different windows — a window for typing the program, another window for running the program, and maybe a third window to keep track of all the code that you've written. An IDE seamlessly combines all this functionality into one well-organized application.

Java has its share of integrated development environments. Some of the more popular products include Eclipse, IntelliJ IDEA, and NetBeans. Some fancy environments even have drag-and-drop components so that you can design your graphical interface visually. (See Figure 2-3. For more info on the neat-o Jigloo graphical user interface builder shown here, check out `www.cloud garden.com/jigloo/index.html`.)

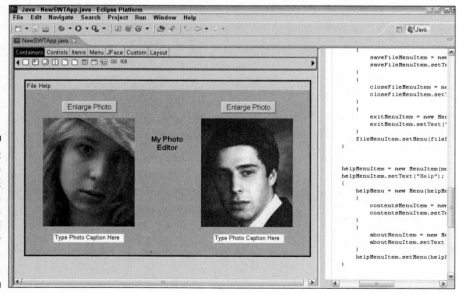

Figure 2-3: Using the Eclipse IDE with the Jigloo graphical user interface builder.

JCreator

The programs in this book work with almost any Java IDE. But in this chapter, I show you how to use JCreator LE (Lite Edition). I chose JCreator LE over other IDEs for several reasons:

- ✔ JCreator LE is free.

- ✔ Among all the Java IDEs, JCreator represents a nice compromise between power and simplicity.

- ✔ Unlike some other Java IDEs, JCreator works with almost any version of Java, from the ancient version 1.0.2 to the new Java SE 6, and onward to Java SE 7 beta.

- ✔ JCreator LE is free. (It's worth mentioning twice.)

If you're the kind of person who prefers plain old text editors and command prompts over IDEs, visit this book's Web site. On that site, I've posted instructions for writing and running Java programs without an IDE.

This book's CD-ROM has a special version of JCreator LE — a version that's customized especially for readers of *Java For Dummies,* 4th Edition! So please install JCreator LE from the CD-ROM. (Who knows? You may like it a lot, and buy JCreator Pro!)

For help installing materials from the CD-ROM, see Appendix A.

Running JCreator for the first time

The first time you run JCreator, the program asks for some configuration information. Just follow these steps:

1. **If you haven't already done so, launch JCreator.**

   The JCreator Setup Wizard appears on your screen. The wizard's first page is for File Associations.

2. **Accept the File Associations defaults and click Next.**

   The wizard's next page (the JDK Home Directory page) appears.

3. **Look at the text field on the JDK Home Directory page. Make sure that this field displays the name of your Java home directory. (See Figure 2-4.)**

   If the wrong directory name appears in the text field, just click the Browse button and navigate to your computer's Java home directory.

JDK Home Directory listing

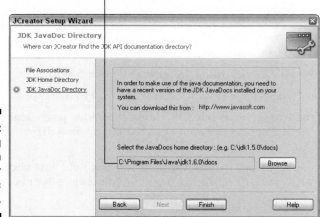

Figure 2-4:
Confirming
the location
of your
Java home
directory.

For information on your computer's Java home directory, see Step 4 of this chapter's "Downloading and Installing the Java Development Kit (JDK)" section, or Step 4 of this chapter's "Installing Java on your computer" section.

 4. **When you're happy with the name in the home directory text field, click Next.**

 The wizard's last page (the JDK JavaDoc Directory page) appears.

 5. **Look at the text field on the JDK JavaDoc Directory page. Make sure that this field displays the name of your JavaDoc directory. (See Figure 2-5.)**

JDK JavaDoc Directory listing

Figure 2-5:
Confirming
the location
of your
JavaDoc
directory.

Normally, your JavaDoc directory's name is the name of your Java home directory, followed by \docs. For information on your computer's Javadoc directory, see Step 6 of this chapter's "Downloading and Installing the Java Development Kit (JDK)" section, or Step 7 of this chapter's "Installing Java on your computer" section.

If the wrong directory name appears in the text field, just click the Browse button and navigate to your computer's JavaDoc directory.

If you do anything wrong in Steps 3 or 4, you can correct your mistake later. See this book's Web site for details.

6. **Click Finish.**

At this point, the JCreator Start Page appears. (See Figure 2-6.)

Running Java Programs

In this section, you run three Java programs — programs I wrote to help you practice running some Java code. Each program computes the monthly payment on a home mortgage, but each program interacts with the user in its own unique way. After you make your way through this section, you'll know how to run three kinds of programs: a text-based program, a stand-alone GUI program, and a Java applet.

Figure 2-6:
JCreator's
Start Page.

Running a text-based program

The first mortgage-calculating program doesn't open its own window. Instead, the program runs in JCreator's General Output pane. (See Figure 2-7.) A program that operates completely in this General Output pane is called a *text-based program.*

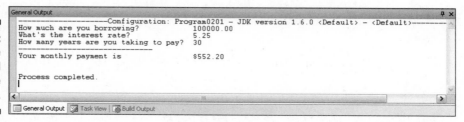

Figure 2-7: A run of the text-based mortgage program.

If you're using Linux, Unix, Mac, or some other non-Windows system, the instructions in this section don't apply to you. Visit this book's Web site for an alternative set of instructions.

Actually, as you run the mortgage program, you see two things in the General Output pane:

- ✔ **Messages and results that the mortgage program sends to you.** Messages include things like How much are you borrowing? Results include lines like Your monthly payment is $552.20.

- ✔ **Responses that you give to the mortgage program while it runs.** If you type **100000.00** in response to the program's question about how much you're borrowing, you see that number echoed in the General Output pane.

Running the mortgage program is easy. Here's how you do it:

1. **Make sure that you've followed the previous instructions in this chapter — instructions for installing the Java JDK and configuring JCreator.**

   Thank goodness! You don't have to follow those instructions more than once.

2. **Launch JCreator.**

   The big JCreator Start Page stares at you from your computer screen. (Refer to Figure 2-6.)

   If this is your first time running JCreator, you don't see JCreator's Start Page. Instead you see the JCreator Setup Wizard. To get past the Setup Wizard, follow the instructions in the section entitled "Running JCreator for the first time" in this chapter.

3. **In JCreator's menu bar, choose File⇨Open Workspace from the main menu.**

   Don't choose File⇨*Open*. Instead, choose File⇨*Open Workspace*.

   A familiar-looking Open dialog box appears. This dialog box looks in your `MyProjects` directory. This `MyProjects` directory is a subdirectory of the directory in which JCreator is installed.

   The `MyProjects` directory has subdirectories named `Program0201`, `Listing0302`, and so on. The `MyProjects` directory also has files with names like `Chapter02` and `Chapter03`. If you set your computer so that it doesn't hide file extensions for known file types, then the names of the files are `Chapter02.jcw`, `Chapter03.jcw`, and so on. (See the sidebar entitled "Those pesky filename extensions.")

   If you install the custom version of JCreator from this book's CD-ROM, then the `MyProjects` directory has subdirectories named `Program0201`, `Listing0302`, and so on. The regular version of JCreator (downloaded from the `www.jcreator.com` Web site) doesn't have these subdirectories.

4. **Select the file named *Chapter02* (or *Chapter02.jcw*), and then click Open.**

   In response to your click, JCreator displays its main work area. (See Figure 2-8.)

Those pesky filename extensions

The filenames displayed in My Computer or in Windows Explorer can be misleading. You may visit the `MyProjects\Program0203` directory and see the name `MyWebPage`. Instead of just `MyWebPage`, the file's full name is `MyWeb Page.html`. You may see two `Mortgage Applet` files. What you don't see is that one file's real name is `MortgageApplet.java`, and the other file's real name is `Mortgage Applet.class`.

The ugly truth is that My Computer and Windows Explorer can hide a file's extensions. This awful feature tends to confuse Java programmers. So, if you don't want to be confused, modify the Windows Hide Extensions feature. To do this, you have to open the Folder Options dialog box. Here's how:

✔ **In Windows XP with the control panel's default (category) view:** Choose Start⇨ Control Panel⇨Appearance and Themes⇨ Folder Options.

✔ **In Windows Vista with the control panel's default (category) view:** Choose Start⇨ Control Panel⇨Appearance and Personalization ⇨Folder Options.

✔ **In Windows XP or Windows Vista with the control panel's classic view:** Choose Start⇨Control Panel⇨Folder Options.

In the Folder Options dialog box, click the View tab. Then look for the Hide File Extensions For Known File Types option. Make sure that this check box is *not* selected.

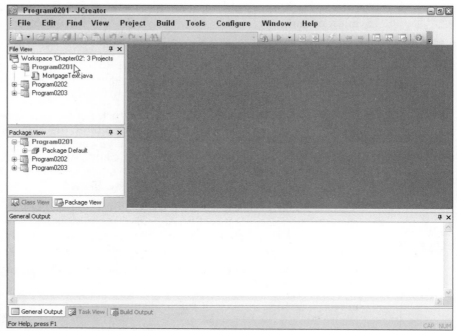

Figure 2-8:
JCreator's
work area.

In this book I refer to the window in Figure 2-8 (the menu bar, the toolbar, the File View, General Output pane, and so on) as the *JCreator work area.* But JCreator's help files use slightly different terminology. In JCreator's help files, the window in Figure 2-8 is called the *workspace,* not the *work area.* Elsewhere in these help files, JCreator reuses the word *workspace* to mean something entirely different. To avoid any confusion, I use two different terms. I use *work area* for the window in Figure 2-8, and I use *workspace* for that other, entirely different thing. (I explain that entirely different thing in the next paragraph.)

JCreator divides Java programs into *workspaces.* Each workspace is further subdivided into *projects.* To organize this book's examples, I made a workspace for each chapter, and then made a project for each complete Java program. When you open `Chapter02.jcw`, you get my Chapter02 workspace — a workspace that contains three projects. The projects' names are `Program0201`, `Program0202`, and `Program0203`. That's why, in JCreator's File View pane, you see a `Chapter02` tree with branches labeled `Program0201`, `Program0202`, and `Program0203`. (See Figure 2-8.)

Clicking Open in Step 4 may coax out a message box asking if you want to "Save the workspace modifications?" If so, click Yes. Clicking Open may coax out another box asking if you want to ". . . close all document Windows?" If so, click Yes.

5. **In the File View's tree, right-click the branch labeled *Program0201*. In the resulting context menu, choose Sets As Active Project. (See Figure 2-9.)**

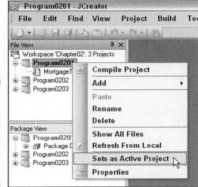

Figure 2-9:
Setting a particular project to be the active project.

Choosing Sets As Active Project makes `Program0201` the *active project.*

In JCreator, only one project at a time can be the active project. To run a particular program, the program's code has to be in whatever project is currently active. In JCreator's File View, you can tell which project is active by looking for the project whose name is displayed in boldface. On some systems, the active project's name is a hazy, light-gray boldface.

If a particular program isn't in the active project, you can't run that program, but you can do some other things with that program. For instance, you can see the program in one of JCreator's panes, make changes to the program, save the program, and so on. For this reason, it's really easy to get confused and forget which project is active. So always keep the active project in the forefront of your mind. If your code doesn't do what you think it should do, check to make sure that the project you want to run is the active project.

6. **Choose Build➪Compile Project from the main menu.**

Choosing Compile Project does exactly what it says. It *compiles* the project's code. (To find out what *compile* means, see the sidebar entitled "Compiling and running a Java program.")

After some pleasant chirping sounds from your hard drive, JCreator's bottom pane displays a `Process completed` message. (See Figure 2-10.)

7. **Choose Build➪Execute Project from the main menu.**

When you choose Execute Project, the computer runs the project's code. (That is, the computer runs a Java program that I wrote.) As part of the run, the message `How much are you borrowing?` appears in JCreator's General Output pane. (Refer to Figure 2-7.)

Figure 2-10:
The
compiling
process is
completed.

8. **Click anywhere inside JCreator's General Output pane, and then type a number, like** 100000.00, **and press Enter.**

When you type a number in Step 8, don't include your country's currency symbol and don't use a grouping separator. (U.S. residents, don't type a dollar sign and don't use commas.) Things like $100000.00 or 100,000.00 cause the program to crash. You see a NumberFormatException message in the General Output pane.

After you press Enter, the Java program displays another message (What's the interest rate?) in JCreator's General Output pane.

9. **In response to the interest rate question, type a number, like** 5.25, **and press Enter.**

After you press Enter, the Java program displays another message (How many years . . . ?) in JCreator's General Output pane.

10. **Type a number, like** 30, **and press Enter.**

In response to the numbers that you've typed, the Java program displays a monthly payment amount. Again, refer to Figure 2-7. (Disclaimer: Your local mortgage company will charge you much more than the amount that my Java program calculates.)

When you type a number in Step 10, don't include a decimal point. Things like 30.0 cause the program to crash. You see a NumberFormatException message in the General Output pane.

Occasionally you decide in the middle of a program's run that you've made a mistake of some kind. You want to stop the program's run dead in its tracks. To do this, choose Tools⇨Stop Tool from the main menu.

Running a GUI on its own

In the previous section, you go through all the steps for compiling and running a text-based Java program. In this section, you go through the same steps for a GUI. The term *GUI* stands for *Graphical User Interface.* It's the term used for a program that displays windows, buttons, and other nice-looking stuff. GUI programs are good because, unlike text-based programs, they don't look like they're running on your grandparents' computers.

Compiling and running a Java program

What does it mean for JCreator to "compile your project?" A *compiler* is a tool that translates code from one form to another. For instance, in my `Program0201` project directory, I have a file named `MortgageText.java`. If you look inside the `Mortgage Text.java` file, you see code like this:

```
import java.io.*;
import
  java.text.NumberFormat;
public class MortgageText {
    public static void
  main(String args[]) throws
  IOException
```

Although this code isn't easy reading, it certainly uses letters and other characters that English-speaking people can understand. This file, `MortgageText.java`, is called Java *source code*. It's the kind of code that you find out how to write by reading this book. It's the code that you have before you've done any compiling — before you choose Build⇨Compile Project from JCreator's main menu.

When you choose Build⇨Compile Project, the computer takes your source code and translates it into something called *bytecode*. The newly created bytecode file is automatically given a name like *MortgageText.class.* (You can open My Computer and look for the new `.class` file in your `Program0201` directory.) Unlike the original `.java` file, the new `.class` file has no recognizable characters in it and isn't suitable for human consumption. Instead, the `.class` file is streamlined so that the computer can carry out your program's commands quickly and easily.

In the way that it compiles code, Java represents a strict departure from most other programming languages. When you compile a program in another language (COBOL or C++, for instance), you create a file that can be run on only one operating system. For example, if you compile a C++ program on a Windows computer and then move the translated file to a Mac, the Mac treats the translated file as pure garbage. The Mac can't interpret any of the instructions in the translated file. This is bad for many reasons. One of the most striking reasons is that you can't send this kind of code over the World Wide Web and expect anyone with a different kind of computer to be able to run the code.

But with Java, you can take a bytecode file that you created with a Windows computer, copy the bytecode to who-knows-what kind of computer, and then run the bytecode with no trouble at all. That's one of the many reasons why Java has become popular so quickly. This outstanding feature, which gives you the ability to run code on many different kinds of computers, is called *portability.*

After compiling your Java project, choose Build⇨Execute from the main menu. At this point, I normally say that your computer starts running a Java program. But to be really picky, your computer never actually "runs a Java program." Instead, your computer runs something called the *Java Virtual Machine* (JVM). The use of a virtual machine is another way in which Java is different from other computer programming languages.

The Java Virtual Machine is a piece of software. Think of the JVM as a proxy, an errand boy, a go-between. The JVM serves as an interpreter between Java's run-anywhere bytecode and your computer's own system. As it runs, the JVM walks your computer through the execution of bytecode instructions. The JVM examines your bytecode, bit by bit, and carries out the instructions described in the bytecode. The JVM interprets bytecode for your Windows system, your Mac, your Linux box, or whatever kind of computer you're using. That's a good thing. It's what makes Java programs more portable than programs in any other language.

If you installed JCreator from this book's CD-ROM, you can find a GUI version of the mortgage-calculating program in a project named `Program0202`. To run the program, just follow these instructions:

1. **If you haven't already done so, follow Steps 1 to 4 from the section entitled "Running a text-based program."**

   When you finish with these steps, the Chapter02 workspace is open.

   JCreator can remember which workspace is open from one launch to another. That way, whenever you restart JCreator, you can skip the steps for opening a workspace (Steps 3 and 4 in the text-based program section). To make JCreator remember, choose Configure⇨Options in the JCreator menu bar. Then, in the resulting Options dialog, select Workspace⇨Start Up. In the At Startup drop-down box, select Open Last Workspace. (See Figure 2-11.) Finally, click OK to dismiss the Options dialog.

2. **In the File View's tree, right-click the branch labeled *Program0202*. In the resulting context menu, choose Sets As Active Project.**

   This makes `Program0202` the active project.

3. **Follow Steps 6 and 7 in the "Running a text-based program" section.**

   This compiles and runs the `Program0202` project's code. The code displays a window like the one shown in Figure 2-12. In the window, you can experiment and type your own values for the principal, the interest rate, and the number of years of the loan. Whenever you change a value, the program responds instantly by updating the value in the Payment field.

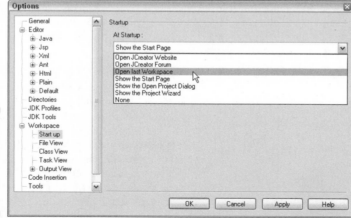

Figure 2-11:
Telling JCreator to automatically open a workspace.

Figure 2-12:
A run of
the GUI
mortgage
program.

🍵 Mortgage Payment Calculator	▢▢⊠
Principal $	100000.00
Rate (%)	5.25
Years	30
Payment $	552.20

Running a GUI on a Web page (a Java applet)

Java's big splash onto the scene came in the mid-1990s. The people at Sun Microsystems had managed to work Java programs into Web pages, and the results were dazzling. The infusion of Java into the Web was powerful, efficient, portable, and secure. The trick was to create a part of a program, called an *applet* and to display the applet inside a rectangle on the Web page.

These days, applets are passé. Real Java programmers roll their eyes when they hear the word *applet*. Three reasons for this are:

✔ Since the mid-1990s, better technologies have emerged for putting eye-catching content onto Web pages.

✔ Microsoft, the maker of the world's most powerful Web browser, refused to give its browser the most up-to-date Java tools.

✔ For Java programmers, the real money isn't in creating glittery Web pages. The real money is in business applications with Java EE.

For more information on Java EE, see Chapter 3.

Passé or not, some people still want to create applets. So in this section, you run a simple Java applet. Just follow these steps:

1. **If you haven't already done so, follow Steps 1 to 4 from the section entitled "Running a text-based program."**

   When you finish with these steps, the Chapter02 workspace is open.

2. **In the File View's tree, right-click the branch labeled *Program0203*. In the resulting context menu, choose Sets As Active Project.**

   This makes `Program0203` the active project.

Running an applet

In this chapter, you can find a sidebar entitled "Compiling and running a Java program." The sidebar describes the execution of a Java project. To execute a project, your computer runs a Java Virtual Machine (JVM), and this JVM carries a Java program's instructions. That's how it works for a project that *doesn't* involve applets. But when your project involves an applet, the story is a bit different.

If you've worked with Web pages, you may be familiar with something called *HTML* — the *Hypertext Markup Language.* It's the universal language for the World Wide Web. Almost every Web page starts with an HTML file. That's why, when you expand Program0203 in JCreator's File View pane, you see something named MyWebPage.html.

When JCreator executes the Program0203 project, it finds this MyWebPage.html file and opens this file with Microsoft Internet Explorer. At this point, Internet Explorer takes on the full burden of running your code. Internet Explorer acts on the commands (the *tags*) in the MyWebPage.html file. In particular, Internet Explorer finds the following tag inside the MyWebPage.html file:

```
<applet code="MortgageApplet"
    width=300
    height=200></applet>
```

This tag instructs Internet Explorer to look for the Java program named MortgageApplet. When it finds the program, Internet Explorer displays the applet (the text fields, the words *Principal, Rate, Payment,* and other stuff) in the browser window.

So that's what JCreator does when you want an applet to be executed. JCreator doesn't run the JVM directly. Instead, JCreator tells Internet Explorer to visit an HTML document. Then Internet Explorer runs the JVM and displays the applet on a Web page. Have you read about all the lawsuits between Microsoft and Sun Microsystems? At the heart of these lawsuits is the use of an outdated JVM in the Internet Explorer browser.

By the way, JCreator may be configured to use Sun's appletviewer instead of Internet Explorer. The *appletviewer* is a small browser that's designed specifically for viewing Java applets. The appletviewer displays nothing but applets (no hyperlinks, no images, no text other than the applet's text) so you can't use appletviewer to preview a complete Web page. For tips on switching between the appletviewer and Internet Explorer, see this book's Web site.

3. **Follow Steps 6 and 7 in the "Running a text-based program" section.**

   This compiles and runs the Program0203 project's code. You see a new Web page containing a mortgage applet in the Web browser window. (See Figure 2-13.)

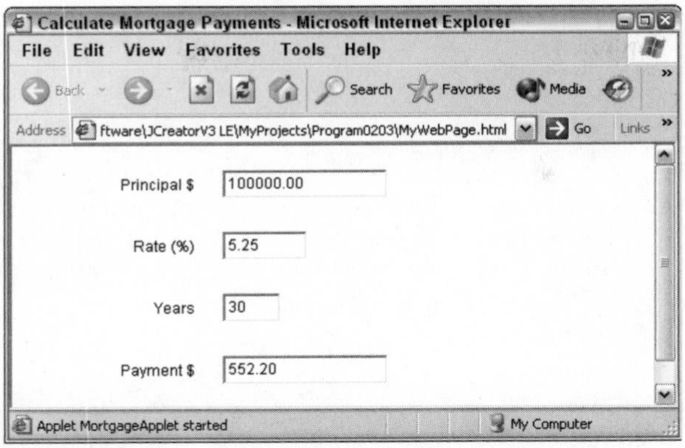

Figure 2-13:
The
mortgage
applet runs
in your
browser
window.

If you follow the steps in this section and you don't see the mortgage applet running in your Web browser, you can do a few things:

✔ **Check your Web browser's settings to make sure that the display of Java applets is enabled.**

✔ **Close any browser windows that you have open. Then return to JCreator and choose Build⇨Execute Project again.**

Sometimes this helps.

✔ **Skip the whole applet business and move on to Chapter 3.**

Hardly anyone uses Java applets these days, anyway.

Chapter 3

Using the Basic Building Blocks

"All great ideas are simple."

— Leo Tolstoy

The quotation applies to all kinds of things — things like life, love, and computer programming. That's why this chapter takes a multilayered approach. In this chapter, you get your first blast of details about Java programming. But in discovering details, you see the simplicities.

Speaking the Java Language

If you try to picture in your mind the whole English language, what do you see? Maybe you see words, words, words. (That's what Hamlet saw.) Looking at the language under a microscope, you see one word after another. The bunch-of-words image is fine, but if you step back a bit, you may see two other things:

▶ The language's grammar

▶ Thousands of expressions, sayings, idioms, and historical names

The first category (the grammar) includes rules like, "The verb agrees with the noun in number and person." The second category (expressions, sayings, and stuff) includes knowledge like, "Julius Caesar was a famous Roman emperor, so don't name your son Julius Caesar, unless you want him to get beat up every day after school."

The Java programming language has all the aspects of a spoken language like English. Java has words, grammar, commonly used names, stylistic idioms, and other such things.

The grammar and the common names

The people at Sun Microsystems who created Java thought of Java as coming in two parts. Just as English has its grammar and commonly used names, the Java programming language has its specification (its grammar) and its Application Programming Interface (its commonly used names). Whenever I write Java programs, I keep two important pieces of documentation — one for each part of the language — on my desk:

- ✔ **The Java Language Specification:** This includes rules like, "Always put an open parenthesis after the word *for*" and "Use an asterisk to multiply two numbers."

- ✔ **The Application Programming Interface:** Java's *Application Programming Interface* (API) contains thousands of tools that were added to Java after the language's grammar was defined. These tools range from the commonplace to the exotic. For instance, the tools include a routine named *pow* that can raise 5 to the 10th power for you. A more razzle-dazzle tool (named *JFrame*) displays a window on your computer's screen. Other tools listen for the user's button clicks, query databases, and do all kinds of useful things.

You can download the Language Specification, the API documents, and all the other Java documentation (or view the documents online) by poking around at `java.sun.com/javase/downloads`. But watch out! This Web page is a moving target. By the time you read this book, the links in this paragraph will probably be out of date. The safest thing to do is to start at `java.sun.com`, and then look for links to things like "Java SE" and "documentation."

The first part of Java, the Language Specification, is relatively small. That doesn't mean you won't take plenty of time finding out how to use the rules in the Language Specification. Other programming languages, however, have double, triple, or ten times the number of rules.

The second part of Java — the API — can be intimidating because it's so large. The API contains at least 3,000 tools and keeps growing with each new Java language release. Pretty scary, eh? Well, the good news is that you don't have to memorize anything in the API. Nothing. None of it. You can look up the stuff you need to use in the documentation and ignore the stuff you don't need. What you use often, you'll remember. What you don't use often, you'll forget (like any other programmer).

For information on how to find things in Java's API documentation, see the section entitled "Finding javadoc pages," later in this chapter.

No one knows all there is to know about the Java API. If you're a Java programmer who frequently writes programs that open new windows, you know how to use the API `Frame` class. If you seldom write programs that open windows, the first few times you need to create a window, you can look up the `Frame` class in the API documentation. My guess is that if you took a typical Java programmer and kept that programmer from looking up anything in the API documentation, the programmer would be able to use less than 2 percent of all the tools in the Java API.

Sure, you may love the *For Dummies* style. But unfortunately, Java's official API documentation isn't written that way. The API documentation is both concise and precise. For some help deciphering the API documentation's language and style, see this book's Web site.

In a way, nothing about the Java API is special. Whenever you write a Java program — even the smallest, simplest Java program — you create a class that's on par with any of the classes defined in the official Java API. The API is just a set of classes and other tools that were created by ordinary programmers who happen to participate in the official JCP — the *Java Community Process*. Unlike the tools that you create yourself, the tools in the API are distributed with every version of Java. (I'm assuming that you, the reader, are not a participant in the Java Community Process. But then, with a fine book like *Java For Dummies*, 4th Edition, one never knows.)

If you're interested in the JCP's activities, visit `www.jcp.org`.

The folks at the JCP don't keep the Java programs in the official Java API a secret. If you want, you can look at all these programs. When you install Java on your computer, the installation puts a file named `src.zip` on your hard drive. You can open `src.zip` with your favorite unzipping program. There, before your eyes, is all the Java API code.

The words in a Java program

A hard-core Javateer will say that the Java programming language has two different kinds of words: keywords and identifiers. This is true. But the bare truth, without any other explanation, is sometimes misleading. So I recommend dressing up the truth a bit and thinking in terms of three kinds of words: keywords, identifiers that ordinary programmers like you and me create, and identifiers from the API.

The differences among these three kinds of words are similar to the differences among words in the English language. In the sentence "Sam is a person," the word *person* is like a Java keyword. No matter who uses the word *person,* the word always means roughly the same thing. (Sure, you can think of bizarre exceptions in English usage, but please don't.)

The word *Sam* is like a Java identifier because Sam is a name for a particular person. Words like *Sam, Dinswald,* and *McGillimaroo* don't come prepacked with meaning in the English language. These words apply to different people depending on the context and become names when parents pick one for their newborn kid.

Now consider the sentence "Julius Caesar is a person." If you utter this sentence, you're probably talking about the fellow who ruled Rome until the Ides of March. Although the name *Julius Caesar* isn't hard-wired into the English language, almost everyone uses the name to refer to the same person. If English were a programming language, the name *Julius Caesar* would be an API identifier.

So here's how I, in my own mind, divide the words in a Java program into categories:

✔ **Keywords:** A *keyword* is a word that has its own special meaning in the Java programming language, and that meaning doesn't change from one program to another. Examples of keywords in Java include if, else, and do. The Cheat Sheet in the front of this book has a complete list of Java keywords.

The JCP committee members, who have the final say on what constitutes a Java program, have chosen all Java's keywords. If you think about the two parts of Java, which I discuss in "The grammar and the common names" section earlier in this chapter, the Java keywords belong solidly to the Language Specification.

✔ **Identifiers:** An *identifier* is a name for something. The identifier's meaning can change from one program to another, but some identifiers' meanings tend to change more than others.

- **Identifiers created by you and me:** As a Java programmer (yes, even as a novice Java programmer), you create new names for classes and other things that you describe in your programs. Of course, you may name something Prime, and the guy writing code two cubicles down the hall can name something else Prime. That's okay because Java doesn't have a predetermined meaning for the word Prime. In your program, you can make Prime stand for the Federal Reserve's prime rate. And the guy down the hall can make Prime stand for the "bread, roll, preserves, and prime rib." A conflict doesn't arise, because you and your co-worker are writing two different Java programs.

- **Identifiers from the API:** The JCP members have created names for many things and thrown at least 3,000 of these names into the Java API. The API comes with each version of Java, so these names are available to anyone who writes a Java program. Examples of such names are String, Integer, JWindow, JButton, JTextField, and File.

Strictly speaking, the meanings of the identifiers in the Java API are not cast in stone. Although you can make up your own meanings for the words like JButton or JWindow, this isn't a good idea. If you did, you would confuse the dickens out of other programmers, who are used to the standard API meanings for these familiar identifier names. But even worse, when your code assigns a new meaning to an identifier like JButton, you lose any computational power that was created for the identifier in the API code. The programmers at Sun Microsystems did all the work writing Java code to handle buttons. If you assign your own meaning to the word JButton, you're turning your back on all the progress made in creating the API.

Checking Out Java Code for the First Time

The first time you look at somebody else's Java program, you tend to feel a bit queasy. The realization that you don't understand something (or many things) in the code can make you nervous. I've written hundreds (maybe thousands) of Java programs, but I still feel insecure when I start reading someone else's code.

The truth is that finding out about a Java program is a bootstrapping experience. First you gawk in awe of the program. Then you run the program to see what it does. Then you stare at the program for a while or read someone's explanation of the program and its parts. Then you gawk a little more and run the program again. Eventually, you come to terms with the program. (Don't believe the wise guys who say they never go through these steps. Even the experienced programmers approach a new project slowly and carefully.)

In Listing 3-1, you get a blast of Java code. (Like all novice programmers, you're expected to gawk humbly at the code.) Hidden in the code, I've placed some important ideas, which I explain in detail in the next section. These ideas include the use of classes, methods, and Java statements.

Listing 3-1:   The Simplest Java Program

```
class Displayer {

    public static void main(String args[]) {
        System.out.println("You'll love Java!");
    }
}
```

To see the code of Listing 3-1 in the JCreator work area, follow these steps:

1. **Open the Chapter03 workspace and, within that workspace, make `Listing0301` the active project. (See Chapter 2 for details.)**

   In the File View pane's tree, the name `Listing0301` is set in boldface. Under `Listing0301`, you see a branch labeled `Displayer.java`.

2. **Double-click the `Displayer.java` branch in the File View pane's tree.**

   JCreator's Editor pane appears on the right side of the work area. The Editor pane contains the code in Listing 3-1.

After following the first step, you can run the code in Listing 3-1 by choosing Build⇨Compile Project, and then choosing Build⇨Execute Project. (See Chapter 2 for details.)

When you run the program from Listing 3-1, the computer displays `You'll love Java!` (See Figure 3-1.) Now, I admit that writing and running a Java program is a lot of work just to get `You'll love Java!` to appear on somebody's computer screen, but every endeavor has to start somewhere.

Figure 3-1:
Running the program in Listing 3-1.

```
General Output                                                                      ₽ ×
---------------------Configuration: Listing0301 - JDK version 1.6.0 <Default> - <Default>---------
You'll love Java!

Process completed.



General Output    Task View    Build Output
```

After following this section's steps, you may see a lot more than just `You'll love Java!` in JCreator's General Output pane. The General Output pane may display previous runs (runs of some examples from Chapter 2) in addition to this most recent `Displayer.java` run. To dispose of previous runs, start right-clicking the General Output pane. Then, in the resulting context menu, select Clear.

In the following section, you do more than just run the program and admire the program's output. After you read the following section, you actually understand what makes the program in Listing 3-1 work.

Understanding a Simple Java Program

This section presents, explains, analyzes, dissects, and otherwise demystifies the Java program shown previously in Listing 3-1.

The Java class

Because Java is an object-oriented programming language, your primary goal is to describe classes and objects. (If you're not convinced about this, read the sections on object-oriented programming in Chapter 1.)

On those special days when I'm feeling sentimental, I tell people that Java is more pure in its object-orientation than most other so-called object-oriented languages. I say this because, in Java, you can't do anything until you've created a class of some kind. It's like being on *Jeopardy!*; hearing Alex Trebec say, "Let's go to a commercial;" and then interrupting him by saying, "I'm sorry, Alex. You can't issue an instruction without putting your instruction inside a class."

In Java, the entire program is a class. I wrote the program, so I get to make up a name for my new class. I chose the name `Displayer,` because the program displays a line of text on the computer screen. That's why the code in Listing 3-1 starts with `class Displayer`. (See Figure 3-2.)

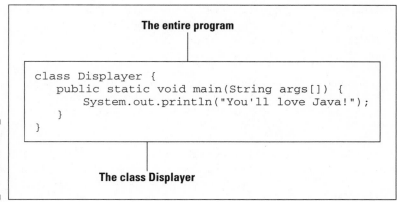

The entire program

```
class Displayer {
    public static void main(String args[]) {
        System.out.println("You'll love Java!");
    }
}
```

The class Displayer

Figure 3-2:
A Java program is a class.

The first word in Listing 3-1, the word `class`, is a Java keyword. (See the section "The words in a Java program," earlier in this chapter.) No matter who writes a Java program, the word `class` is always used the same way. On the other hand, the word `Displayer` in Listing 3-1 is an identifier. I made up the word `Displayer` while I was writing this chapter. The word `Displayer` is the name of a particular class — the class that I'm creating by writing this program.

The Java programming language is *case-sensitive*. This means that if you change a lowercase letter in a word to an uppercase letter, you change the word's meaning. Changing case can make the entire word go from being meaningful to being meaningless. In the first line of Listing 3-1, you can't replace `class` with `Class`. If you do, the whole program stops working.

The Java method

You're working as an auto mechanic in an upscale garage. Your boss, who's always in a hurry and has a habit of running words together, says, "FixTheAlternator on that junkyOldFord." Mentally, you run through a list of tasks. "Drive the car into the bay, lift the hood, get a wrench, loosen the alternator belt," and so on. Three things are going on here:

✔ **You have a name for the thing you're supposed to do.** The name is *FixTheAlternator.*

✔ **In your mind, you have a list of tasks associated with the name *FixTheAlternator.*** The list includes "Drive the car into the bay, lift the hood, get a wrench, loosen the alternator belt," and so on.

✔ **You have a grumpy boss who's telling you to do all this work.** Your boss gets you working by saying, "FixTheAlternator." In other words, your boss gets you working by saying the name of the thing you're supposed to do.

In this scenario, using the word *method* wouldn't be a big stretch. You have a method for doing something with an alternator. Your boss calls that method into action, and you respond by doing all the things in the list of instructions that you've associated with the method.

If you believe all that (and I hope you do), then you're ready to read about Java methods. In Java, a *method* is a list of things to do. Every method has a name, and you tell the computer to do the things in the list by using the method's name in your program.

I've never written a program to get a robot to fix an alternator. But, if I did, the program may include a `FixTheAlternator` method. The list of instructions in my `FixTheAlternator` method would look something like the text in Listing 3-2.

Listing 3-2:   A Method Declaration

```
void FixTheAlternator() {
    DriveInto(car, bay);
    Lift(hood);
    Get(wrench);
    Loosen(alternatorBelt);
    ...
}
```

Somewhere else in my Java code (somewhere outside of Listing 3-2), I need an instruction to call my `FixTheAlternator` method into action. The instruction to call the `FixTheAlternator` method into action may look like the line in Listing 3-3.

Listing 3-3:   A Method Call

```
FixTheAlternator(junkyOldFord);
```

Don't scrutinize Listings 3-2 and 3-3 too carefully. All the code in Listings 3-2 and 3-3 is fake! I made up this code so that it looks a lot like real Java code, but it's not real. What's more important, the code in Listings 3-2 and 3-3 isn't meant to illustrate all the rules about Java. So, if you have a grain of salt handy, take it with Listings 3-2 and 3-3.

Now that you have a basic understanding of what a method is and how it works, you can dig a little deeper into some useful terminology:

- ✔ If I'm being lazy, I refer to the code in Listing 3-2 as a *method*. If I'm not being lazy, I refer to this code as a *method declaration*.

- ✔ The method declaration in Listing 3-2 has two parts. The first line (the part with `FixTheAlternator` in it, up to but not including the open curly brace) is called a *method header*. The rest of Listing 3-3 (the part surrounded by curly braces) is a *method body*.

- ✔ The term *method declaration* distinguishes the list of instructions in Listing 3-2 from the instruction in Listing 3-3, which is known as a *method call*.

A *method's declaration* tells the computer what happens if you call the method into action. A *method call* (a separate piece of code) tells the computer to actually call the method into action. A method's declaration and the method's call tend to be in different parts of the Java program.

The main method in a program

Figure 3-3 has a copy of the code from Listing 3-1. The bulk of the code contains the declaration of a method named `main`. (Just look for the word *main* in the code's method header.) For now, don't worry about the other words in the method header — the words `public`, `static`, `void`, `String`, and `args`. I explain these words in the next several chapters.

Like any Java method, the `main` method is a recipe.

```
How to make biscuits:
    Heat the oven.
    Roll the dough.
    Bake the rolled dough.
```

or

```
How to follow the main instructions for a Displayer:
    Print "You'll love Java!" on the screen.
```

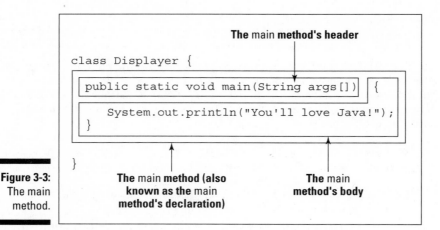

The main method's header

```
class Displayer {
    public static void main(String args[])  {
        System.out.println("You'll love Java!");
    }
}
```

Figure 3-3:
The main
method.

The main **method (also known as the** main **method's declaration)**

The main **method's body**

The word *main* plays a special role in Java. In particular, you never write code that explicitly calls a main method into action. The word *main* is the name of the method that is called into action automatically when the program begins running.

So look back at Figure 3-1. From within JCreator you choose Build⇨Execute Project to run the Displayer program. When the Displayer program runs, the computer automatically finds the program's main method and executes any instructions inside the method's body. In the Displayer program, the main method's body has only one instruction. That instruction tells the computer to print You'll love Java! on the screen. So in Figure 3-1, You'll love Java! appears in JCreator's General Output pane.

None of the instructions in a method is executed until the method is called into action. But, if you give a method the name *main,* that method is called into action automatically.

Almost every computer programming language has something akin to Java's methods. If you've worked with other languages, you may remember things like subprograms, procedures, functions, subroutines, subprocedures, or PERFORM statements. Whatever you call it in your favorite programming language, a method is a bunch of instructions collected and given a new name.

How you finally tell the computer to do something

Buried deep in the heart of Listing 3-1 is the single line that actually issues a direct instruction to the computer. The line, which is highlighted in Figure 3-4, tells the computer to display You'll love Java! This line is known as a statement. In Java, a *statement* is a direct instruction that tells the computer to do something (for example, display this text, put 7 in that memory location, make a window appear).

```
class Displayer {
    public static void main(String args[]) {
        System.out.println("You'll love Java!");
    }
}
```

Figure 3-4:
A Java
statement.

A statement (a call to the
System.out.println **method)**

Of course, Java has different kinds of statements. A method call, which I introduce in "The Java method," earlier in this chapter, is one of the many kinds of Java statements. Listing 3-3 shows you what a method call looks like, and Figure 3-4 also contains a method call that looks like this:

```
System.out.println("You'll love Java!");
```

When the computer starts executing this statement, the computer calls a method named System.out.println into action. (Yes, in Java, a name can have dots in it. The dots mean something.)

To learn the meaning behind the dots in Java names, see Chapter 7.

Figure 3-5 illustrates the System.out.println situation. Actually, two methods play active roles in the running of the Displayer program. Here's how they work:

- ✔ **There's a declaration for a main method.** I wrote the main method myself. This main method is called automatically whenever I start running the Displayer program.

- ✔ **There's a call to the System.out.println method.** The method call for the System.out.println method is the only statement in the body of the main method. In other words, calling the System.out.println method is the only thing on the main method's to-do list.

  The declaration for the System.out.println method is buried inside the official Java API. For a refresher on the Java API, see the sections, "The grammar and the common names" and "The words in a Java program," earlier in this chapter.

When I say things like "System.out.println is buried inside the API," I'm not doing justice to the API. True, you can ignore all the nitty-gritty Java code inside the API. All you need to remember is that System.out.println is defined somewhere inside that code. But I'm not being fair when I make the API code sound like something magical. The API is just another bunch of Java code. The statements in the API that tell the computer what it means to carry out a call to System.out.println look a lot like the Java code in Listing 3-1.

In Java, each statement (like the boxed line in Figure 3-4) ends with a semi-colon. Other lines in Figure 3-4 don't end with semicolons, because the other lines in Figure 3-4 aren't statements. For instance, the method header (the line with the word *main* in it) doesn't directly tell the computer to do anything. The method header announces, "Just in case you ever want to do main, the next few lines of code tell you how you'll do it."

Every complete Java statement ends with a semicolon.

```
101010000111000...
```

The computer calls your main
method automatically, then...

```
class Displayer {
    public static void main(String args[]) {
        System.out.println("You'll love Java!");
    }
}
```

...a statement in your main **method**
calls the System.out.println **method.**

Somewhere
inside the
JavaAPI...

```
public void println(String s) {
    ensureOpen();
    textOut.write(s);
    textOut.flushBuffer();
    ...
}
```

Figure 3-5:
Calling the
System.
out.
println
method.

Curly braces

Long ago, or maybe not so long ago, your schoolteachers told you how useful outlines are. With an outline, you can organize thoughts and ideas, help people see forests instead of trees, and generally show that you're a member of the Tidy Persons Club. Well, a Java program is like an outline. The program in Listing 3-1 starts with a big header line that says, "Here comes a class named `Displayer`." After that first big header is a subheader that announces, "Here comes a method named `main`."

Now, if a Java program is like an outline, why doesn't a program look like an outline? What takes the place of the Roman numerals, capital letters, and other things? The answer is twofold:

✔ In a Java program, curly braces enclose meaningful units of code.

✔ You, the programmer, can (and should) indent lines so that other programmers can see the outline form of your code at a glance.

In an outline, everything is subordinate to the item in Roman numeral I. In a Java program, everything is subordinate to the top line — the line with the word `class` in it. To indicate that everything else in the code is subordinate to this `class` line, you use curly braces. Everything else in the code goes inside these curly braces. (See Listing 3-4.)

Listing 3-4:   Curly Braces for a Java Class

```
class Displayer {

    public static void main(String args[]) {
        System.out.println("You'll love Java!");
    }
}
```

In an outline, some stuff is subordinate to a capital letter *A* item. In a Java program, some lines are subordinate to the method header. To indicate that something is subordinate to a method header, you use curly braces. (See Listing 3-5.)

Listing 3-5:   Curly Braces for a Java Method

```
class Displayer {

    public static void main(String args[]) {
        System.out.println("You'll love Java!");
    }
}
```

In an outline, some items are at the bottom of the food chain. In the `Displayer` class, the corresponding line is the line that begins with `System.out.println`. Accordingly, this `System.out.println` line goes inside all the other curly braces and is indented more than anything else.

Never lose sight of the fact that a Java program is, first and foremost, an outline.

If you put curly braces in the wrong places or omit curly braces where the braces should be, your program probably won't work at all. If your program works, it'll probably work incorrectly.

If you don't indent lines of code in an informative manner, your program will still work correctly, but neither you nor any other programmer will be able to figure out what you were thinking when you wrote the code.

If you're one of those visual thinkers, you could picture outlines of Java programs in your head. One friend of mine visualizes an actual numbered outline morphing into a Java program. (See Figure 3-6.) Another person, who shall remain nameless, uses more bizarre imagery. (See Figure 3-7.)

I. The Displayer **class**
    A. The main **method**
        1. Print "You'll love Java!"

I. class Displayer
    A. public static void main(String args[])
        1. System.out.println("You'll love Java!");

```
class Displayer {
    public static void main(String args[]) {
        System.out.println("You'll love Java!");
    }
}
```

Figure 3-6:
An outline turns into a Java program.

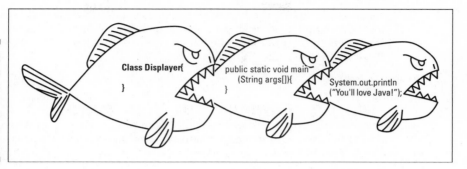

Figure 3-7:
A class is
bigger than
a method; a
method is
bigger than
a statement.

Class Displayer{

}

public static void main
(String args[]){

}

System.out.println
("You'll love Java!");

And Now, a Few Comments

People gather around campfires to hear the old legend about a programmer whose laziness got her into trouble. To maintain this programmer's anonymity, I call her Jane Pro. Jane worked many months to create the holy grail of computing — a program that thinks on its own. If completed, this program could work independently, learning new things without human intervention. Day after day, night after night, she labored to give the program that spark of creative, independent thought.

One day, when she was almost finished with the project, she received a disturbing piece of paper mail from her health insurance company. No, the mail wasn't about a serious illness. It was about a routine office visit. The insurance company's claim form had a place for her date of birth, as if her date of birth had changed since the last time she sent in a claim. She had absentmindedly scribbled 2006 as her year of birth, so the insurance company refused to pay the bill.

Jane dialed the insurance company's phone number. Within twenty minutes she was talking to a live person. "I'm sorry," said the live person. "To resolve this issue you must dial a different number." Well, you can guess what happened next. "I'm sorry. The other operator gave you the wrong number." And then "I'm sorry. You must call back the original phone number."

Five months later, Jane's ear ached, but after 800 hours on the phone she had finally gotten a tentative promise that the insurance company would eventually reprocess the claim. Elated as she was, she was anxious to get back to her computer programming project. Could she remember what all those lines of code were supposed to be doing?

No, she couldn't. She stared and stared at her own work and, like a dream that doesn't make sense the next morning, the code was now completely meaningless to her. She had written a million lines of code and not one line was accompanied by an informative explanatory comment. She had left no clues to help her understand what she'd been thinking; so in frustration, she abandoned the whole project.

Adding comments to your code

Listing 3-6 has an enhanced version of this chapter's sample program. In addition to all the keywords, identifiers, and punctuation, Listing 3-6 has text that's meant for human beings to read.

Listing 3-6:   Three Kinds of Comments

```
/*
 * Listing 3-6 in "Java For Dummies"
 *
 * Copyright 2006 Wiley Publishing, Inc. All rights reserved.
 */

/**
 * The Displayer class displays text on the computer screen.
 *
 * @author  Barry Burd
 * @version 1.6 02/21/06
 * @see     java.lang.System
 */
class Displayer {

    /**
     * Execution of the program starts at this main method.
     *
     * @param  args   (See Chapter 11.)
     */
    public static void main(String args[]) {
        System.out.println("I love Java!");  //Changed to "I"
    }
}
```

A *comment* is a special section of text inside a program. It is text whose purpose is to help people understand the program. A comment is part of a good program's documentation.

The Java programming language has three different kinds of comments:

- ✔ **Traditional comments:** The first five lines of Listing 3-6 form one *traditional* comment. The comment begins with /* and ends with */. Everything between the opening /* and the closing */ is for human eyes only. No information about "Java For Dummies" or Wiley Publishing, Inc. is translated by the compiler.

  To read about compilers, see Chapter 2.

  The second, third, and fourth lines in Listing 3-6 have extra asterisks (*). I call them extra because these asterisks aren't required when you create a comment. They just make the comment look pretty. I include them in Listing 3-6 because, for some reason that I don't entirely understand, most Java programmers add these extra asterisks.

- ✔ **End-of-line comments:** The text //Changed to "I" in Listing 3-6 is an *end-of-line* comment. An end-of-line comment starts with two slashes, and goes to the end of a line of type. Once again, no text inside the end-of-line comment gets translated by the compiler.

- ✔ **Javadoc comments:** A *javadoc* comment begins with a slash and two asterisks (/**). Listing 3-6 has two javadoc comments — one with text The Displayer class . . . and another with text Execution of the program. . . .

  A javadoc comment is a special kind of traditional comment. A javadoc comment is meant to be read by people who never even look at the Java code. But that doesn't make sense. How can you see the javadoc comments in Listing 3-6 if you never look at Listing 3-6?

  Well, a certain program called *javadoc* (what else?) can find all the javadoc comments in Listing 3-6 and turn these comments into a nice-looking Web page. The page is shown in Figure 3-8.

Javadoc comments are great. Here are several great things about them:

- ✔ The only person who has to look at a piece of Java code is the programmer who writes the code. Other people who use the code can find out what the code does by viewing the automatically generated Web page.

- ✔ Because other people don't look at the Java code, other people don't make changes to the Java code. (In other words, other people don't introduce errors into the existing Java code.)

- ✔ Because other people don't look at the Java code, other people don't have to decipher the inner workings of the Java code. All these people need to know about the code is what they read in the code's Web page.

✔ The programmer doesn't create two separate things — some Java code over here and some documentation about the code over there. Instead, the programmer creates one piece of Java code and embeds the documentation (in the form of javadoc comments) right inside the code.

✔ Best of all, the generation of Web pages from javadoc comments is done automatically. So everyone's documentation has the same format. No matter whose Java code you use, you find out about that code by reading a page like the one in Figure 3-8. That's good because the format in Figure 3-8 is familiar to anyone who uses Java.

You can generate your own Web pages from the javadoc comments that you put in your code. To discover how, visit this book's Web site.

Package **Class** Tree Deprecated Index Help
PREV CLASS   NEXT CLASS   FRAMES   NO FRAMES   All Classes
SUMMARY: NESTED | FIELD | CONSTR | METHOD   DETAIL: FIELD | CONSTR | METHOD

Class Displayer

java.lang.Object
 └ **Displayer**

---

class **Displayer**
extends Object

The Displayer class displays text on the computer screen.

See Also:
    System

Constructor Summary

Displayer()

Method Summary

static void | **main**(String[] args)
             Execution of the program starts at this main method.

Methods inherited from class java.lang.Object

clone, equals, finalize, getClass, hashCode, notify, notifyAll, toString, wait, wait, wait

---

Constructor Detail

Displayer

Displayer()

Method Detail

main

public static void **main**(String[] args)

    Execution of the program starts at this main method.

    Parameters:
        args - (See Chapter 11.)

Package **Class** Tree Deprecated Index Help
PREV CLASS   NEXT CLASS   FRAMES   NO FRAMES   All Classes
SUMMARY: NESTED | FIELD | CONSTR | METHOD   DETAIL: FIELD | CONSTR | METHOD

Figure 3-8:
The javadoc page generated from the code in Listing 3-6.

What's Barry's excuse?

For years, I've been telling my students to put comments in their code, and for years I've been creating sample code (like the code in Listing 3-1) with no comments in it. Why?

Three little words: "Know your audience." When you write complicated, real-life code, your audience is other programmers, information technology managers, and people who need help deciphering what you've done. When I write simple samples of code for this book, my audience is you — the novice Java programmer. Instead of reading my comments, your best strategy is to stare at my Java statements — the statements that Java's compiler deciphers. That's why I put so few comments in this book's listings.

Besides, I'm a little lazy.

Finding javadoc pages

In Chapter 2, I encourage you to download a copy of the official Java API documentation. This API documentation is a huge collection of Web pages created automatically from javadoc comments. To access this documentation, do the following:

1. **Follow Steps 1 and 2 in the step list that comes immediately after Listing 3-1 in this chapter.**

   The code of Listing 3-1 appears in JCreator's Editor pane.

2. **In the Editor pane, right-click the word** System. **In the resulting context menu, choose Show JDK Help.**

   The javadoc page for System appears in JCreator's Editor pane. To see more of this page, use the pane's scrollbar. The stuff on this page may not make much sense to you now, but as you read more of this book, things become clearer.

   For tips on reading and understanding Java's API documentation, see this book's Web site.

3. **Click the Displayer.java tab at the top of the Editor pane.**

   The code of Listing 3-1 appears once again.

4. **In the Editor pane, right-click the word** println, **and choose Show JDK Help from the context menu that appears.**

   A dialog box appears. The dialog box shows you a list of things in the Java API, each having the same name println.

5. **In the dialog box's list, double-click the item labeled** println(String - Method in java.io.PrintStream.

The documentation for the `println` method appears in the Editor pane.

Using comments to experiment with your code

You may hear programmers talk about *commenting out* certain parts of their code. When you're writing a program and something's not working correctly, it often helps to try removing some of the code. If nothing else, you find out what happens when that suspicious code is removed. Of course, you may not like what happens when the code is removed, so you don't want to delete the code completely. Instead, you turn your ordinary Java statements into comments. For instance, you turn the statement

```
System.out.println("I love Java!");
```

into the comment

```
// System.out.println("I love Java!");
```

This keeps the Java compiler from seeing the code while you try to figure out what's wrong with your program.

Traditional comments aren't very useful for commenting out code. The big problem is that you can't put one traditional comment inside of another. For instance, suppose you want to comment out the following statements:

```
System.out.println("Parents,");
System.out.println("pick your");
/*
 * Intentionally displays on four separate lines
 */
System.out.println("battles");
System.out.println("carefully!");
```

If you try to turn this code into one traditional comment, you get the following mess:

```
/*
  System.out.println("Parents,");
  System.out.println("pick your");
  /*
   * Intentionally displays on four separate lines
   */
  System.out.println("battles");
  System.out.println("carefully!");
*/
```

The first */ (after Intentionally displays) ends the traditional comment prematurely. Then the battles and carefully statements aren't commented out, and the last */ chokes the compiler.

So the best way to comment out code is to use end-of-line comments. But typing two slashes for each of ten lines can be tedious. Fortunately, JCreator has a good shortcut. Here's how it works:

1. **Select the lines that you want to comment out.**

2. **From the JCreator menu bar, choose Edit⇨Format⇨Increase Comment Indent.**

When you do this, each selected line becomes an end-of-line comment. End-of-line comments can contain traditional comments (and end-of-line comments can contain other end-of-line comments) so you can comment out the Parents, pick your battles carefully! code with no unwanted side effects. If you decide later to uncomment the code, that's easy, too:

1. **Select the lines that you no longer want to be commented out.**

2. **From the JCreator menu bar, choose Edit⇨Format⇨Decrease Comment Indent.**

Typing Your Own Code

Chapter 2 is about running someone else's Java code (code that you download from this book's Web site). But eventually, you'll write code on your own. This section shows you how to create code with the JCreator development environment.

The version of JCreator on this book's CD-ROM has a specially customized MyProjects directory. The MyProjects directory contains several ready-made workspaces. One of these workspaces (named *MyWorkspace*) has no projects in it. Here's how you create a project in MyWorkspace:

1. **Launch JCreator.**

2. **From JCreator's menu bar, choose File⇨Open Workspace.**

   An Open dialog box appears.

3. **In the Open dialog box, select MyWorkspace.jcw (or simply MyWorkspace). Then click Open.**

   Clicking Open may coax out a message box asking whether you want to "Save the workspace modifications?" If so, click Yes. Clicking Open may coax out another box asking if you want to ". . . close all document Windows?" If so, click Yes.

In `MyWorkspace.jcw`, the extension `.jcw` stands for "JCreator workspace."

After clicking Open, you see MyWorkspace in JCreator's File View pane. The next step is to create a new project within MyWorkspace.

4. **In the File View pane, right-click MyWorkspace. Then choose Add New Project from the context menu that appears, as shown in Figure 3-9.**

   JCreator's Project Wizard opens. (See Figure 3-10.)

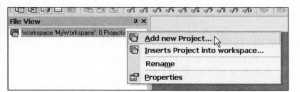

Figure 3-9: Getting JCreator to add a new project.

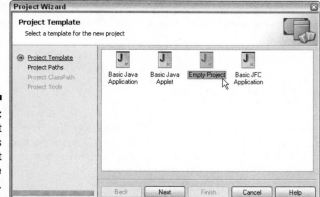

Figure 3-10: The Project Wizard's Project Template tab.

5. **In the wizard's Project Template tab, select the Empty Project icon, and then click Next.**

   After clicking Next, you see the wizard's Project Paths tab, as shown in Figure 3-11.

6. **In the Name field, type** MyFirstProject.

   You can add blank spaces, making the name My First Project, but I don't recommend it.

7. **Make sure that the Add to Current Workspace and Local Folder System radio buttons are selected, and then click Finish.**

   You may have to click Finish twice — once to tell JCreator to create the project, and a second time to tell JCreator to close the Project Wizard.

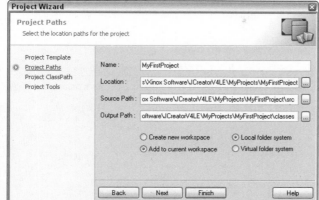

Figure 3-11:
The Project
Wizard's
Project
Paths tab.

If you click Next instead of Finish, you see some other options that you don't need right now. So to avoid any confusion, just click Finish.

Clicking Finish brings you back to JCreator's work area, with MyFirstProject set in bold. The bold typeface means that MyFirstProject is the active project. The next step is to create a new Java source code file.

8. **In the File View pane, right-click MyFirstProject. Then choose Add⇨ New Class from the context menu that appears, as shown in Figure 3-12.**

   JCreator's Class Wizard opens. (See Figure 3-13.)

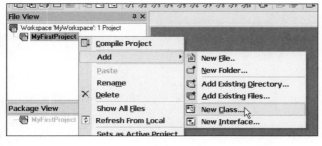

Figure 3-12:
Getting
JCreator
to add a
new class.

Like every other windowed environment, JCreator provides many ways to accomplish the same task. Instead of right-clicking MyFirstProject, you can go to the menu bar and choose File⇨New⇨Class. But right-clicking a project has a small benefit. If you right-click the name of a project, the newly created class is without a doubt in that project. If you use the menu bar instead, the newly created class goes in whichever project happens to be the active project. So if your workspace contains many projects, you can accidentally put the new class into the wrong project.

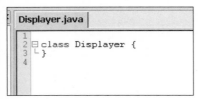

Figure 3-13:
The Class
Wizard's
Class
Settings tab.

9. **In the Class Wizard's Name field, type the name of your new class.**

   For this first project, I highly recommend the name `Displayer`. To be safe, use an uppercase letter *D* and lowercase letters for all the other characters. (Refer to Figure 3-13.)

10. **Skip everything in the Class Wizard except the Name field. (In other words, click Finish.)**

    Clicking Finish brings you back to JCreator's work area. Now the Editor pane has a tab named `Displayer.java`. For your convenience, the `Displayer.java` tab already has a tiny bit of code in it. (See Figure 3-14.)

Figure 3-14:
JCreator
writes a bit
of code in
the Editor
pane.

```
Displayer.java

1
2  class Displayer {
3  }
4
```

11. **Type your new Java program.**

    Add your code to the code in JCreator's Editor pane. For this first project, I recommend copying the code in Listing 3-1 exactly as you see it.

    • Spell each word exactly the way I spell it in Listing 3-1.

    • Capitalize each word exactly the way I do in Listing 3-1.

    • Include all the punctuation symbols — the curly braces, the semicolon, everything.

12. From the menu bar, choose Build⇨Compile Project.

If you typed everything correctly, you see the comforting `Process completed` message, with no error messages, at the bottom of JCreator's work area. The text appears in JCreator's Build Output pane, which now covers up the old General Output pane. (See Figure 3-15.)

Figure 3-15:
The result of
a successful
compilation.

```
Build Output                                                                              ⁊ ×
----------------------Configuration: MyThirdProject - JDK version 1.6.0 <Default> - <Default>------
Process completed.
```

When you choose Build⇨Compile Project, JCreator compiles whichever project is currently active. Only one project at a time is active. So if your workspace contains several projects, make sure that the project you want to compile is currently the active project.

13. Check for error messages at the bottom of JCreator's work area.

If, in Step 11, you didn't type the code exactly as it's shown in Listing 3-1, you see some error messages in the Task List pane. (Like so many other things, the Task List pane appears at the bottom of JCreator's work area.)

Each error message refers to a specific place in your Java code. To jump the cursor to that place in the Editor pane, double-click the message in the Task List pane. Compare everything you see, character by character, with my code in Listing 3-1. Don't miss a single detail, including spelling, punctuation, and uppercase versus lowercase.

14. Make any changes or corrections to the code in the Editor pane. Then repeat Steps 12 and 13.

When at last you see the `Process completed` message with no error messages, you're ready to run the program.

15. From the menu bar choose Build⇨Execute Project.

That does the trick. Your new Java program runs in JCreator's General Output pane. If you're running the code in Listing 3-1, you see the `You'll love Java!` message in Figure 3-1. And believe me; messages like this are never wrong.

Part II
Writing Your Own Java Programs

The 5th Wave   By Rich Tennant

"We met on the Internet and I absolutely fell in love with his syntax."

In this part . . .

In this part, you dig in and get dirty by writing some programs and finding out what Java really feels like. Some of the stuff in this part is specific to Java, but lots of the material is just plain-old, generic, computer programming. Here you concentrate on details — details about data, logic, and program flow. After you've read this part and practiced some of the techniques, you can write all kinds of interesting Java programs.

Chapter 4

Making the Most of Variables and Their Values

● ●

In This Chapter

▶ Assigning values to things

▶ Making things store certain types of values

▶ Applying operators to get new values

● ●

*T*he following conversation between Van Doren and Vieira never took place:

> *Charles:* A sea squirt eats its brain, turning itself from an animal into a plant.
>
> *Meredith:* Is that your final answer, Charles?
>
> *Charles:* Yes, it is.
>
> *Meredith:* How much money do you have in your account today, Charles?
>
> *Charles:* I have fifty dollars and twenty-two cents in my checking account.
>
> *Meredith:* Well, you better call the IRS, because I'm putting another million dollars in your account. What do you think of that, Charles?
>
> *Charles:* I owe it all to honesty, diligence, and hard work, Meredith.

Some aspects of this dialogue can be represented in Java by a few lines of code.

Varying a Variable

No matter how you acquire your million dollars, you can use a variable to tally your wealth. The code is shown in Listing 4-1.

Listing 4-1:   Using a Variable

```
amountInAccount = 50.22;
amountInAccount = amountInAccount + 1000000.00;
```

The code in Listing 4-1 makes use of the `amountInAccount` variable. A *variable* is a placeholder. You can stick a number like 50.22 into a variable. After you place a number in the variable, you can change your mind and put a different number into the variable. (That's what varies in a variable.) Of course, when you put a new number in a variable, the old number is no longer there. If you didn't save the old number somewhere else, the old number is gone.

Figure 4-1 gives a before-and-after picture of the code in Listing 4-1. After the first statement in Listing 4-1 is executed, the variable `amountInAccount` has the number 50.22 in it. Then, after the second statement of Listing 4-1 is executed, the `amountInAccount` variable suddenly has 1000050.22 in it. When you think about a variable, picture a place in the computer's memory where wires and transistors store 50.22, 1000050.22, or whatever. In the left side of Figure 4-1, imagine that the box with the number 50.22 in it is surrounded by millions of other such boxes.

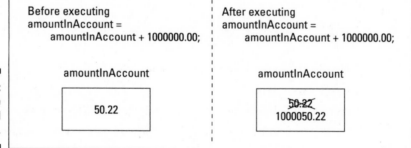

Figure 4-1:
A variable
(before and
after).

Now you need some terminology. The thing stored in a variable is called a *value*. A variable's value can change during the run of a program (when Meredith gives you a million bucks, for instance). The value that's stored in a variable isn't necessarily a number. (You can, for instance, create a variable that always stores a letter.) The kind of value that's stored in a variable is a variable's *type*.

You can read more about types in the section "Understanding the Types of Values That Variables May Have," later in this chapter.

A subtle, almost unnoticeable difference exists between a variable and a variable's *name*. Even in formal writing, I often use the word *variable* when I mean *variable name*. Strictly speaking, `amountInAccount` is a variable name, and all the memory storage associated with `amountInAccount` (including the type that `amountInAccount` has and whatever value `amountInAccount` currently represents) is the variable itself. If you think this distinction between *variable* and *variable name* is too subtle for you to worry about, join the club.

Every variable name is an identifier — a name that you can make up in your own code. In preparing Listing 4-1, I made up the name *amountInAccount*.

For more information on the kinds of names in a Java program, see Chapter 3.

Before the sun sets on Listing 4-1, you need to notice one more part of the listing. The listing has `50.22` and `1000000.00` in it. Anybody in his or her right mind would call these things *numbers,* but in a Java program it helps to call these things *literals*.

And what's so literal about `50.22` and `1000000.00`? Well, think about the variable `amountInAccount` in Listing 4-1. The variable `amountInAccount` stands for 50.22 some of the time, but it stands for 1000050.22 the rest of the time. You could sort of use the word *number* to talk about `amountInAccount`. But really, what `amountInAccount` stands for depends on the fashion of the moment. On the other hand, `50.22` literally stands for the value $50^{22}/_{100}$.

A variable's value changes; a literal's value doesn't.

Assignment Statements

Statements like the ones in Listing 4-1 are called *assignment statements*. In an assignment statement, you assign a value to something. In many cases, this something is a variable.

I recommend getting into the habit of reading assignment statements from right to left. For instance, the first line in Listing 4-1 says,

```
                          "Assign 50.22...
amountInAccount    =      50.22;
...to the
amountInAccount
variable."
```

The second line in Listing 4-1 is just a bit more complicated. Reading the second line from right to left, you get

```
                   "Add 1000000.00 to the value that's
                   already in the amountInAccount
                   variable...
```

```
amountInAccount    =    amountInAccount + 1000000.00;
...and make
that number
(1000050.22) be
the new value of the
amountInAccount variable."
```

In an assignment statement, the thing being assigned a value is always on the left side of the equal sign.

Understanding the Types of Values That Variables May Have

Have you seen the TV commercials that make you think you're flying around among the circuits inside a computer? Pretty cool, eh? These commercials show 0s (zeros) and 1s sailing by because 0s and 1s are the only things that computers can really deal with. When you think a computer is storing the letter *J,* the computer is really storing 01001010. Everything inside the computer is a sequence of 0s and 1s. As every computer geek knows, a 0 or 1 is called a *bit.*

As it turns out, the sequence 01001010, which stands for the letter *J,* can also stand for the number 74. The same sequence can also stand for $1.0369608636003646 \times 10^{-43}$. In fact, if the bits are interpreted as screen pixels, the same sequence can be used to represent the dots shown in Figure 4-2. The meaning of 01001010 depends on the way the software interprets this sequence of 0s and 1s.

Figure 4-2:
An extreme close-up of eight black-and-white screen pixels.

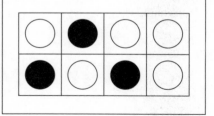

So how do you tell the computer what 01001010 stands for? The answer is in the concept of *type.* The type of a variable is the range of values that the variable is permitted to store.

I copied the lines from Listing 4-1 and put them into a complete Java program. The program is in Listing 4-2. When I run the program in Listing 4-2, I get the output shown in Figure 4-3.

Listing 4-2:   A Program Uses amountInAccount

```
import static java.lang.System.out;

class Millionaire {
    public static void main(String args[]) {
        double amountInAccount;

        amountInAccount = 50.22;
        amountInAccount = amountInAccount + 1000000.00;

        out.print("You have $");
        out.print(amountInAccount);
        out.println(" in your account.");
    }
}
```

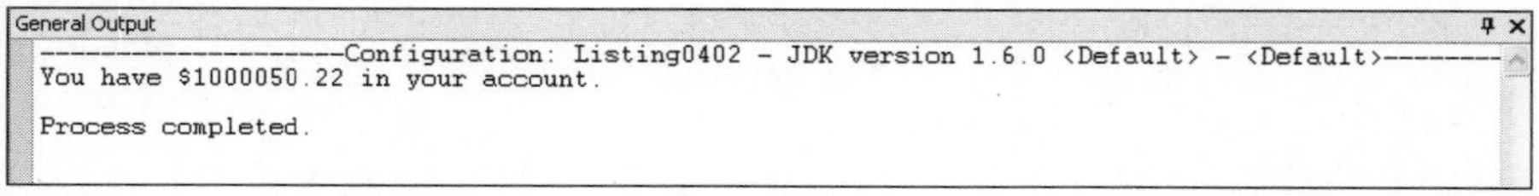

Figure 4-3:
Running the
program in
Listing 4-2.

```
General Output                                                                                      ╪ ×
-----------------------Configuration: Listing0402 - JDK version 1.6.0 <Default> - <Default>---------
You have $1000050.22 in your account.

Process completed.
```

In Listing 4-2, look at the first line in the body of the `main` method.

```
double amountInAccount;
```

This line is called a *variable declaration.* Putting this line in your program is like saying, "I'm declaring my intention to have a variable named *amountIn Account* in my program." This line reserves the name *amountInAccount* for your use in the program.

In this variable declaration, the word *double* is a Java keyword. This word *double* tells the computer what kinds of values you intend to store in `amountInAccount`. In particular, the word *double* stands for numbers between -1.8×10^{308} and 1.8×10^{308}. (These are enormous numbers with 308 zeros before the decimal point. Only the world's richest people write checks with 308 zeros in them. The second of these numbers is one-point-eight gazazzo-zillion-kaskillion. The number 1.8×10^{308}, a constant defined by the International Bureau of Weights and Measures, is the number of eccentric computer programmers between Sunnyvale, California, and the M31 Andromeda Galaxy.)

Digits beyond the decimal point

Java has two different types that have digits beyond the decimal point: type `double` and type `float`. So what's the difference? When you declare a variable to be of type `double`, you're telling the computer to keep track of 64 bits when it stores the variable's values. When you declare a variable to be of type `float`, the computer keeps track of only 32 bits.

You could change Listing 4-2 and declare `amountInAccount` to be of type `float`.

```
float amountInAccount;
```

Surely, 32 bits are enough to store a small number like 50.22? Well, they are and they aren't. You could easily store 50.00 with only 32 bits. Heck, you could store 50.00 with only 6 bits. The size of the number doesn't matter. It's the accuracy that matters. In a 64-bit double variable, you're using most of the bits to store stuff beyond the decimal point. To store the .22 part of 50.22, you need more than the measly 32 bits that you get with type `float`.

Do you really believe what you just read — that it takes more than 32 bits to store .22? To help convince you, I made a few changes to the code in Listing 4-2. I made `amountInAccount` be of type `float`, and the output I got was

```
You have $1000050.25 in your
   account.
```

Compare this with the output in Figure 4-3. When I switch from type `double` to type `float`, Charles has an extra three cents in his account. By changing to the 32-bit `float` type, I've clobbered the accuracy in the `amountInAccount` variable's hundredths place. That's bad.

Another difficulty with `float` values is purely cosmetic. Look again at the literals, `50.22` and `1000000.00`, in Listing 4-2. The Laws of Java say that literals like these take up 64 bits each. This means that if you declare `amountInAccount` to be of type `float`, you're going to run into trouble. You'll have trouble stuffing those 64-bit literals into your little 32-bit `amountInAccount` variable. To compensate, you can switch from `double` literals to `float` literals by adding an `F` to each double literal, but a number with an extra `F` at the end looks funny.

```
float amountInAccount;
    amountInAccount =
  50.22F;
    amountInAccount =
  amountInAccount +
  1000000.00F;
```

To experiment with numbers, visit `http://babbage.cs.qc.edu/courses/cs341/IEEE-754.html`. The page takes any number that you enter and shows you how the number would be represented as 32 bits and as 64 bits.

More important than the humongous range of the double keyword's numbers is the fact that a `double` value can have digits beyond the decimal point. After you declare `amountInAccount` to be of type `double`, you can store all sorts of numbers in `amountInAccount`. You can store 50.22, 0.02398479, or −3.0. In Listing 4-2, if I hadn't declared `amountInAccount` to be of type `double`, I may not have been able to store 50.22. Instead, I would have had to store plain old 50, without any digits beyond the decimal point.

Another type — type `float` — also allows you to have numbers after the decimal point, but this type isn't as accurate. (See the sidebar, "Digits beyond the decimal point," for the full story.) Don't sweat the choice between `float` and `double`. For most programs, just use `double`.

An Import Declaration

It's always good to announce your intentions up front. Consider the following classroom lecture:

> *"Today, in our History of Film course, we'll be discussing the career of actor* **Lionel Herbert Blythe Barrymore**.
>
> *"Born in Philadelphia,* **Barrymore** *appeared in more than 200 films, including* It's a Wonderful Life, Key Largo, *and* Dr. Kildare's Wedding Day. *In addition,* **Barrymore** *was a writer, composer, and director.* **Barrymore** *did the voice of Ebenezer Scrooge every year on radio. . . ."*

Interesting stuff, heh? Now compare the paragraphs above with a lecture in which the instructor doesn't begin by introducing the subject:

> *"Welcome once again to the History of Film.*
>
> *"Born in Philadelphia,* **Lionel Barrymore** *appeared in more than 200 films, including* It's a Wonderful Life, Key Largo, *and* Dr. Kildare's Wedding Day. *In addition,* **Barrymore (not Ethel, John, or Drew)** *was a writer, composer, and director.* **Lionel Barrymore** *did the voice of Ebenezer Scrooge every year on radio. . . ."*

Without a proper introduction, a speaker may have to remind you constantly that the discussion is about Lionel Barrymore and not about some other Barrymore. The same is true in a Java program. Compare some code from Listings 3-1 and 4-2. From Listing 3-1:

```
class Displayer {

        System.out.println("You'll love Java!");
```

and from Listing 4-2:

```
import static java.lang.System.out;

class Millionaire {

        out.print("You have $");
        out.print(amountInAccount);
        out.println(" in your account.");
```

In Listing 4-2, you announce in the introduction (in the *import declaration*) that you're using `System.out` in your Java class. You clarify what you mean by `System` with the full name `java.lang.System`. (Hey! Didn't the first lecturer clarify with the full name "Lionel Herbert Blythe Barrymore?") After having announced your intentions in the import declaration, you can use the abbreviated name *out* in your Java class code.

The details of this import stuff can be pretty nasty. So for now, just paste the import declaration in Listing 4-2 at the top of your Java programs. (Don't bother pasting this import declaration into a program that doesn't use `System.out`. It probably wouldn't hurt anything, but it would look very strange to a veteran Java programmer.)

No single section in this book can present the entire story about import declarations. To begin untangling some of the import declaration's subtleties, see Chapters 5, 9, and 10.

Displaying Text

The last three statements in Listing 4-2 use a neat formatting trick. You want to display several different things on a single line on the screen. You put these things in separate statements. All but the last of the statements are calls to `out.print`. (The last statement is a call to `out.println`.) Calls to `out.print` display text on part of a line and then leave the cursor at the end of the current line. After executing `out.print`, the cursor is still at the end of the same line, so the next `out.whatever` can continue printing on that same line. With several calls to print capped off by a single call to `println`, the result is just one nice-looking line of output. (Refer to Figure 4-3.)

A call to `out.print` writes some things and leaves the cursor sitting at the end of the line of output. A call to `out.println` writes things and then finishes the job by moving the cursor to the start of a brand new line of output.

Numbers without Decimal Points

"In 1995, the average family had 2.3 children."

At this point, a wise guy always remarks that no real family has exactly 2.3 children. Clearly, whole numbers have a role in this world. So, in Java, you can declare a variable to store nothing but whole numbers. Listing 4-3 shows a program that uses whole number variables.

Listing 4-3:   Using the int Type

```
import static java.lang.System.out;

class ElevatorFitter {

    public static void main(String args[]) {
        int weightOfAPerson;
        int elevatorWeightLimit;
        int numberOfPeople;

        weightOfAPerson = 150;
        elevatorWeightLimit = 1400;
        numberOfPeople =
            elevatorWeightLimit / weightOfAPerson;

        out.print("You can fit ");
        out.print(numberOfPeople);
        out.println(" people on the elevator.");
    }
}
```

The story behind the program in Listing 4-3 takes some heavy-duty explaining. So here goes:

You have a hotel elevator whose weight capacity is 1,400 pounds. One weekend, the hotel hosts the Brickenchicker family reunion. A certain branch of the Brickenchicker family has been blessed with identical dectuplets (ten siblings, all with the same physical characteristics). Normally, each of the Brickenchicker dectuplets weighs exactly 145 pounds. But on Saturday, the family has a big catered lunch, and, because lunch included strawberry shortcake, each of the Brickenchicker dectuplets now weighs 150 pounds. Immediately after lunch, all ten of the Brickenchicker dectuplets arrive at the elevator at exactly the same time. (Why not? All ten of them think alike.) So, the question is, how many of the dectuplets can fit on the elevator?

Now remember, if you put one ounce more than 1,400 pounds of weight on the elevator, the elevator cable breaks, plunging all dectuplets on the elevator to their sudden (and costly) deaths.

The answer to the Brickenchicker riddle (the output of the program of Listing 4-3) is shown in Figure 4-4.

Figure 4-4: Save the Brickenchickers.

```
General Output                                                                    ᄆ x
----------------------Configuration: Listing0403 - JDK version 1.6.0 <Default> - <Default>---------
You can fit 9 people on the elevator.

Process completed.
```

Four ways to store whole numbers

Java has four different types of whole numbers. The types are called `byte`, `short`, `int`, and `long`. Unlike the complicated story about the accuracy of types `float` and `double`, the only thing that matters when you choose among the whole number types is the size of the number that you're trying to store. If you want to use numbers larger than 127, don't use `byte`.

To store numbers larger than 32767, don't use `short`.

Most of the time, you'll use `int`. But if you need to store numbers larger than 2147483647, forsake `int` in favor of `long`. (A long number can be as big as 9223372036854775807.) For the whole story, see Table 4-1.

At the core of the Brickenchicker elevator problem, you've got whole numbers — numbers with no digits beyond the decimal point. When you divide 1,400 by 150, you get 9⅓, but you shouldn't take the ⅓ seriously. No matter how hard you try, you can't squeeze an extra 50 pounds worth of Brickenchicker dectuplet onto the elevator. This fact is reflected nicely in Java. In Listing 4-3, all three variables (`weightOfAPerson`, `elevatorWeightLimit`, and `numberOfPeople`) are of type `int`. An `int` value is a whole number. When you divide one `int` value by another (as you do with the slash in Listing 4-3), you get another `int`. When you divide 1,400 by 150, you get 9 — not 9⅓. You see this in Figure 4-4. Taken together, the following statements put the number 9 on the computer screen:

```
numberOfPeople =
    elevatorWeightLimit / weightOfAPerson;

out.print(numberOfPeople);
```

Combining Declarations and Initializing Variables

Look back at Listing 4-3. In that listing, you see three variable declarations — one for each of the program's three `int` variables. I could have done the same thing with just one declaration:

```
int weightOfAPerson, elevatorWeightLimit, numberOfPeople;
```

If two variables have completely different types, you can't create both variables in the same declaration. For instance, to create an `int` variable named *weightOfFred* and a `double` variable named *amountInFredsAccount,* you need two separate variable declarations.

You can give variables their starting values in a declaration. In Listing 4-3 for instance, one declaration can replace several lines in the `main` method (all but the calls to `print` and `println`).

```
int weightOfAPerson = 150, elevatorWeightLimit = 1400,
    numberOfPeople = elevatorWeightLimit /
        weightOfAPerson;
```

When you do this, you don't say that you're assigning values to variables. The pieces of the declarations with equal signs in them aren't really called assignment statements. Instead, you say that you're *initializing* the variables. Believe it or not, keeping this distinction in mind is helpful.

Like everything else in life, initializing a variable has advantages and disadvantages:

- ✔ **When you combine six lines of Listing 4-3 into just one declaration, the code becomes more concise.** Sometimes, concise code is easier to read. Sometimes it's not. As a programmer, it's your judgment call.

- ✔ **By initializing a variable, you may automatically avoid certain programming errors.** For an example, see Chapter 7.

- ✔ **In some situations, you have no choice. The nature of your code forces you either to initialize or not to initialize.** For an example that doesn't lend itself to variable initialization, see the deleting-evidence program in Chapter 6.

The Atoms: Java's Primitive Types

The words *int* and *double,* which I describe in the previous sections, are examples of *primitive types* (also known as *simple* types) in Java. The Java language has exactly eight primitive types. As a newcomer to Java, you can pretty much ignore all but four of these types. (As programming languages go, Java is nice and compact that way.) The complete list of primitive types is shown in Table 4-1.

Table 4-1	Java's Primitive Types	
Type Name	*What a Literal Looks Like*	*Range of Values*
Whole number types		
byte	(byte)42	−128 to 127
short	(short)42	−32768 to 32767

(continued)

Table 4-1 *(continued)*

Type Name	What a Literal Looks Like	Range of Values
int	42	–2147483648 to 2147483647
long	42L	–9223372036854775808 to 9223372036854775807
Decimal number types		
float	42.0F	-3.4×10^{38} to 3.4×10^{38}
double	42.0	-1.8×10^{308} to 1.8×10^{308}
Character type		
char	'A'	Thousands of characters, glyphs, and symbols
Logical type		
boolean	true	true, false

The types that you shouldn't ignore are int, double, char, and boolean. Previous sections in this chapter cover the int and double types. So, this section covers char and boolean types.

The char type

Not so long ago, people thought computers existed only for doing big number-crunching calculations. Nowadays, with word processors, nobody thinks that way anymore. So, if you haven't been in a cryogenic freezing chamber for the last 20 years, you know that computers store letters, punctuation symbols, and other characters.

The Java type that's used to store characters is called *char*. Listing 4-4 has a simple program that uses the char type. The output of the program of Listing 4-4 is shown in Figure 4-5.

Listing 4-4: Using the char Type

```
class CharDemo {

    public static void main(String args[]) {
        char myLittleChar = 'b';
        char myBigChar = Character.toUpperCase(myLittleChar);
        System.out.println(myBigChar);
    }
}
```

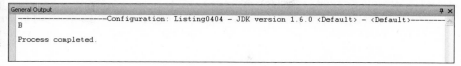

Figure 4-5:
An exciting
run of the
program of
Listing 4-4.

```
General Output                                                                    ⊐ ×
-----------------------Configuration: Listing0404 – JDK version 1.6.0 <Default> – <Default>--------
B

Process completed.
```

In Listing 4-4, the first initialization stores the letter *b* in the variable
`myLittleChar`. In the initialization, notice how *b* is surrounded by single
quote marks. In Java, every `char` literal starts and ends with a single quote
mark.

In a Java program, single quote marks surround the letter in a `char` literal.

If you need help sorting out the terms *assignment, declaration,* and *initialization,* see the "Combining Declarations and Initializing Variables" section, earlier in this chapter.

In the second initialization of Listing 4-4, the program calls an API method
whose name is *Character.toUpperCase*. The `Character.toUpperCase`
method does just what its name suggests — the method produces the uppercase equivalent of the letter *b*. This uppercase equivalent (the letter *B*) is
assigned to the `myBigChar` variable, and the *B* that's in `myBigChar` is
printed on the screen.

For an introduction to the Java Application Programming Interface (API), see
Chapter 3.

If you're tempted to write the following statement,

```
char myLittleChars = 'barry';   //Don't do this
```

please resist the temptation. You can't store more than one letter at a time in
a `char` variable, and you can't put more than one letter between a pair of
single quotes. If you're trying to store words or sentences (not just single letters), you need to use something called a *String*.

For a look at Java's `String` type, see the section, "The Molecules and
Compounds: Reference Types," later in this chapter.

If you're used to writing programs in other languages, you may be aware of
something called ASCII Character Encoding. Most languages use ASCII; Java
uses Unicode. In the old ASCII representation, each character takes up only 8
bits, but in Unicode, each character takes up 8, 16, or 32 bits. Whereas ASCII
stores the letters of the familiar Roman (English) alphabet, Unicode has room
for characters from most of the world's commonly spoken languages. The

only problem is that some of the Java API methods are geared specially toward 16-bit Unicode. Occasionally, this bites you in the back (or it bytes you in the back, as the case may be). If you're using a method to write `Hello` on the screen and `H e l l o` shows up instead, check the method's documentation for mention of Unicode characters.

It's worth noticing that the two methods, `Character.toUpperCase` and `System.out.println`, are used quite differently in Listing 4-4. The method `Character.toUpperCase` is called as part of an initialization or an assignment statement, but the method `System.out.println` is called on its own. To find out more about this, see Chapter 7.

The boolean type

A variable of type `boolean` stores one of two values — `true` or `false`. Listing 4-5 demonstrates the use of a `boolean` variable. The output of the program in Listing 4-5 is shown in Figure 4-6.

Listing 4-5:   Using the boolean Type

```
import static java.lang.System.out;

class ElevatorFitter2 {

    public static void main(String args[]) {
        out.println("True or False?");
        out.println("You can fit all ten of the");
        out.println("Brickenchicker dectuplets");
        out.println("on the elevator:");
        out.println();

        int weightOfAPerson = 150;
        int elevatorWeightLimit = 1400;
        int numberOfPeople =
            elevatorWeightLimit / weightOfAPerson;

        boolean allTenOkay = numberOfPeople >= 10;

        out.println(allTenOkay);
    }
}
```

Figure 4-6:
The
Bricken-
chicker
dectuplets
strike again.

```
General Output                                                                    ₽ ×
-----------------Configuration: Listing0405 - JDK version 1.6.0 <Default> - <Default>-------
True or False?
You can fit all ten of the
Brickenchicker dectuplets
on the elevator:

false

Process completed.
```

In Listing 4-5, the `allTenOkay` variable is of type `boolean`. To find a value for the `allTenOkay` variable, the program checks to see whether `numberOfPeople` is greater than or equal to ten. (The symbols >= stand for *greater than or equal to*.)

At this point, becoming fussy about terminology pays. Any part of a Java program that has a value is called an *expression*. If you write

```
weightOfAPerson = 150;
```

then `150` is an expression (an expression whose value is the quantity 150). If you write

```
numberOfEggs = 2 + 2;
```

then `2 + 2` is an expression (because 2 + 2 has the value 4). If you write

```
int numberOfPeople =
    elevatorWeightLimit / weightOfAPerson;
```

then `elevatorWeightLimit / weightOfAPerson` is an expression. (The value of the expression `elevatorWeightLimit / weightOfAPerson` depends on whatever values the variables `elevatorWeightLimit` and `weightOfAPerson` have when the code containing the expression is executed.)

Any part of a Java program that has a value is called an *expression*.

In Listing 4-5, the code `numberOfPeople >= 10` is an expression. The expression's value depends on the value stored in the `numberOfPeople` variable. But, as you know from seeing the strawberry shortcake at the Bricken-chicker family's catered lunch, the value of `numberOfPeople` isn't greater than or equal to ten. This makes the value of `numberOfPeople >= 10` to be `false`. So, in the statement in Listing 4-5, in which `allTenOkay` is assigned a value, the `allTenOkay` variable is assigned a `false` value.

TIP

In Listing 4-5, I call `out.println()` with nothing inside the parentheses. When I do this, Java adds a line break to the program's output. In Listing 4-5, `out.println()` tells the program to display a blank line.

The Molecules and Compounds: Reference Types

By combining simple things, you get more complicated things. That's the way it always goes. Take some of Java's primitive types, whip them together to make a primitive type stew, and what do you get? A more complicated type called a *reference type*.

The program in Listing 4-6 uses reference types. Figure 4-7 shows you what happens when you run the program in Listing 4-6.

Listing 4-6:   Using Reference Types

```
import javax.swing.JFrame;

class ShowAFrame {

    public static void main(String args[]) {
        JFrame myFrame = new JFrame();
        String myTitle = "Blank Frame";

        myFrame.setTitle(myTitle);
        myFrame.setSize(200, 200);
        myFrame.setDefaultCloseOperation
            (JFrame.EXIT_ON_CLOSE);
        myFrame.setVisible(true);
    }
}
```

Figure 4-7:
An empty frame.

The program in Listing 4-6 uses two references types. Both these types are defined in the Java API. One of the types (the one that you'll use all the time) is called *String*. The other type (the one that you can use to create GUIs) is called *JFrame*.

A `String` is a bunch of characters. It's like having several `char` values in a row. So, with the `myTitle` variable declared to be of type `String`, assigning `"Blank Frame"` to the `myTitle` variable makes sense in Listing 4-6. The `String` class is declared in the Java API.

In a Java program, double quote marks surround the letters in a `String` literal.

A Java *JFrame* is a lot like a window. (The only difference is that you call it a JFrame instead of a window.) To keep Listing 4-6 short and sweet, I decided not to put anything in my frame — no buttons, no fields, nothing.

Even with a completely empty frame, Listing 4-6 uses tricks that I don't describe until later in this book. So don't try reading and interpreting every word of Listing 4-6. The big thing to get from Listing 4-6 is that the program has two variable declarations. In writing the program, I made up two variable names — `myTitle` and `myFrame`. According to the declarations, `myTitle` is of type `String`, and `myFrame` is of type `JFrame`.

You can look up `String` and `JFrame` in Java's API documentation. But, even before you do, I can tell you what you'll find. You'll find that `String` and `JFrame` are the names of Java classes. So, that's the big news. Every class is the name of a reference type. You can reserve `amountInAccount` for `double` values by writing

```
double amountInAccount;
```

or by writing

```
double amountInAccount = 50.22;
```

You can also reserve `myFrame` for a `JFrame` value by writing

```
JFrame myFrame;
```

or by writing

```
JFrame myFrame = new JFrame();
```

To review the notion of a Java class, see the sections on object-oriented programming (OOP) in Chapter 1.

Every Java class is a reference type. If you declare a variable to have some type that's not a primitive type, the variable's type is (most of the time) the name of a Java class.

Now, when you declare a variable to have type `int`, you can visualize what that declaration means in a fairly straightforward way. It means that, somewhere inside the computer's memory, a storage location is reserved for that variable's value. In that storage location is a bunch of bits. The arrangement of the bits assures that a certain whole number is represented.

That explanation is fine for primitive types like `int` or `double`, but what does it mean when you declare a variable to have a reference type? What does it mean to declare variable `myFrame` to be of type `JFrame`?

Well, what does it mean to declare *i thank You God* to be an E. E. Cummings poem? What would it mean to write the following declaration?

```
EECummingsPoem ithankYouGod;
```

It means that a class of things is `EECummingsPoem`, and `ithankYouGod` refers to an instance of that class. In other words, `ithankYouGod` is an object belonging to the `EECummingsPoem` class.

Because `JFrame` is a class, you can create objects from that class. (See Chapter 1.) Each such object (each instance of the `JFrame` class) is an actual frame — a window that appears on the screen when you run the code in Listing 4-6. By declaring the variable `myFrame` to be of type `JFrame`, you're reserving the use of the name `myFrame`. This reservation tells the computer that `myFrame` can refer to an actual `JFrame`-type object. In other words, `myFrame` can become a nickname for one of the windows that appears on the computer screen. The situation is illustrated in Figure 4-8.

When you declare `ClassName variableName;`, you're saying that a certain variable can refer to an instance of a particular class.

In Listing 4-6, the phrase `JFrame myFrame` reserves the use of the name `myFrame`. On that same line of code, the phrase `new JFrame()` creates a new object (an instance of the `JFrame` class). Finally, that line's equal sign makes `myFrame` refer to the new object. Knowing that the two words `new JFrame()` create an object can be very important. For a more thorough explanation of objects, see Chapter 7.

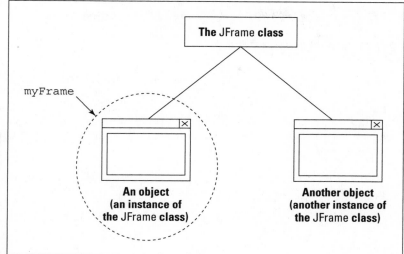

Figure 4-8:
The variable
myFrame
refers to an
instance of
the JFrame
class.

Primitive type stew

While I'm on the subject of frames, what's a frame anyway? A *frame* is a window that has a certain height and width and a certain location on your computer's screen. So, deep inside the declaration of the Frame class, you can find variable declarations that look something like this:

```
int width;
int height;
int x;
int y;
```

Here's another example — Time. An instance of the Time class may have an hour (a number from 1 to 12), a number of minutes (from 0 to 59), and a letter (*a* for a.m.; *p* for p.m.).

```
int hour;
int minutes;
char amOrPm;
```

So notice that this high and mighty thing called a Java API class is neither high nor mighty. A class is just a collection of declarations. Some of those declarations are the declarations of variables. Some of those variable declarations use primitive types, and other variable declarations use reference types. These reference types, however, come from other classes, and the declarations of those classes have variables. The chain goes on and on. Ultimately, everything comes, in one way or another, from the primitive types.

Creating New Values by Applying Operators

What could be more comforting than your old friend, the plus sign? It was the first thing that you learned about in elementary school math. Almost everybody knows how to add 2 and 2. In fact, in English usage, adding 2 and 2 is a metaphor for something that's easy to do. Whenever you see a plus sign, a cell in your brain says, "Thank goodness — it could be something much more complicated."

So Java has a plus sign. You can use it for several different purposes. You can use the plus sign to add two numbers, like this:

```
int apples, oranges, fruit;
apples = 5;
oranges = 16;
fruit = apples + oranges;
```

You can also use the plus sign to paste `String` values together:

```
String startOfChapter =
    "It's three in the morning. I'm dreaming about the "+
    "history course that I failed in high school.";
System.out.println(startOfChapter);
```

This can be handy because in Java, you're not allowed to make a `String` straddle from one line to another. In other words, the following code wouldn't work at all:

```
String thisIsBadCode =
    "It's three in the morning. I'm dreaming about the
     history course that I failed in high school.";
System.out.println(thisIsBadCode);
```

The correct way to say that you're pasting `String` values together is to say that you're *concatenating* `String` values.

You can even use the plus sign to paste numbers next to `String` values.

```
int apples, oranges, fruit;
apples = 5;
oranges = 16;
fruit = apples + oranges;
System.out.println("You have " + fruit +
                   " pieces of fruit.");
```

Of course, the old minus sign is available too (but not for `String` values).

```
apples = fruit - oranges;
```

Use an asterisk (*) for multiplication and a forward slash (/) for division.

```
double rate, pay;
int hours;

rate = 6.25;
hours = 35;
pay = rate * hours;
System.out.println(pay);
```

For an example using division, refer to Listing 4-3.

When you divide an `int` value by another `int` value, you get an `int` value. The computer doesn't round. Instead, the computer chops off any remainder. If you put `System.out.println(11 / 4)` in your program, the computer prints 2, not 2.75. To get past this, make either (or both) of the numbers you're dividing `double` values. If you put `System.out.println(11.0 / 4)` in your program, the computer prints 2.75.

Another useful arithmetic operator is called the *remainder* operator. The symbol for the remainder operator is the percent sign (%). When you put `System.out.println(11 % 4)` in your program, the computer prints 3. It does this because 4 goes into 11 who-cares-how-many times with a remainder of 3. The remainder operator turns out to be fairly useful. Listing 4-7 has an example.

Listing 4-7: Making Change

```
import static java.lang.System.out;

class MakeChange {

    public static void main(String args[]) {
        int total = 248;
        int quarters = total / 25;
        int whatsLeft = total % 25;

        int dimes = whatsLeft / 10;
        whatsLeft = whatsLeft % 10;

        int nickels = whatsLeft / 5;
        whatsLeft = whatsLeft % 5;

        int cents = whatsLeft;

        out.println("From " + total + " cents you get");
```

(continued)

Listing 4-7: (continued)

```
        out.println(quarters + " quarters");
        out.println(dimes + " dimes");
        out.println(nickels + " nickels");
        out.println(cents + " cents");
    }
}
```

A run of the code in Listing 4-7 is shown in Figure 4-9. You start with a total of 248 cents. Then

```
quarters = total / 25
```

divides 248 by 25, giving 9. That means you can make 9 quarters from 248 cents. Next,

```
whatsLeft = total % 25
```

divides 248 by 25 again, and puts only the remainder, 23, into whatsLeft. Now you're ready for the next step, which is to take as many dimes as you can out of 23 cents.

Figure 4-9:
Change for
$2.48.

```
9 quarters
2 dimes
0 nickels
3 cents
```

Initialize once, assign often

Listing 4-7 has three lines that put values into the variable whatsLeft:

```
int whatsLeft = total % 25;

whatsLeft = whatsLeft % 10;

whatsLeft = whatsLeft % 5;
```

Only one of these lines is a declaration. The other two lines are assignment statements. That's good because you can't declare the same variable more than once (not without creating something called a *block*). If you goof and write

```
int whatsLeft = total % 25;

int whatsLeft = whatsLeft % 10;
```

in Listing 4-7, you see an error message (whatsLeft is already defined) when you try to compile your code.

To find out what a block is, see Chapter 5. Then, for some honest talk about redeclaring variables, see Chapter 10.

The increment and decrement operators

Java has some neat little operators that make life easier (for the computer's processor, for your brain, and for your fingers). Altogether, four such operators exist — two increment operators and two decrement operators. The increment operators add 1, and the decrement operators subtract 1. The increment operators use double plus signs (++), and the decrement operators use double minus signs (−−). To see how they work, you need some examples. The first example is in Figure 4-10.

A run of the program in Figure 4-10 is shown in Figure 4-11. In this horribly uneventful run, the count of bunnies is printed three times.

The double plus signs go by two different names, depending on where you put them. When you put the ++ before a variable, the ++ is called the *preincrement* operator. (The *pre* stands for *before*.)

```
import static java.lang.System.out;
class preIncrementDemo {
        public static void main(String args[]) {
                int numberOfBunnies = 27;

                ++numberOfBunnies;
                out.println(numberOfBunnies);
                out.println(++numberOfBunnies);
                out.println(numberOfBunnies);
        }
}
```

> numberOfBunnies **becomes 28.**
>
> **28 gets printed.**
>
> numberOfBunnies **becomes 29, and 29 gets printed.**
>
> **29 gets printed again.**

Figure 4-10: Using preincrement.

```
28
29
29
Process completed.
```

Figure 4-11: A run of the code in Figure 4-10.

The word *before* has two different meanings:

- ✔ You put ++ before the variable.
- ✔ The computer adds 1 to the variable's value before the variable is used in any other part of the statement.

To understand this, look at the bold line in Figure 4-10. The computer adds 1 to numberOfBunnies (raising the value of numberOfBunnies to 29), and then the computer prints the number 29 on-screen.

With out.println(++numberOfBunnies), the computer adds 1 to numberOfBunnies before printing the new value of numberOfBunnies on-screen.

An alternative to preincrement is *postincrement*. (The *post* stands for *after*.) The word *after* has two different meanings:

- ✔ You put ++ after the variable.
- ✔ The computer adds 1 to the variable's value after the variable is used in any other part of the statement.

To see more clearly how postincrement works, look at the bold line in Figure 4-12. The computer prints the old value of numberOfBunnies (which is 28) on the screen, and then the computer adds 1 to numberOfBunnies, which raises the value of numberOfBunnies to 29.

Figure 4-12:
Using
postincre-
ment.

```
import static java.lang.System.out;
class preIncrementDemo {
    public static void main(String args[]) {
        int numberOfBunnies = 27;

        numberOfBunnies++;
        out.println(numberOfBunnies);
        out.println(numberOfBunnies++);
        out.println(numberOfBunnies);
    }
}
```

| numberOfBunnies becomes 28. |
| 28 gets printed. |
| 28 gets printed, and then numberOfBunnies becomes 29. |
| 29 gets printed. |

With out.println(numberOfBunnies++), the computer adds 1 to numberOfBunnies after printing the old value that numberOfBunnies already had.

A run of the code in Figure 4-12 is shown in Figure 4-13. Compare Figure 4-13 with the run in Figure 4-11:

- With preincrement in Figure 4-11, the second number is 29.

- With postincrement in Figure 4-13, the second number is 28.

    In Figure 4-13, the number 29 doesn't show up on-screen until the end of the run, when the computer executes one last `out.println` `(numberOfBunnies)`.

Figure 4-13:
A run of the code in Figure 4-12.

```
28
28
29
Process completed.
```

Are you trying to decide between using preincrement or postincrement? Try no longer. Most programmers use postincrement. In a typical Java program, you often see things like `numberOfBunnies++`. You seldom see things like `++numberOfBunnies`.

In addition to preincrement and postincrement, Java has two operators that use `--`. These operators are called *predecrement* and *postdecrement*.

- With predecrement (`--numberOfBunnies`), the computer subtracts 1 from the variable's value before the variable is used in the rest of the statement.

- With postdecrement (`numberOfBunnies--`), the computer subtracts 1 from the variable's value after the variable is used in the rest of the statement.

Instead of writing `++numberOfBunnies`, you could achieve the same effect by writing `numberOfBunnies = numberOfBunnies + 1`. So some people conclude that Java's `++` and `--` operators are for saving keystrokes — to keep those poor fingers from overworking themselves. This is entirely incorrect. The best reason for using `++` is to avoid the inefficient and error-prone practice of writing the same variable name, such as `numberOfBunnies`, twice in the same statement. If you write `numberOfBunnies` only once (as you do when you use `++` or `--`), the computer has to figure out what `numberOfBunnies` means only once. On top of that, when you write `numberOfBunnies` only once, you have only one chance (instead of two chances) to type the variable name incorrectly. With simple expressions like `numberOfBunnies++`, these advantages hardly make a difference. But with more complicated expressions, like `inventoryItems[(quantityReceived--*itemsPerBox+17)]++`, the efficiency and accuracy that you gain by using `++` and `--` are significant.

Statements and expressions

You can describe the pre- and postincrement and pre- and postdecrement operators in two ways: the way everyone understands them and the right way. The way that I explain the concept in most of this section (in terms of time, with *before* and *after*) is the way that everyone understands it. Unfortunately, the way everyone understands the concept isn't really the right way. When you see `++` or `--`, you can think in terms of time sequence. But occasionally some programmer uses `++` or `--` in a convoluted way, and the notions of *before* and *after* break down. So, if you're ever in a tight spot, think about these operators in terms of statements and expressions.

First, remember that a statement tells the computer to do something, and an expression has a value. (I discuss statements in Chapter 3, and I describe expressions elsewhere in this chapter.) Which category does `numberOfBunnies++` belong to? The surprising answer is both. The Java code `numberOfBunnies++` is both a statement and an expression.

Assume that, before the computer executes the code `out.println(numberOfBunnies++)`, the value of `numberOfBunnies` is 28.

✔ As a statement, `numberOfBunnies++` tells the computer to add 1 to `numberOfBunnies`.

✔ As an expression, the value of `numberOfBunnies++` is 28, not 29.

So, even though the computer adds 1 to `numberOfBunnies`, the code `out.println(numberOfBunnies++)` really means `out.println(28)`.

Now, almost everything you just read about `numberOfBunnies++` is true about `++numberOfBunnies`. The only difference is that as an expression, `++numberOfBunnies` behaves in a more intuitive way.

✔ As a statement, `++numberOfBunnies` tells the computer to add 1 to `numberOfBunnies`.

✔ As an expression, the value of `++numberOfBunnies` is 29.

So, with `out.println(++numberOfBunnies)`, the computer adds 1 to the variable `numberOfBunnies`, and the code `out.println(++numberOfBunnies)` really means `out.println(29)`.

Assignment operators

If you read the preceding section, which is about operators that add 1, you may be wondering whether you can manipulate these operators to add 2 or add 5 or add 1000000. Can you write `numberOfBunnies++++` and still call yourself a Java programmer? Well, you can't. If you try it, an error message appears when you try to compile your code.

So what can you do? As luck would have it, Java has plenty of assignment operators that you can use. With an *assignment operator,* you can add, subtract, multiply, or divide by anything you want. You can do other cool operations, too. Listing 4-8 has a smorgasbord of assignment operators (the things with equal signs). Figure 4-14 shows the output from running Listing 4-8.

Listing 4-8:   Assignment Operators

```
import static java.lang.System.out;

class UseAssignmentOperators {

    public static void main(String args[]) {
        int numberOfBunnies = 27;
        int numberExtra = 53;

        numberOfBunnies += 1;
        out.println(numberOfBunnies);

        numberOfBunnies += 5;
        out.println(numberOfBunnies);

        numberOfBunnies += numberExtra;
        out.println(numberOfBunnies);

        numberOfBunnies *= 2;
        out.println(numberOfBunnies);

        out.println(numberOfBunnies -= 7);

        out.println(numberOfBunnies = 100);
    }
}
```

Figure 4-14:
A run of the
code in
Listing 4-8.

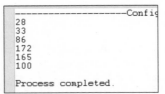

```
----------------------Config
28
33
86
172
165
100

Process completed.
```

Listing 4-8 shows how versatile Java's assignment operators are. With the assignment operators, you can add, subtract, multiply, or divide a variable by any number. Notice how += 5 adds 5 to numberOfBunnies, and how *= 2 multiplies numberOfBunnies by 2. You can even use another expression's value (in Listing 4-8, numberExtra) as the number to be applied.

The last two lines in Listing 4-8 demonstrate a special feature of Java's assignment operators. You can use an assignment operator as part of a larger Java statement. In the next to last line of Listing 4-8, the operator subtracts 7 from numberOfBunnies, decreasing the value of numberOfBunnies from 172 to 165. But then the whole assignment business is stuffed into a call to out.println, so the number 165 is printed on the computer screen.

Lo and behold, the last line of Listing 4-8 shows how you can do the same thing with Java's plain old equal sign. The thing that I call an assignment statement near the start of this chapter is really one of the assignment operators that I describe in this section. So, whenever you assign a value to something, you can make that assignment be part of a larger statement.

Each use of an assignment operator does double duty as both a statement and an expression. In all cases, the expression's value equals whatever value you assign. For example, before executing the code out.println (numberOfBunnies -= 7), the value of numberOfBunnies is 172. As a statement, numberOfBunnies -= 7 tells the computer to subtract 7 from numberOfBunnies (so the value of numberOfBunnies goes from 172 down to 165). As an expression, the value of numberOfBunnies -= 7 is 165. So the code out.println(numberOfBunnies -= 7) really means out.println(165). The number 165 is displayed on the computer screen.

For a richer explanation of this kind of thing, see the sidebar, "Statements and expressions," earlier in this chapter.

Chapter 5

Controlling Program Flow with Decision-Making Statements

The TV show *Dennis the Menace* aired on CBS from 1959 to 1963. I remember one episode in which Mr. Wilson was having trouble making an important decision. I think it was something about changing jobs or moving to a new town. Anyway, I can still see that shot of Mr. Wilson sitting in his yard, sipping lemonade, and staring into nowhere for the whole afternoon. Of course, the annoying character Dennis was constantly interrupting Mr. Wilson's peace and quiet. That's what made this situation funny.

What impressed me about this episode (the reason why I remember it so clearly even now) was Mr. Wilson's dogged intent in making the decision. This guy wasn't going about his everyday business, roaming around the neighborhood, while thoughts about the decision wandered in and out of his mind. He was sitting quietly in his yard, making marks carefully and logically on his mental balance sheet. How many people actually make decisions this way?

At that time, I was still pretty young. I'd never faced the responsibility of having to make a big decision that affected my family and me. But I wondered what such a decision-making process would be like. Would it help to sit there like a stump for hours on end? Would I make my decisions by the careful weighing and tallying of options? Or would I shoot in the dark, take risks, and act on impulse? Only time would tell.

Making Decisions (Java if Statements)

When you're writing computer programs, you're constantly hitting forks in roads. Did the user correctly type his or her password? If yes, let the user work; if no, kick the bum out. So the Java programming language needs a way of making a program branch in one of two directions. Fortunately, the language has a way. It's called an *if statement*.

Guess the number

The use of an `if` statement is illustrated in Listing 5-1. Two runs of the program in Listing 5-1 are shown in Figure 5-1.

Listing 5-1:   A Guessing Game

```java
import static java.lang.System.out;
import java.util.Scanner;
import java.util.Random;

class GuessingGame {

    public static void main(String args[]) {
        Scanner myScanner = new Scanner(System.in);

        out.print("Enter an int from 1 to 10: ");

        int inputNumber = myScanner.nextInt();
        int randomNumber = new Random().nextInt(10) + 1;

        if (inputNumber == randomNumber) {
            out.println("**********");
            out.println("*You win.*");
            out.println("**********");
        } else {
            out.println("You lose.");
            out.print("The random number was ");
            out.println(randomNumber + ".");
        }

        out.println("Thank you for playing.");
    }
}
```

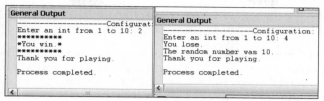

Figure 5-1:
Two runs of
the guessing
game.

The program in Listing 5-1 plays a guessing game with the user. The program gets a number (a guess) from the user and then generates a random number between 1 and 10. If the number that the user entered is the same as the random number, the user wins. Otherwise, the user loses. In either case, the program tells the user what the random number was.

She controlled keystrokes from the keyboard

Taken together, the lines

```
import java.util.Scanner;

        Scanner myScanner = new Scanner(System.in);

        int inputNumber = myScanner.nextInt();
```

in Listing 5-1 get whatever number the user types on the keyboard. The last of the three lines puts this number into a variable named *inputNumber*. If these lines look complicated, don't worry. You can copy these lines almost word for word whenever you want to read from the keyboard. Include the first two lines (the `import` and `Scanner` lines) just once in your program. Later in your program, wherever the user types an `int` value, include a line with a call to `nextInt` (as in the last of the preceding three lines of code).

Of all the names in these three lines of code, the only two names that I coined myself are *inputNumber* and *myScanner*. All the other names are part of Java. So, if I want to be creative, I can write the lines this way:

```
import java.util.Scanner;

        Scanner readingThingie = new Scanner(System.in);

        int valueTypedIn = readingThingie.nextInt();
```

I can also beef up my program's `import` declarations, as I do in Listings 5-2 and 5-3. Other than that, I have very little leeway.

As you read on in this book, you'll start recognizing the patterns behind these three lines of code, so I don't clutter up this section with all the details. For now, you can just copy these three lines and keep the following in mind:

✔ **When you import `java.util.Scanner`, you don't use the word _static_.**

Importing `Scanner` is different from importing `System.out`. When you import `java.lang.System.out`, you use the word _static_. (See Listing 5-1.)

For the real story on the word _static,_ see Chapter 10.

✔ **The name _System.in_ stands for the keyboard.**

To get characters from someplace other than the keyboard, you can type something other than `System.in` inside the parentheses.

What else can you put inside the parentheses? For some ideas, see Chapter 8.

✔ **When you expect the user to type an `int` value (a whole number of some kind), use `nextInt()`.**

If you expect the user to type a `double` value (a number containing a decimal point), use `nextDouble()`. If you expect the user to type **true** or **false**, use `nextBoolean()`. If you expect the user to type a word (a word like _Barry, Java,_ or _Hello_), use `next()`.

For an example in which the user types a word, see Listing 5-3. For an example in which the user types a single character, see Listing 6-4 in Chapter 6. For an example in which a program reads an entire line of text (all in one big gulp), see Chapter 8.

✔ **You can get several values from the keyboard, one after another.**

To do this, use the `myScanner.nextInt()` code several times.

To see a program that reads more than one value from the keyboard, go to Listing 5-4.

Creating randomness

Achieving real randomness is surprisingly difficult. Mathematician Persi Diaconis says that if you flip a coin several times, always starting with the head side up, you're likely to toss heads more often than tails. If you toss several more times, always starting with the tail side up, you're likely to toss tails more often than heads. In other words, coin tossing isn't really fair.*

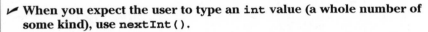

* Diaconis, Persi. "The Search for Randomness." American Association for the Advancement of Science annual meeting. Seattle. 14 Feb. 2004.

Computers aren't much better than coins and human thumbs. A computer mimics the generation of random sequences but, in the end, the computer just does what it's told and does all this in a purely deterministic fashion. So in Listing 5-1, when the computer executes

```
import java.util.Random;

        int randomNumber = new Random().nextInt(10) + 1;
```

the computer appears to give us a randomly generated number — a whole number between 1 and 10. But it's all a fake. The computer just follows instructions. It's not really random, but without bending a computer over backwards, it's the best that anyone can do.

Once again, I ask you to take this code on blind faith. Don't worry about what new Random().nextInt means until you have more experience with Java. Just copy this code into your own programs and have fun with it. And if the numbers from 1 to 10 aren't in your flight plans, don't fret. To roll an imaginary die, write the statement

```
int rollEmBaby = new Random().nextInt(6) + 1;
```

With the execution of this statement, the variable rollEmBaby gets a value from 1 to 6.

The if statement

At the core of Listing 5-1 is a Java if statement. This if statement represents a fork in the road. (See Figure 5-2.) The computer follows one of two prongs — the prong that prints You win or the prong that prints You lose. The computer decides which prong to take by testing the truth or falsehood of a *condition*. In Listing 5-1, the condition being tested is

```
inputNumber == randomNumber
```

Does the value of inputNumber equal the value of randomNumber? When the condition is true, the computer does the stuff between the condition and the word *else*. When the condition turns out to be false, the computer does the stuff after the word *else*. Either way, the computer goes on to execute the last println call, which displays Thank you for playing.

The condition in an if statement must be enclosed in parentheses. However, a line like if (inputNumber == randomNumber) is not a complete statement (just as "If I had a hammer" isn't a complete sentence). So this line if (inputNumber == randomNumber) shouldn't end with a semicolon.

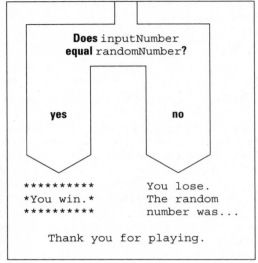

Figure 5-2:
An if
statement is
like a fork in
the road.

```
* * * * * * * * * *        You lose.
*You win.*                 The random
* * * * * * * * * *        number was...

   Thank you for playing.
```

Sometimes, when I'm writing about a condition that's being tested, I slip into using the word *expression* instead of *condition*. That's okay, because every condition is an expression. An expression is something that has a value and, sure enough, every condition has a value. The condition's value is either `true` or `false`. (For revealing information about expressions and values like `true` and `false`, see Chapter 4.)

The double equal sign

In Listing 5-1, in the `if` statement's condition, notice the use of the double equal sign. Comparing two numbers to see whether they're the same isn't the same as setting something equal to something else. That's why the symbol to compare for equality isn't the same as the symbol that's used in an assignment or an initialization. In an `if` statement's condition, you can't replace the double equal sign with a single equal sign. If you do, your program just won't work. (You almost always get an error message when you try to compile your code.)

On the other hand, if you never make the mistake of using a single equal sign in a condition, you're not normal. Not long ago, while I was teaching an introductory Java course, I promised that I'd swallow my laser pointer if no one made the single equal sign mistake during any of the lab sessions. This wasn't an idle promise. I knew I'd never have to keep it. As it turned out, even if I had ignored the first ten times anybody made the single equal sign mistake during those lab sessions, I would still be laser-pointer free. Everybody mistakenly uses the single equal sign several times in his or her programming career. The trick is not to avoid making the mistake; the trick is to catch the mistake whenever you make it.

Brace yourself

The if statement in Listing 5-1 has two halves — a top half and a bottom half. I have names for these two parts of an if statement. I call them the *if part* (the top half) and the *else part* (the bottom half).

The if part in Listing 5-1 seems to have more than one statement in it. I make this happen by enclosing the three statements of the if part in a pair of curly braces. When I do this, I form a *block.* A block is a bunch of statements scrunched together by a pair of curly braces.

With this block, three calls to println are tucked away safely inside the if part. With the curly braces, the rows of asterisks and the words You win are displayed only when the user's guess is correct.

This business with blocks and curly braces applies to the else part as well. In Listing 5-1, whenever inputNumber doesn't equal randomNumber, the computer executes three print/println calls. To convince the computer that all three of these calls are inside the else clause, I put these calls into a block. That is, I enclose these three calls in a pair of curly braces.

Strictly speaking, Listing 5-1 has only one statement between the if and the else statements and only one statement after the else statement. The trick is that when you place a bunch of statements inside curly braces, you get a block; and a block behaves, in all respects, like a single statement. In fact, the official Java documentation lists blocks as one of the many kinds of statements. So, in Listing 5-1, the block that prints You win and asterisks is a single statement. It's a statement that has, within it, three smaller statements.

Indenting if statements in your code

Notice how, in Listing 5-1, the print and println calls inside the if statement are indented. (This includes both the You win and You lose statements. The print and println calls that come after the word *else* are still part of the if statement.) Strictly speaking, you don't have to indent the statements that are inside an if statement. For all the compiler cares, you can write your whole program on a single line or place all your statements in an artful, misshapen zigzag. The problem is that if you don't indent your statements in some logical fashion, neither you nor anyone else can make sense of your code. In Listing 5-1, the indenting of the print and println statements helps your eye (and brain) see quickly that these statements are subordinate to the overall if/else flow.

In a small program, unindented or poorly indented code is barely tolerable. But in a complicated program, indentation that doesn't follow a neat, logical pattern is a big, ugly nightmare.

When you write `if` statements, you may be tempted to chuck all the rules about curly braces out the window and just rely on indentation. Unfortunately, this seldom works. If you indent three statements after the word *else* and forget to enclose those statements in curly braces, the computer thinks that the `else` part includes only the first of the three statements. What's worse, the indentation misleads you into believing that the `else` part includes all three statements. This makes it more difficult for you to figure out why your code isn't behaving the way you think it should behave. So watch those braces!

Elseless in 1frica

Okay, so the title of this section is contrived. Big deal! The idea is that you can create an `if` statement without the `else` part. Take, for instance, the code in Listing 5-1. Maybe you'd rather not rub it in whenever the user loses the game. The modified code in Listing 5-2 shows you how to do this (and Figure 5-3 shows you the result).

Listing 5-2:   A Kinder, Gentler Guessing Game

```
import static java.lang.System.in;
import static java.lang.System.out;
import java.util.Scanner;
import java.util.Random;

class DontTellThemTheyLost {

    public static void main(String args[]) {
        Scanner myScanner = new Scanner(in);

        out.print("Enter an int from 1 to 10: ");

        int inputNumber = myScanner.nextInt();
        int randomNumber = new Random().nextInt(10) + 1;

        if (inputNumber == randomNumber) {
            out.println("*You win.*");
        }

        out.println("That was a very good guess :-)");
        out.print("The random number was ");
        out.println(randomNumber + ".");
        out.println("Thank you for playing.");
    }
}
```

The `if` statement in Listing 5-2 has no `else` part. When `inputNumber` is the same as `randomNumber`, the computer prints `You win`. When `inputNumber` is different from `randomNumber`, the computer doesn't print `You win`.

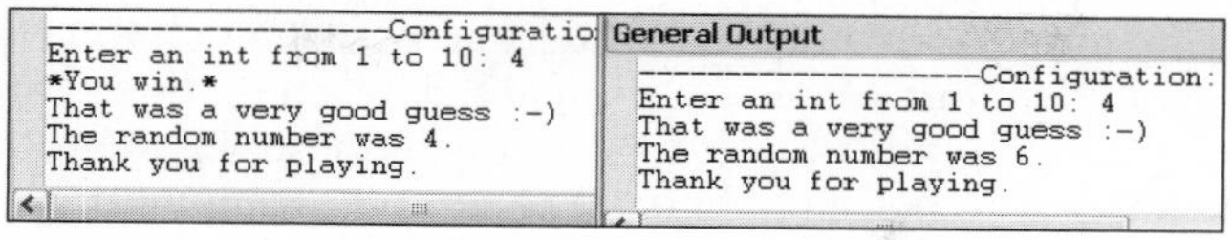

Figure 5-3:
Two runs of
the game in
Listing 5-2.

```
-------------------Configuratio
Enter an int from 1 to 10: 4
*You win.*
That was a very good guess :-)
The random number was 4.
Thank you for playing.
```

```
General Output
-------------------Configuration:
Enter an int from 1 to 10: 4
That was a very good guess :-)
The random number was 6.
Thank you for playing.
```

Listing 5-2 illustrates another new idea. With an `import` declaration for `System.in`, I can reduce `new Scanner(System.in)` to the shorter `new Scanner(in)`. Adding this `import` declaration is hardly worth the effort. In fact, I do more typing with the `import` declaration than without it. Nevertheless, the code in Listing 5-2 demonstrates that it's possible to import `System.in`.

Forming Conditions with Comparisons and Logical Operators

The Java programming language has plenty of little squiggles and doodads for your various condition-forming needs. This section tells you all about them.

Comparing numbers; comparing characters

Table 5-1 shows you the operators that you can use to compare one thing with another.

Table 5-1	Comparison Operators	
Operator Symbol	*Meaning*	*Example*
==	is equal to	`numberOfCows == 5`
!=	is not equal to	`buttonClicked != panicButton`
<	is less than	`numberOfCows < 5`
>	is greater than	`myInitial > 'B'`
<=	is less than or equal to	`numberOfCows <= 5`
>=	is greater than or equal to	`myInitial >= 'B'`

You can use all Java's comparison operators to compare numbers and characters. When you compare numbers, things go pretty much the way you think they should go. But when you compare characters, things are a little strange. Comparing uppercase letters with one another is no problem. Because the letter *B* comes alphabetically before *H,* the condition 'B' < 'H' is true. Comparing lowercase letters with one another is also okay. What's strange is that when you compare an uppercase letter with a lowercase letter, the uppercase letter is always smaller. So, even though 'Z' < 'A' is false, 'Z' < 'a' is true.

Under the hood, the letters *A* through *Z* are stored with numeric codes 65 through 90. The letters *a* through *z* are stored with codes 97 through 122. That's why each uppercase letter is smaller than each lowercase letter.

Be careful when you compare two numbers for equality (with ==) or inequality (with !=). After doing some calculations and obtaining two `double` values or two `float` values, the values that you have are seldom dead-on equal to one another. (The problem comes from those pesky digits beyond the decimal point.) For instance, the Fahrenheit equivalent of 21 degrees Celsius is 69.8, and when you calculate 9.0 / 5 * 21 + 32 by hand, you get 69.8. But the condition 9.0 / 5 * 21 + 32 == 69.8 turns out to be false. That's because, when the computer calculates 9.0 / 5 * 21 + 32, it gets 69.80000000000001, not 69.8.

Comparing objects

When you start working with objects, you find that you can use == and != to compare objects with one another. For instance, a button that you see on the computer screen is an object. You can ask whether the thing that was just mouse-clicked is a particular button on your screen. You do this with Java's equality operator.

```
if (e.getSource() == bCopy) {
    clipboard.setText(which.getText());
```

To find out more about responding to button clicks, read Chapter 16 on this book's CD-ROM.

The big gotcha with Java's comparison scheme comes when you compare two strings. (For a word or two about Java's `String` type, see the section about reference types in Chapter 4.) When you compare two strings with one another, you don't want to use the double equal sign. Using the double equal sign would ask, "Is this string stored in exactly the same place in memory as that other string?" That's usually not what you want to ask. Instead, you usually want to ask, "Does this string have the same characters in it as that other string?" To ask the second question (the more appropriate question) Java's `String` type has a method named *equals*. (Like everything else in the known universe, this `equals` method is defined in the Java API, short for Application Programming Interface.) The `equals` method compares two strings to see whether they have the same characters in them. For an example using Java's `equals` method, see Listing 5-3. (A run of the program in Listing 5-3 is shown in Figure 5-4.)

Listing 5-3:   Checking a Password

```java
import static java.lang.System.*;
import java.util.Scanner;

class CheckPassword {

    public static void main(String args[]) {

        out.print("What's the password? ");

        Scanner myScanner = new Scanner(in);
        String password = myScanner.next();

        out.println("You typed >>" + password + "<<");
        out.println();

        if (password == "swordfish") {
            out.println("The word you typed is stored");
            out.println("in the same place as the real");
            out.println("password. You must be a");
            out.println("hacker.");
        } else {
            out.println("The word you typed is not");
            out.println("stored in the same place as");
            out.println("the real password, but that's");
            out.println("no big deal.");
        }
        out.println();

        if (password.equals("swordfish")) {
            out.println("The word you typed has the");
            out.println("same characters as the real");
            out.println("password. You can use our");
            out.println("precious system.");
        } else {
            out.println("The word you typed doesn't");
            out.println("have the same characters as");
            out.println("the real password. You can't");
            out.println("use our precious system.");
        }
    }
}
```

Figure 5-4:
The result of using == and using Java's equals method.

```
----------------------Configuration: Li
What's the password? swordfish
You typed >>swordfish<<

The word you typed is not
stored in the same place as
the real password, but that's
no big deal.

The word you typed has the
same characters as the real
password. You can use our
precious system.

Process completed.
```

In Listing 5-3, the call myScanner.next() grabs whatever word the user types on the computer keyboard. The code shoves this word into the variable named *password*. Then the program's if statements use two different techniques to compare password with "swordfish".

The more appropriate of the two techniques uses Java's equals method. The equals method looks funny because when you call it you put a dot after one string and put the other string in parentheses. But that's the way you have to do it.

In calling Java's equals method, it doesn't matter which string gets the dot and which gets the parentheses. For instance, in Listing 5-3, you could have written

```
if ("swordfish".equals(password))
```

The method would work just as well.

A call to Java's equals method looks imbalanced, but it's not. There's a reason behind the apparent imbalance between the dot and the parentheses. The idea is that you have two objects: the password object and the "swordfish" object. Each of these two objects is of type String. (However, password is a variable of type String, and "swordfish" is a String literal.) When you write password.equals("swordfish"), you're calling an equals method that belongs to the password object. As you call that method, you're feeding "swordfish" to the method as the method's parameter (pun intended).

You can read more about methods belonging to objects in Chapter 7.

When comparing strings with one another, use the equals method — not the double equal sign.

Importing everything in one fell swoop

The first line of Listing 5-3 illustrates a lazy way of importing both System. out and System.in. To import everything that System has to offer, you use the asterisk wildcard character (*). In fact, importing java.lang.System.* is like having about 30 separate import declarations, including System.in, System.out, System.err, System.nanoTime, and many other System things.

The use of an asterisk in an import declaration is generally considered bad programming practice, so I don't do it often in this book's examples. But for larger programs — programs that use dozens of names from the Java API — the lazy asterisk trick is handy.

You can't toss an asterisk anywhere you want inside an import declaration. For example, you can't import everything starting with java by writing import java.*. You can substitute an asterisk only for the name of a class or for the name of something static that's tucked away inside a class. For more information about asterisks in import declarations, see Chapter 9. For information about static things, see Chapter 10.

Java's logical operators

Mr. Spock would be pleased. Java has all the operators that you need for mixing and matching logical tests. The operators are shown in Table 5-2.

Table 5-2		Logical Operators
Operator Symbol	*Meaning*	*Example*
&&	and	5 < x && x < 10
||	or	x < 5 || 10 < x
!	not	!password.equals("swordfish")

You can use these operators to form all kinds of elaborate conditions. Listing 5-4 has an example.

Some runs of the program of Listing 5-4 are shown in Figure 5-5. When the username is *bburd* and the password is *swordfish* or when the username is *hritter* and the password is *preakston,* the user gets a nice message. Otherwise, the user is a bum who gets the nasty message that he or she deserves.

Listing 5-4: **Checking Username and Password**

```
import static java.lang.System.out;
import java.util.Scanner;

class Authenticator {

    public static void main(String args[]) {

        Scanner myScanner = new Scanner(System.in);

        out.print("Username: ");
        String username = myScanner.next();

        out.print("Password: ");
        String password = myScanner.next();

        if (
            (username.equals("bburd") &&
             password.equals("swordfish")) ||
            (username.equals("hritter") &&
             password.equals("preakston"))
            )
        {
            out.println("You're in.");
        } else {
            out.println("You're suspicious.");
        }
    }
}
```

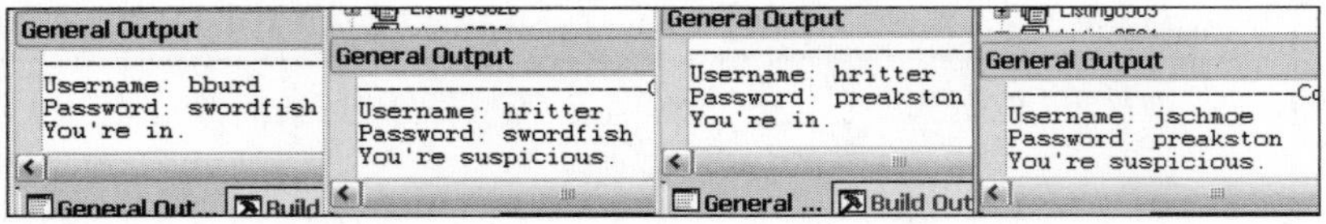

Figure 5-5:
Using
logical
operators.

General Output

Username: bburd
Password: swordfish
You're in.

General Output

Username: hritter
Password: swordfish
You're suspicious.

General Output

Username: hritter
Password: preakston
You're in.

General Output

Username: jschmoe
Password: preakston
You're suspicious.

Keep an eye on those parentheses! When you're combining comparisons with logical operators, it's better to waste typing effort and add unneeded parentheses than to goof up your result by using too few parentheses. Take, for example, the expression

```
2 < 5 || 100 < 6 && 27 < 1
```

By misreading this expression, you may come to the conclusion that the expression is false. That is, you could wrongly read the expression as meaning (*something-or-other*) && 27 < 1. Because 27 < 1 is false, you would conclude that the whole expression is false. The fact is that, in Java, any `&&` operator is evaluated before any `||` operator. So the expression really asks if `2 < 5 || (something-or-other)`. Because 2 < 5 is true, the whole expression is true.

To change the expression's value from `true` to `false`, you can put the expression's first two comparisons in parentheses, like this:

```
(2 < 5 || 100 < 6) && 27 < 1
```

Java's `||` operator is *inclusive*. This means that you get a `true` value whenever the thing on the left side is true, the thing on the right side is true, or both things are true. For instance, the expression `2 < 10 || 20 < 30` is true.

In Java, you can't combine comparisons the way you do in ordinary English. In English, you may say, "We'll have between three and ten people at the dinner table." But in Java, you get an error message if you write `3 <= people <= 10`. To do this comparison, you need something like `3 <= people && people <= 10`.

Building a Nest

Have you seen those cute Russian Matryoshka nesting dolls? Open up one, and another one is inside. Open up the second, and a third one is inside it. You can do the same thing with Java's `if` statements. (Talk about fun!) Listing 5-5 shows you how.

Listing 5-5: Nested if Statements

```java
import static java.lang.System.out;
import java.util.Scanner;

class Authenticator2 {

    public static void main(String args[]) {
        Scanner myScanner = new Scanner(System.in);

        out.print("Username: ");
        String username = myScanner.next();

        if (username.equals("bburd")) {
            out.print("Password: ");
            String password = myScanner.next();

            if (password.equals("swordfish")) {
```

(continued)

Listing 5-5 (continued)

```
            out.println("You're in.");
        } else {
            out.println("Incorrect password");
        }

    } else {
        out.println("Unknown user");
    }
  }
}
```

Figure 5-6 shows several runs of the code in Listing 5-5. The main idea is that to log on, you have to pass two tests. (In other words, two conditions must be true.) The first condition tests for a valid username; the second condition tests for the correct password. If you pass the first test (the username test), you march right into another `if` statement that performs a second test (the password test). If you fail the first test, you never make it to the second test. The overall plan is shown in Figure 5-7.

Figure 5-6:
Authen-
ticating a
user.

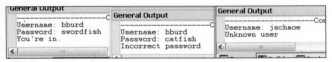

The code in Listing 5-5 does a good job with nested `if` statements, but it does a terrible job with real-world user authentication. First of all, never show a password in plain view (without asterisks to masquerade the password). Second, don't handle passwords without encrypting them. Third, don't tell the malicious user which of the two words (the username or the password) was entered incorrectly. Fourth . . . well I could go on and on. The code in Listing 5-5 just isn't meant to illustrate good username/password practices.

Choosing among Many Alternatives (Java switch Statements)

I'm the first to admit that I hate making decisions. If things go wrong, I would rather have the problem be someone else's fault. Writing the previous sections (on making decisions with Java's `if` statement) knocked the stuffing right out of me. That's why my mind boggles as I begin this section on choosing among many alternatives. What a relief it is to have that confession out of the way!

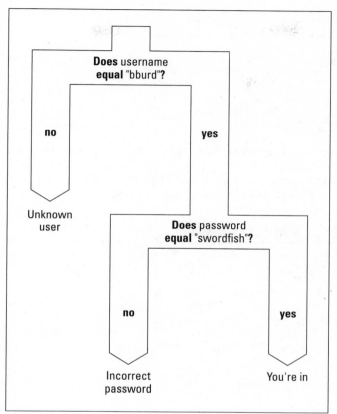

Figure 5-7:
Don't try
eating with
this fork.

Your basic switch statement

Now, it's time to explore situations in which you have a decision with many branches. Take, for instance, the popular campfire song "Al's All Wet." (For a review of the lyrics, see the sidebar.) You're eager to write code that prints this song's lyrics. Fortunately, you don't have to type all the words over and over again. Instead, you can take advantage of the repetition in the lyrics.

A complete program to display the "Al's All Wet" lyrics won't come until Chapter 6. In the meantime, assume that you have a variable named *verse*. The value of verse is 1, 2, 3, or 4, depending on which verse of "Al's All Wet" you're trying to print. You could have a big, clumsy bunch of if statements that checks each possible verse number.

```
if (verse == 1) {
    out.println("That's because he has no brain.");
}
if (verse == 2) {
    out.println("That's because he is a pain.");
}
if (verse == 3) {
    out.println("'Cause this is the last refrain.");
}
```

But that approach seems wasteful. Why not create a statement that checks the value of `verse` just once and then takes an action based on the value that it finds? Fortunately, just such a statement exists. It's called a *switch* statement. Listing 5-6 has an example of a `switch` statement.

Listing 5-6:   A switch Statement

```
import static java.lang.System.out;
import java.util.Scanner;

class JustSwitchIt {

    public static void main(String args[]) {
        Scanner myScanner = new Scanner(System.in);
        out.print("Which verse? ");
        int verse = myScanner.nextInt();

        switch (verse) {
        case 1:
            out.println("That's because he has no brain.");
            break;
        case 2:
            out.println("That's because he is a pain.");
            break;
        case 3:
            out.println("'Cause this is the last
          refrain.");
            break;
        default:
            out.println("No such verse. Please try
          again.");
            break;
        }

        out.println("Ohhhhhhh. . . .");
    }
}
```

Figure 5-8 shows two runs of the program in Listing 5-6. (The overall idea behind the program is illustrated in Figure 5-9.) First, the user types a number, like the number 2. Then, execution of the program reaches the top of the switch statement. The computer checks the value of the verse variable. When the computer determines that the verse variable's value is 2, the computer checks each case of the switch statement. The value 2 doesn't match the topmost case, so the computer proceeds on to the middle of the three cases. The value posted for the middle case (the number 2) matches the value of the verse variable, so the computer executes the statements that come immediately after case 2. These two statements are

```
out.println("That's because he is a pain.");
break;
```

The first of the two statements displays the line That's because he is a pain. on the screen. The second statement is called a *break* statement. (What a surprise!) When the computer encounters a break statement, the computer jumps out of whatever switch statement it's in. So, in Listing 5-6, the computer skips right past the case that would display 'Cause this is the last refrain. In fact, the computer jumps out of the entire switch statement and goes straight to the statement just after the end of the switch statement. The computer displays Ohhhhhhhh. . . . because that's what the statement after the switch statement tells the computer to do.

Figure 5-8:
Running the
code of
Listing 5-6.

```
General Output
------------------------Configura
Which verse? 2
That's because he is a pain.
Ohhhhhhhh. . . .
```
```
General Output
------------------------Configuration:
Which verse? 6
No such verse. Please try again.
Ohhhhhhhh. . . .
```

If the pesky user asks for verse 6, the computer responds by dropping past cases 1, 2, and 3. Instead, the computer does the default. In the default, the computer displays No such verse. Please try again, and then breaks out of the switch statement. After the computer is out of the switch statement, the computer displays Ohhhhhhhh. . . .

You don't really need to put a break at the very end of a switch statement. In Listing 5-6, the last break (the break that's part of the default) is just for the sake of overall tidiness.

"Al's All Wet"

Sung to the tune of "Gentille Alouette":

Al's all wet. Oh, why is Al all wet? Oh,
Al's all wet 'cause he's standing in the
rain.
Why is Al out in the rain?
That's because he has no brain.
Has no brain, has no brain,
In the rain, in the rain.
Ohhhhhhhh. . . .

Al's all wet. Oh, why is Al all wet? Oh,
Al's all wet 'cause he's standing in the
rain.
Why is Al out in the rain?
That's because he is a pain.
He's a pain, he's a pain,
Has no brain, has no brain,

In the rain, in the rain.
Ohhhhhhhh. . . .

Al's all wet. Oh, why is Al all wet? Oh,
Al's all wet 'cause he's standing in the
rain.
Why is Al out in the rain?
'Cause this is the last refrain.
Last refrain, last refrain,
He's a pain, he's a pain,
Has no brain, has no brain,
In the rain, in the rain.
Ohhhhhhhh. . . .

Al's all wet. Oh, why is Al all wet? Oh,
Al's all wet 'cause he's standing in the
rain.

—Harriet Ritter and Barry Burd

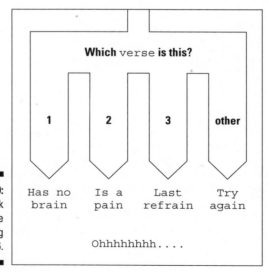

Figure 5-9:
The big fork
in the code
of Listing
5-6.

To break or not to break

In every Java programmer's life, a time comes when he or she forgets to use break statements. At first, the resulting output is confusing, but then the programmer remembers fall-through. The term *fall-through* describes what happens when you end a case without a break statement. What happens is that execution of the code falls right through to the next case in line. Execution keeps falling through until you eventually reach a break statement or the end of the entire switch statement.

Usually, when you're using a switch statement, you don't want fall-through, so you pepper break statements throughout the switch statements. But, occasionally, fall-through is just the thing you need. Take, for instance, the "Al's All Wet" song. (The classy lyrics are shown in the sidebar bearing the song's name.) Each verse of "Al's All Wet" adds new lines in addition to the lines from previous verses. This situation (accumulating lines from one verse to another) cries out for a switch statement with fall-through. Listing 5-7 demonstrates the idea.

Listing 5-7: A switch Statement with Fall-Through

```java
import static java.lang.System.out;
import java.util.Scanner;

class FallingForYou {

    public static void main(String args[]) {
        Scanner myScanner = new Scanner(System.in);
        out.print("Which verse? ");
        int verse = myScanner.nextInt();

        switch (verse) {
        case 3:
            out.print("Last refrain, ");
            out.println("last refrain,");
        case 2:
            out.print("He's a pain, ");
            out.println("he's a pain,");
        case 1:
            out.print("Has no brain, ");
            out.println("has no brain,");
        }

        out.println("In the rain, in the rain.");
        out.println("Ohhhhhhhh...");
        out.println();
    }
}
```

Figure 5-10 shows several runs of the program in Listing 5-7. Because the switch has no `break` statements in it, fall-through happens all over the place. For instance, when the user selects verse 2, the computer executes the two statements in case 2:

```
out.print   ("He's a pain, ");
out.println("he's a pain,");
```

Then, the computer marches right on to execute the two statements in case 1:

```
out.print   ("Has no brain, ");
out.println("has no brain,");
```

That's good, because the song's second verse has all these lines in it.

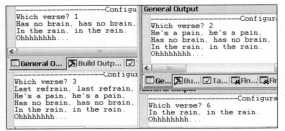

Figure 5-10:
Running the
code of
Listing 5-7.

Notice what happens when the user asks for verse 6. The `switch` statement in Listing 5-7 has no case 6 and no default, so none of the actions inside the `switch` statement are executed. Even so, with statements that print `In the rain, in the rain` and `Ohhhhhhhh` right after the `switch` statement, the computer displays something when the user asks for verse 6.

Chapter 6

Controlling Program Flow with Loops

. . . .

In This Chapter
▶ Using basic looping
▶ Counting as you loop
▶ Impressing your friends with Java's enhanced loops

. . . .

*I*n 1966, the company that brings you Head & Shoulders shampoo made history. On the back of the bottle, the directions for using the shampoo read, "LATHER-RINSE-REPEAT." Never before had a complete set of directions (for doing anything, let alone shampooing your hair) been summarized so succinctly. People in the direction-writing business hailed this as a monumental achievement. Directions like these stood in stark contrast to others of the time. (For instance, the first sentence on a can of bug spray read, "Turn this can so that it points away from your face." Duh!)

Aside from their brevity, the thing that made the Head & Shoulders directions so cool was that, with three simple words, they managed to capture a notion that's at the heart of all instruction-giving — the notion of repetition. That last word, *REPEAT,* took an otherwise bland instructional drone and turned it into a sophisticated recipe for action.

The fundamental idea is that when you're following directions, you don't just follow one instruction after another. Instead, you take turns in the road. You make decisions ("If HAIR IS DRY, then USE CONDITIONER,") and you go into loops ("LATHER-RINSE, and then LATHER-RINSE again."). In computer programming, you use decision making and looping all the time. This chapter explores looping in Java.

Repeating Instructions Over and Over Again (Java while Statements)

Here's a guessing game for you. The computer generates a random number from 1 to 10. The computer asks you to guess the number. If you guess incorrectly, the game continues. As soon as you guess correctly, the game is over. The program to play the game is shown in Listing 6-1, and a round of play is shown in Figure 6-1.

Listing 6-1:   A Repeating Guessing Game

```
import static java.lang.System.out;
import java.util.Scanner;
import java.util.Random;

class GuessAgain {

    public static void main(String args[]) {
        Scanner myScanner = new Scanner(System.in);

        int numGuesses = 0;
        int randomNumber = new Random().nextInt(10) + 1;

        out.println("      ************      ");
        out.println("Welcome to the Guessing Game");
        out.println("      ************      ");
        out.println();

        out.print("Enter an int from 1 to 10: ");
        int inputNumber = myScanner.nextInt();
        numGuesses++;

        while (inputNumber != randomNumber) {
            out.println();
            out.println("Try again...");
            out.print("Enter an int from 1 to 10: ");
            inputNumber = myScanner.nextInt();
            numGuesses++;
        }

        out.print("You win after ");
        out.println(numGuesses + " guesses.");
    }
}
```

```
-----------------------Configuratic
           ************
Welcome to the Guessing Game
           ************

Enter an int from 1 to 10: 2

Try again...
Enter an int from 1 to 10: 5

Try again...
Enter an int from 1 to 10: 8

Try again...
Enter an int from 1 to 10: 3
You win after 4 guesses.
```

Figure 6-1:
Play until
you drop.

In Figure 6-1, the user makes four guesses. Each time around, the computer checks to see whether the guess is correct. An incorrect guess generates a request to try again. For a correct guess, the user gets a rousing `You win`, along with a tally of the number of guesses he or she made. The computer repeats several statements over and over again, checking each time through to see whether the user's guess is the same as a certain randomly generated number. Each time the user makes a guess, the computer adds 1 to its tally of guesses. When the user makes the correct guess, the computer displays that tally. The flow of action is illustrated in Figure 6-2.

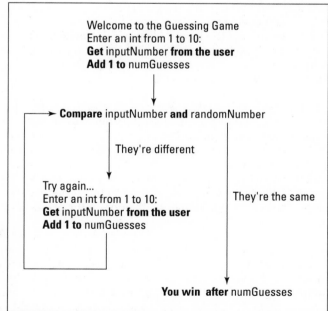

Figure 6-2:
Around and
around
you go.

When you look over Listing 6-1, you see the code that does all this work. At the core of the code is a thing called a *while statement* (also known as a *while loop*). Rephrased in English, the `while` statement says:

```
while the inputNumber is not equal to the randomNumber
keep doing all the stuff in curly braces: {



}
```

The stuff in curly braces (the stuff that repeats over and over again) is the code that prints `Try again, Enter an int . . .`, gets a value from the keyboard and adds 1 to the count of the user's guesses.

When you're dealing with counters, like `numGuesses` in Listing 6-1, you may easily become confused and be off by 1 in either direction. You can avoid this headache by making sure that the `++` statements stay close to the statements whose events you're counting. For example, in Listing 6-1, the variable `numGuesses` starts off with a value of `0`. That's because, when the program starts running, the user hasn't made any guesses. Later in the program, right after each call to `myScanner.nextInt`, is a `numGuesses++` statement. That's how you do it — you increment the counter as soon as the user enters another guess.

The statements in curly braces are repeated as long as `inputNumber != randomNumber` keeps being true. Each repetition of the statements in the loop is called an *iteration* of the loop. In Figure 6-1, the loop undergoes three iterations. (If you don't believe that Figure 6-1 has exactly three iterations, count the number of `Try again` printings in the program's output. A `Try again` appears for each incorrect guess.)

When, at long last, the user enters the correct guess, the computer goes back to the top of the `while` statement, checks the condition in parentheses, and finds itself in double negative land. The not equal (`!=`) relationship between `inputNumber` and `randomNumber` no longer holds. In other words, the `while` statement's condition, `inputNumber != randomNumber`, has become false. Because the `while` statement's condition is false, the computer jumps past the `while` loop and goes on to the statements just below the `while` loop. In these two statements, the computer prints `You win after 4 guesses.`

With code of the kind shown in Listing 6-1, the computer never jumps out in mid-loop. When the computer finds that `inputNumber` isn't equal to `randomNumber`, the computer marches on and executes all five statements inside the loop's curly braces. The computer performs the test again (to see whether `inputNumber` is still not equal to `randomNumber`) only after it fully executes all five statements in the loop.

Repeating a Certain Number of Times (Java for Statements)

"Write 'I will not talk in class' on the blackboard 100 times."

What your teacher really meant was,

```
Set the count to 0.
As long as the count is less than 100,
    Write 'I will not talk in class' on the blackboard,
    Add 1 to the count.
```

Fortunately, you didn't know about loops and counters at the time. If you pointed out all this stuff to your teacher, you'd have gotten into a lot more trouble than you were already in.

One way or another, life is filled with examples of counting loops. And computer programming mirrors life — or is it the other way around? When you tell a computer what to do, you're often telling the computer to print three lines, process ten accounts, dial a million phone numbers, or whatever. Because counting loops are so common in programming, the people who create programming languages have developed statements just for loops of this kind. In Java, the statement that repeats something a certain number of times is called a *for statement*. The use of the `for` statement is illustrated in Listings 6-2 and 6-3. Listing 6-2 has a rock-bottom simple example, and Listing 6-3 has a more exotic example. Take your pick.

Listing 6-2:   The World's Most Boring for Loop

```java
import static java.lang.System.out;

class Yawn {

    public static void main(String args[]) {

        for (int count = 1; count <= 10; count++) {
            out.print("The value of count is ");
            out.print(count);
            out.println(".");
        }

        out.println("Done!");
    }
}
```

Figure 6-3 shows you what you get when you run the program of Listing 6-2. (You get exactly what you deserve.) The `for` statement in Listing 6-2 starts by setting the `count` variable equal to 1. Then the statement tests to make sure that `count` is less than or equal to 10 (which it certainly is). Then the `for` statement dives ahead and executes the printing statements between the curly braces. (At this early stage of the game, the computer prints `The value of count is 1`.) Finally, the `for` statement does that last thing inside its parentheses — it adds 1 to the value of `count`.

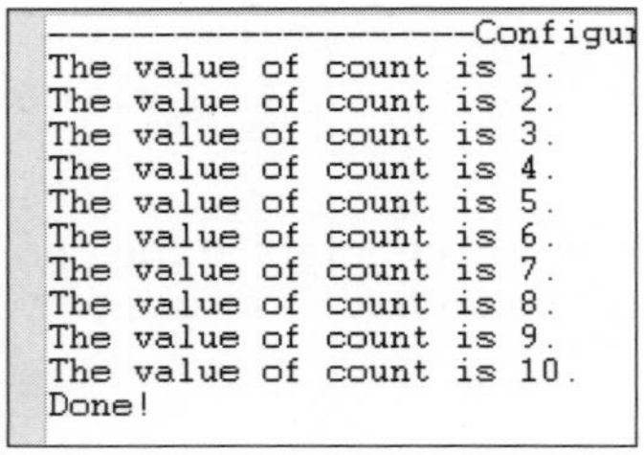

Figure 6-3:
Counting
to ten.

```
--------------------Configu
The value of count is 1.
The value of count is 2.
The value of count is 3.
The value of count is 4.
The value of count is 5.
The value of count is 6.
The value of count is 7.
The value of count is 8.
The value of count is 9.
The value of count is 10.
Done!
```

With `count` now equal to 2, the `for` statement checks again to make sure that `count` is less than or equal to 10. (Yes, 2 is smaller than 10.) Because the test turns out okay, the `for` statement marches back into the curly braced statements and prints `The value of count is 2` on the screen. Finally, the `for` statement does that last thing inside its parentheses — it adds 1 to the value of `count`, increasing the value of `count` to 3.

And so on. This whole thing keeps being repeated over and over again until, after 10 iterations, the value of `count` finally reaches 11. When this happens, the check for `count` being less than or equal to 10 fails, and the loop's execution ends. The computer jumps to whatever statement comes immediately after the `for` statement. In Listing 6-2, the computer prints `Done!` The whole process is illustrated in Figure 6-4.

The anatomy of a for statement

After the word *for,* you always put three things in parentheses. The first of these three things is called an *initialization,* the second is an *expression,* and the third thing is called an *update.*

```
for ( initialization ; expression ; update )
```

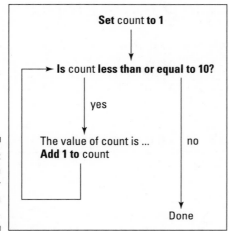

Figure 6-4:
The action
of the for
loop in
Listing 6-2.

Set count **to 1**

Is count **less than or equal to 10?**

yes

The value of count is ...
Add 1 to count

no

Done

Each of the three items in parentheses plays its own distinct role:

- ✔ The **initialization** is executed once, when the run of your program first reaches the for statement.
- ✔ The **expression** is evaluated several times (before each iteration).
- ✔ The **update** is also evaluated several times (at the end of each iteration).

If it helps, think of the loop as if its text is shifted all around:

```
int count = 1
for count <= 10 {
    out.print("The value of count is ");
    out.print(count);
    out.println(".");
    count++
}
```

You can't write a real for statement this way. Even so, this is the order in which the parts of the statement are executed.

If you declare a variable in the initialization of a for loop, you can't use that variable outside the loop. For instance, in Listing 6-2, you get an error message if you try putting out.println(count) after the end of the loop.

Anything that can be done with a for loop can also be done with a while loop. Choosing to use a for loop is a matter of style and convenience, not necessity.

The world premiere of "Al's All Wet"

Listing 6-2 is very nice, but the program in that listing doesn't do anything interesting. For a more eye-catching example, see Listing 6-3. In Listing 6-3, I make good on a promise I made in Chapter 5. The program in Listing 6-3 prints all the lyrics of the hit single, "Al's All Wet." (You can find the lyrics in Chapter 5.)

Listing 6-3:   The Unabridged "Al's All Wet" Song

```java
import static java.lang.System.out;

class AlsAllWet {

    public static void main(String args[]) {

        for (int verse = 1; verse <= 3; verse++) {
            out.print("Al's all wet. ");
            out.println("Oh, why is Al all wet? Oh,");
            out.print("Al's all wet 'cause ");
            out.println("he's standing in the rain.");
            out.println("Why is Al out in the rain?");

            switch (verse) {
            case 1:
                out.println
                    ("That's because he has no brain.");
                break;
            case 2:
                out.println
                    ("That's because he is a pain.");
                break;
            case 3:
                out.println
                    ("'Cause this is the last refrain.");
                break;
            }

            switch (verse) {
            case 3:
                out.println("Last refrain, last
refrain,");
            case 2:
                out.println("He's a pain, he's a pain,");
            case 1:
                out.println("Has no brain, has no
brain,");
            }

            out.println("In the rain, in the rain.");
```

Listing 6-3 (continued)

```
            out.println("Ohhhhhhhh...");
            out.println();
        }

        out.print("Al's all wet. ");
        out.println("Oh, why is Al all wet? Oh,");
        out.print("Al's all wet 'cause ");
        out.println("he's standing in the rain.");
    }
}
```

Listing 6-3 is nice because it combines many of the ideas from Chapters 5 and 6. In Listing 6-3, two `switch` statements are nested inside a `for` loop. One of the `switch` statements uses `break` statements; the other `switch` statement uses fall-through. As the value of the `for` loop's counter variable (`verse`) goes from 1 to 2 and then to 3, all the cases in the `switch` statements are executed. When the program is near the end of its run and execution has dropped out of the `for` loop, the program's last four statements print the song's final verse.

When I boldly declare that a `for` statement is for counting, I'm stretching the truth just a bit. Java's `for` statement is very versatile. You can use a `for` statement in situations that have nothing to do with counting. For instance, a statement with no update part, such as `for (i = 0; i < 10; )`, just keeps on going. The looping ends when some action inside the loop assigns a big number to the variable `i`. You can even create a `for` statement with nothing inside the parentheses. The loop `for ( ; ; )` runs forever, which is good if the loop controls a serious piece of machinery. Usually, when you write a `for` statement, you're counting how many times to repeat something. But, in truth, you can do just about any kind of repetition with a `for` statement.

Listing 6-3 uses `break` statements to jump out of a `switch`. But a `break` statement can also play a role inside a loop. To see an example, visit this book's Web site.

Repeating Until You Get What You Want (Java do Statements)

"Fools rush in where angels fear to tread."

— Alexander Pope

Today, I want to be young and foolish (or, at the very least, foolish). Look back at Figure 6-2 and notice how Java's `while` loop works. As execution enters a `while` loop, the computer checks to make sure that the loop's condition is true. If the condition isn't true, the statements inside the loop are never executed — not even once. In fact, you can easily cook up a `while` loop whose statements are never executed (although I can't think of a reason why you would ever want to do it).

```java
int twoPlusTwo = 2 + 2;

while (twoPlusTwo == 5) {
    out.println("Are you kidding?");
    out.println("2 + 2 doesn't equal 5");
    out.print("Everyone knows that");
    out.println(" 2 + 2 equals 3");
}
```

In spite of this silly `twoPlusTwo` example, the `while` statement turns out to be the most versatile of Java's looping constructs. In particular, the `while` loop is good for situations in which you must look before you leap. For example: "While money is in my account, write a mortgage check every month." When you first encounter this statement, if your account has a zero balance, you don't want to write a mortgage check — not even one check.

But at times (not many), you want to leap before you look. Take, for instance, the situation in which you're asking the user for a response. Maybe the user's response makes sense, but maybe it doesn't. If it doesn't, you want to ask again. Maybe the user's finger slipped, or perhaps the user didn't understand the question.

Figure 6-5 shows some runs of a program to delete a file. Before deleting the file, the program asks the user whether making the deletion is okay. If the user answers *y* or *n,* the program proceeds according to the user's wishes. But if the user enters any other character (any digit, uppercase letter, punctuation symbol, or whatever), the program asks the user for another response.

Figure 6-5:
Checking
before you
delete a file.

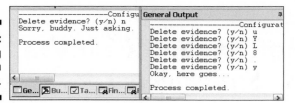

To write this program, you need a loop — a loop that repeatedly asks the user whether the file should be deleted. The loop keeps asking until the user gives a meaningful response. Now, the thing to notice is that the loop doesn't need to check anything before asking the user the first time. Indeed, before the user gives the first response, the loop has nothing to check. The loop doesn't start with "as long as such-and-such is true, then get a response from the user." Instead, the loop just leaps ahead, gets a response from the user, and then checks the response to see if it makes sense.

That's why the program in Listing 6-4 has a *do* loop (also known as a *do . . . while* loop). With a do loop, the program jumps right in, takes action, and then checks a condition to see whether the result of the action makes sense. If the result makes sense, execution of the loop is done. If not, the program goes back to the top of the loop for another go-around.

Listing 6-4:   To Delete or Not to Delete

```
import java.io.File;
import static java.lang.System.out;
import java.util.Scanner;

class DeleteEvidence {

    public static void main(String args[]) {
        File evidence = new File("c:\\cookedBooks.txt");
        Scanner myScanner = new Scanner(System.in);
        char reply;

        do {
            out.print("Delete evidence? (y/n) ");
            reply =
                myScanner.findWithinHorizon(".",0).charAt(0);
        } while (reply != 'y' && reply != 'n');

        if (reply == 'y') {
            out.println("Okay, here goes...");
            evidence.delete();
        } else {
            out.println("Sorry, buddy. Just asking.");
        }
    }
}
```

Figure 6-5 shows two runs of the code in Listing 6-4. The program accepts lowercase letters *y* and *n,* but not the uppercase letters *Y* and *N.* To make the program accept uppercase letters, change the conditions in the code as follows:

```
do {
    out.print("Delete evidence? (y/n) ");
    reply = myScanner.findWithinHorizon(".", 0).charAt(0);
} while (reply! = 'y' && reply != 'Y' &&
        reply != 'n' && reply!='N');

if (reply == 'y' || reply == 'Y')
```

Figure 6-6 shows the flow of control in the loop of Listing 6-4. With a do loop, the situation in the twoPlusTwo program (shown earlier) can never happen. Because the do loop carries out its first action without testing a condition, every do loop is guaranteed to perform at least one iteration.

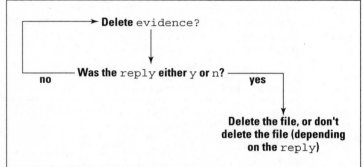

Figure 6-6:
Here we go
loop, do
loop.

Reading a single character

In Listing 5-3, the user types a word on the keyboard. The myScanner.next method grabs the word and places the word into a String variable named *password*. Everything works nicely because a String variable can store many characters at once and the next method can read many characters at once.

But in Listing 6-4, you're not interested in reading several characters. You expect the user to type one letter — either *y* or *n*. So you don't create a String variable to store the user's response. Instead, you create a char variable — a variable that stores just one symbol at a time.

The Java API doesn't have a nextChar method. So to read something suitable for storage in a char variable, you have to improvise. In Listing 6-4, the improvisation looks like this:

```
myScanner.findWithinHorizon(".", 0).charAt(0)
```

You can use this code exactly as it appears in Listing 6-4 whenever you want to read a single character.

A String variable can contain many characters or just one character. But a String variable that contains only one character isn't the same as a char variable. No matter what you put in a String variable, String variables and char variables have to be treated differently.

File handling in Java

In Listing 6-4, the actual file-handling statements deserve some attention. These statements involve the use of classes, objects, and methods. Many of the meaty details about these things are in other chapters, like Chapters 7 and 9. Even so, I can't do any harm by touching on some highlights right here.

So, you can find a class in the Java language API named *java.io.File*. The statement

```
File evidence = new File("c:\\cookedBooks.txt");
```

creates a new object in the computer's memory. This object, formed from the `java.io.File` class, describes everything that the program needs to know about the disk file `c:\cookedBooks.txt`. (In Java, when you want to indicate a backslash inside a double-quoted `String` literal, you use a double backslash instead.) From this point on in Listing 6-4, the variable `evidence` refers to the disk file `c:\cookedBooks.txt`.

After you've got all this `java.io.File` stuff in your head, the only thing left to know is that the `evidence` object, being an instance of the `java.io.File` class, has a `delete` method. (What can I say? It's in the API documentation.) When you call `evidence.delete`, the computer gets rid of the file for you.

Variable declarations and blocks

A bunch of statements surrounded by curly braces form a block. If you declare a variable inside a block, you generally can't use that variable outside the block. For instance, in Listing 6-4, you get an error message if you make the following change:

```
do {
    out.print("Delete evidence? (y/n) ");
    char reply =
        myScanner.findWithinHorizon(".", 0).charAt(0);
} while (reply != 'y' && reply != 'n');

if (reply == 'y')
```

With the declaration `char reply` inside the loop's curly braces, no use of the name `reply` makes sense anywhere outside the braces. When you try to compile this code, you get three error messages — two for the `reply` words in `while (reply != 'y' && reply != 'n')`, and a third for the `if` statement's `reply`.

So in Listing 6-4, your hands are tied. The program's first real use of the `reply` variable is inside the loop. But, to make that variable available after the loop, you have to declare `reply` before the loop. In this situation, you're best off declaring the `reply` variable without initializing the variable. Very interesting!

To read more about variable initializations, see Chapter 4. To read more about blocks, see Chapter 5.

Loops Made Painless

I'll never forget the first time I played *Clue*. We bought the board game during a family vacation in Niagara Falls. (Niagara Falls?) Cousin Alan and I sat in the hotel room playing the game for hours on end. I scribbled complicated assertions in my little detective's notebook.

At one point, I bluffed by suggesting three cards that I had in my hand. Alan took the bait and made an accusation that was wrong on all three counts. Because he'd lost the game, and because I was being so smug about it, he beat the living daylights out of me. It was heaven. If I had the chance, I'd do it all over again.

The material in this section applies to Java 5, Java 6, or whatever higher version number comes along in the next few years. But this section's material doesn't work with older versions of Java — versions such as 1.3, 1.4, and so on. For a bit more about Java's version numbers, see Chapter 2.

Don't need no stinking counters

The `for` loop in Listing 6-2 counts from 1 to 10. And its friend (the `for` loop in Listing 6-3) counts 1, 2, 3. This counting is very nice, but sometimes it's not the most natural way to think about a problem. Take, for instance, the listing of all possible accusations in the board game *Clue*. The suspects aren't numbered from 1 to 6, and neither are the rooms or weapons. You can number all these things, but why bother with numbering when the programming language provides a simpler solution?

Java's *enhanced for loop* lets you cycle through groups of things without creating a counting variable. All you have to do is define the group. Listing 6-5 shows you what to do.

Listing 6-5: "I Accuse . . ."

```java
import static java.lang.System.out;

class Clue {

    enum Suspect {mustard, plum, green,
                    peacock, scarlet, white};

    enum Room {ballroom, kitchen, diningRoom,
                lounge, hall, study, library,
                billiardRoom, conservatory};

    enum Weapon {knife, candlestick, revolver,
                    rope, leadPipe, wrench};

    public static void main(String args[]) {

        for (Suspect mySuspect : Suspect.values()) {
            for (Room myRoom : Room.values()) {
                for (Weapon myWeapon : Weapon.values()) {
                    out.print(mySuspect);
                    out.print(" in the ");
                    out.print(myRoom);
                    out.print(" with a ");
                    out.println(myWeapon);
                }
            }
        }

        Suspect killer = Suspect.peacock;
        Room sceneOfTheCrime = Room.study;
        Weapon murderWeapon = Weapon.leadPipe;

        out.println();
        out.print("I accuse ");
        out.print(killer);
        out.print(" in the ");
        out.print(sceneOfTheCrime);
        out.print(" with a ");
        out.print(murderWeapon);
        out.println(".");
    }
}
```

The output of the code in Listing 6-5 has 324 lines, so I can't show it all to you. But the first several lines appear in Figure 6-7. First, you see Colonel Mustard's ballroom antics. Then you get Mustard's kitchen tricks. Later in the run, when all Mustard's frolics are finished, you see the same possibilities for Professor Plum.

```
----------------------Configuration: Listing0605
mustard in the ballroom with a knife
mustard in the ballroom with a candlestick
mustard in the ballroom with a revolver
mustard in the ballroom with a rope
mustard in the ballroom with a leadPipe
mustard in the ballroom with a wrench
mustard in the kitchen with a knife
mustard in the kitchen with a candlestick
mustard in the kitchen with a revolver
mustard in the kitchen with a rope
mustard in the kitchen with a leadPipe
mustard in the kitchen with a wrench
mustard in the diningRoom with a knife
mustard in the diningRoom with a candlestick
mustard in the diningRoom with a revolver
```

Figure 6-7:
The code in
Listing 6-5
starts
running.

Listing 6-5 has a loop within a loop within a loop.

- ✔ The Room loop is inside of the Suspect loop. Not only do you loop through all the rooms, but you loop through all the rooms six times — once for each of the six suspects. If I count them up, that makes 54 visits to various rooms.

- ✔ The Weapon loop is inside of the Room loop. So every time you visit a room (and you visit a room 54 times), you go through all six of the hideous weapons.

Like the code in Listing 6-3, this section's Clue program nests statements within other statements. In Listing 6-3, I nested switch statements inside a big for statement. But in the Clue program, I nest for statements inside other for statements. It may look at bit tangled at first, but when you get used to it, nesting loop within loop is a really useful technique.

Grouping things together

Java provides lots of ways for you to group things together. In Chapter 11, you can group things into an array or a collection. In this chapter, you group things into an enum type. (Of course, you can't group anything unless you can pronounce enum. The word *enum* is pronounced *ee-noom,* like the first two syllables of the word *enumeration.*)

Creating a complicated enum type isn't easy, but to create a simple enum type, just write a bunch of words inside a pair of curly braces. Listing 6-5 has three enum types. The names of the enum types are Suspect, Room, and Weapon.

When you define an enum type, two important things happen:

- ✔ **You create values.**

    Just as 13 and 151 are int values, mustard and plum are Suspect values.

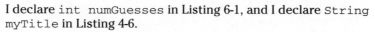

✔ **You can create variables to refer to those values.**

After the `for` loop in Listing 6-5, I declare a variable named *killer*. Just as `int numGuesses` declares a `numGuesses` variable is of type `int`, and just as `String myTitle` declares variable `myTitle` to be of type `String`, so `Suspect killer` declares variable `killer` to be of type `Suspect`.

I declare `int numGuesses` in Listing 6-1, and I declare `String myTitle` in Listing 4-6.

Being of type `Suspect` means that you can have values `mustard`, `plum`, `green`, and so on. So in Listing 6-5, I give the `killer` variable the value `peacock`. (At this point in the code, if I don't type the longer dotted name *Suspect.peacock,* the Java compiler gets confused.)

In a similar way, I create variables `sceneOfTheCrime` and `murderWeapon` toward the end of Listing 6-5. Both these variables have `enum` types, and both are given appropriate values (values like `Room.study` and `Weapon.leadPipe`).

In Listing 6-5, all the `enum` type declarations are *outside* the `main` method. (For example, the line that begins with `enum Suspect` is before the start of the `main` method.) Java doesn't allow you to put an `enum` type declaration inside a method. That's because an `enum` type declaration is really a Java class in disguise. For more insight on `enum` types, see Chapter 9.

Anatomy of an enhanced for loop

The enhanced and un-enhanced `for` loops have a lot in common. Figure 6-8 illustrates the point.

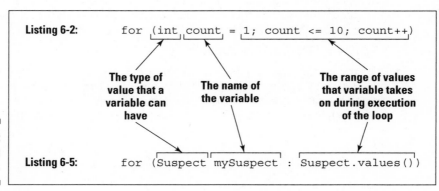

Figure 6-8: Comparing for loops.

✔ **In both kinds of loops, you define a variable.**

The loop in Listing 6-2 defines a variable named *count*. The loop in Listing 6-5 defines a variable named *mySuspect*.

In both listings, the statements inside the loop refer to the newly defined variable. The loop in Listing 6-2 has the statement

```
out.print(count);
```

and the loop in Listing 6-5 has the statement

```
out.print(mySuspect);
```

During successive iterations, the `print` in Listing 6-2 stands for `out.print(1)`, `out.print(2)`, and so on. During successive iterations, the `print` in Listing 6-5 stands for `out.print(mustard)`, `out.print(plum)`, and so on.

✔ **In both kinds of loops, you declare the type of value that the variable can have.**

In Listing 6-2, the variable `count` must store an `int` value (–7, 0, 5, 15, and so on). In Listing 6-5, the variable `mySuspect` must refer to a `Suspect` value (`mustard`, `plum`, `white`, and so on).

In fact, this *declaring the type of value* rule applies everywhere in Java — not only in `for` loops. Every Java variable belongs to one type or another. In Listing 6-1, the line

```
int numGuesses = 0;
```

declares that `numGuesses` must store an `int` value. The line goes on to say that, among all possible `int` values, the starting value for `numGuesses` is 0. Again in Listing 6-1, the line

```
Scanner myScanner = new Scanner(System.in);
```

declares that `myScanner` must refer to a `Scanner` object. Among all such objects, the starting value for `myScanner` is an object that gets keystrokes from the keyboard (from `System.in`).

✔ **In both kinds of loops, you specify a range of values.**

You specify the range of values that the variable takes on during the execution of the loop. In Listing 6-2, you narrow the `count` variable's values to the numbers from 1 to 10. In Listing 6-5, you throw caution to the wind, and say that `mySuspect` gets to be every one of the items in `Suspect.values()`.

You can apply `values()` to the name of any `enum` type. In fact, to create a n enhanced `for` loop with an `enum` type, you have to use something like `values()`. The expression `Suspect.values()` stands for all the items you list in the declaration of the `Suspect` enum type. So, in the loop of Listing 6-5, `mySuspect` becomes `mustard`, then `plum`, then `green`, and so on.

When you apply `values()` to the name of an `enum` type, you get an array of items belonging to that `enum` type. To read all about arrays, see Chapter 11.

Part III

Working with the Big Picture: Object-Oriented Programming

"I asked for software that would biodegrade after it was thrown out, not while it was running."

In this part . . .

Have you read or heard anything about object-oriented programming? Sometimes, all the object-oriented programmers seem to belong to a little club. They have a secret handshake, a secret sign, and a promise not to reveal object-oriented programming concepts to any outsiders. Well, the secrecy is ending. In this part, I take all the mystery out of object-oriented programming. I introduce the concepts step by step and illustrate each concept with a Java program or two.

Chapter 7

Thinking in Terms of Classes and Objects

As a computer book author, I've been told this over and over again — I shouldn't expect people to read sections and chapters in their logical order. People jump around, picking what they need and skipping what they don't feel like reading. With that in mind, I realize that you may have skipped Chapter 1. If that's the case, please don't feel guilty. You can compensate in just sixty seconds by reading the following information from Chapter 1:

> *Because Java is an object-oriented programming language, your primary goal is to describe classes and objects. A class is the idea behind a certain kind of thing. An object is a concrete instance of a class. The programmer defines a class, and from the class definition, the computer makes individual objects.*

Of course, you can certainly choose to skip over the 60-second summary paragraph. If that's the case, you may want to recoup some of your losses. You can do that by reading the following two-word summary of Chapter 1:

> *Classes; objects.*

Defining a Class (What It Means to Be an Account)

What distinguishes one bank account from another? If you ask a banker this question, you hear a long sales pitch. The banker describes interest rates, fees, penalties — the whole routine. Fortunately for you, I'm not interested in all that. Instead, I want to know how my account is different from your account. After all, my account is named *Barry Burd, trading as Burd Brain Consulting,* and your account is named *Jane Q. Reader, trading as Budding Java Expert.* My account has $24.02 in it. How about yours?

When you come right down to it, the differences between one account and another can be summarized as values of variables. Maybe there's a variable named *balance.* For me, the value of `balance` is `24.02`. For you, the value of `balance` is `55.63`. The question is, in writing a computer program to deal with accounts, how do I separate my `balance` variable from your `balance` variable?

The answer is to create two separate objects. Let one `balance` variable live inside one of the objects and let the other `balance` variable live inside the other object. While you're at it, put a `name` variable and an `address` variable in each of the objects. And there you have it. You've got two objects, and each object represents an account. More precisely, each object is an instance of the `Account` class. (See Figure 7-1.)

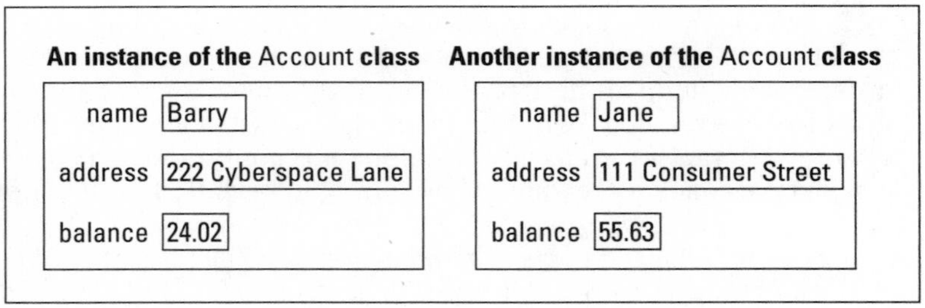

An instance of the Account **class**   **Another instance of the** Account **class**

name Barry	name Jane
address 222 Cyberspace Lane	address 111 Consumer Street
balance 24.02	balance 55.63

Figure 7-1:
Two objects.

So far, so good. But you still haven't solved the original problem. In your computer program, how do you refer to my `balance` variable, as opposed to your `balance` variable? Well, you have two objects sitting around, so maybe you have variables to refer to these two objects. Create one variable named *myAccount* and another variable named *yourAccount.* The `myAccount` variable refers to my object (my instance of the `Account` class) with all the stuff that's inside it. To refer to my balance, write

```
myAccount.balance
```

To refer to my name, write

```
myAccount.name
```

Then `yourAccount.balance` refers to the value in your object's `balance` variable, and `yourAccount.name` refers to the value of your object's `name` variable. To tell the computer how much I have in my account, you can write

```
myAccount.balance = 24.02;
```

To display your name on the screen, you can write

```
out.println(yourAccount.name);
```

These ideas come together in Listings 7-1 and 7-2.

Listing 7-1:   What It Means to Be an Account

```
class Account {
    String name;
    String address;
    double balance;
}
```

Listing 7-2:   Dealing with Account Objects

```
import static java.lang.System.out;

class UseAccount {

    public static void main(String args[]) {
        Account myAccount;
        Account yourAccount;

        myAccount = new Account();
        yourAccount = new Account();

        myAccount.name = "Barry Burd";
        myAccount.address = "222 Cyberspace Lane";
        myAccount.balance = 24.02;

        yourAccount.name = "Jane Q. Public";
        yourAccount.address = "111 Consumer Street";
        yourAccount.balance = 55.63;

        out.print(myAccount.name);
        out.print(" (");
        out.print(myAccount.address);
        out.print(") has $");
        out.print(myAccount.balance);
        out.println();

        out.print(yourAccount.name);
        out.print(" (");
```

(continued)

Listing 7-2 (continued)

```
        out.print(yourAccount.address);
        out.print(") has $");
        out.print(yourAccount.balance);
    }
}
```

Taken together, the two classes — `Account` and `UseAccount` — form one complete program. The `Account` class defines what it means to be an `Account`. The code for the `Account` class tells you that each of the `Account` class's instances has three variables — `name`, `address`, and `balance`. This is consistent with the information in Figure 7-1.

If you've been grappling with the material in Chapters 4 through 6, the code for class `Account` (Listing 7-1) may come as a big shock to you. Can you really define a complete Java class with only four lines of code (give or take a curly brace)? You certainly can. In fact, the `Account` class in Listing 7-1 is quite representative of what Java programmers think of when they think *class*. A class is a grouping of existing things. In the `Account` class of Listing 7-1, those existing things are two `String` values and a `double` value.

The code in Listing 7-2 defines the `UseAccount` class. The code needs a `main` method, and every method has to be in one class or another. So put the `main` method in a class named *UseAccount*. This `main` method has variables of its own — `yourAccount` and `myAccount`.

Declaring variables and creating objects

In a way, the first two lines inside the `main` method of Listing 7-2 are misleading. Some people read `Account yourAccount` as if it's supposed to mean, "yourAccount is an `Account`," or "The variable `yourAccount` refers to an instance of the `Account` class." That's not really what this first line means. Instead, the line `Account yourAccount` means, "If and when I make the variable `yourAccount` refer to something, that something will be an instance of the `Account` class." So, what's the difference?

The difference is that simply declaring `Account yourAccount` doesn't make the `yourAccount` variable refer to an object. All the declaration does is reserve the variable name *yourAccount* so that the name can eventually refer to an instance of the `Account` class. The creation of an actual object doesn't come until later in the code, when the computer executes `new Account()`.

Technically, when the computer executes `new Account()`, you're creating an object by calling the `Account` class's *constructor*. I have more to say about that in Chapter 9.

When the computer executes the assignment yourAccount = new Account(), the computer creates a new object (a new instance of the Account class) and makes the variable yourAccount refer to that new object. (It's the equal sign that makes the variable refer to the new object.) The situation is illustrated in Figure 7-2.

Figure 7-2:
Before and after a constructor is called.

After executing
Account yourAccount;

After executing
yourAccount =
    new Account ();

yourAccount

yourAccount

name

address

balance

To test the claim that I made in the last few paragraphs, I added an extra line to the code of Listing 7-1. I tried to print yourAccount.name after declaring yourAccount, but before calling new Account().

```
Account myAccount;
Account yourAccount;

out.println(yourAccount.name);

myAccount = new Account();
yourAccount = new Account();
```

When I tried to compile the new code, I got this error message: variable yourAccount might not have been initialized. So that settles it. Before you do new Account(), you can't print the name variable of an object; an object doesn't exist.

When a variable has a reference type, simply declaring the variable isn't enough. You don't get an object until you call a constructor and use the keyword new.

For information about reference types, see Chapter 4.

Initializing a variable

In Chapter 4, I announce that you can initialize a primitive type variable as part of the variable's declaration.

```
int weightOfAPerson = 150;
```

You can do the same thing with reference type variables, such as `myAccount` and `yourAccount` in Listing 7-2. You can combine the first four lines in the listing's `main` method into just two lines, like this:

```
Account myAccount = new Account();
Account yourAccount = new Account();
```

If you combine lines this way, you automatically avoid the `variable might not have been initialized` error that I describe in the previous section. Sometimes you find a situation in which you can't initialize a variable. But when you can initialize, it's usually a plus.

Using variables

After you've bitten off and chewed the `main` method's first four lines, the rest of the code in Listing 7-2 is sensible and straightforward. You have three lines that put values in the `myAccount` object's variables, three lines that put values in the `yourAccount` object's variables, and four lines that do some printing. The program's output is shown in Figure 7-3.

Figure 7-3:
Running the
code in
Listings 7-1
and 7-2.

```
----------------------Configuration: Listings0701-02
Barry Burd (222 Cyberspace Lane) has $24.02
Jane Q. Public (111 Consumer Street) has $55.63
Process completed.
```

Compiling and Running More Than One Class

Each program in Chapters 3 to 6 consists of a single class. That's great for a book's introductory chapters. But in real life, a typical program consists of hundreds or even thousands of classes. The program that spans Listings 7-1 and 7-2 consists of two classes. Sure, having two classes isn't like having thousands of classes, but it's a step in that direction.

In practice, most programmers put each class in a file of its own. When you create a program like the one in Listings 7-1 and 7-2, you create two files on your computer's hard drive. So the code that comes from this book's CD-ROM has two separate files — `Account.java` and `UseAccount.java`. (See Figure 7-4.)

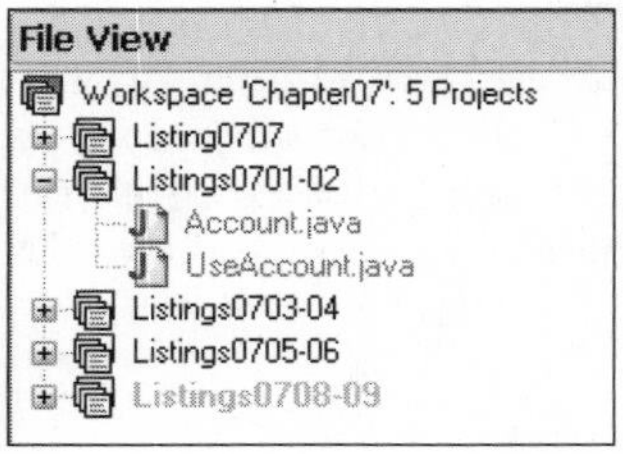

Figure 7-4:
Two files in
one project.

```
File View
  Workspace 'Chapter07': 5 Projects
  ⊞  Listing0707
  ⊟  Listings0701-02
         Account.java
         UseAccount.java
  ⊞  Listings0703-04
  ⊞  Listings0705-06
  ⊞  Listings0708-09
```

To run the code, just do what you do to run any old single-file program:

1. **Open the Chapter07 workspace.**

2. **Set `Listings0701-02` as the active project.**

3. **Choose Build⇨Compile Project.**

4. **Choose Build⇨Execute Project.**

   For details on compiling and running code that's copied from the CD-ROM, see Chapter 2.

Creating a new program with two or more classes is also pretty easy. (All you have to do is flip back and forth a million times between this chapter and Chapter 3.)

1. **Follow Steps 1 through 7 in the "Typing Your Own Code" section of Chapter 3.**

   With these steps, you create a new project.

2. **Follow Steps 8 through 11 (also in the "Typing Your Own Code" section of Chapter 3) to create the first of two or more classes.**

   If you're experimenting with the code in Listings 7-1 and 7-2, this first class is named *Account.*

3. **Follow Steps 8 through 11 again to create another class.**

   If you're experimenting with the code in Listings 7-1 and 7-2, this second class is named *UseAccount.*

   Repeat Steps 8 through 11 once for each of the classes in your Java program.

4. **Follow Steps 12 through 15 in that same section of Chapter 3.**

   When you do, JCreator compiles and runs your program.

When you work with several classes at once, you can easily get the following unfriendly message: `NoSuchMethodError: main`. You see this when you try to execute a class that has no `main` method. For example, the `Account` class in Listing 7-1 has no `main` method. If the `Account` class's code is the front-most code in JCreator's Editor pane, and you choose Build⇨Execute File (instead of Build⇨Execute Project) from JCreator's main menu, you get the dreaded `NoSuchMethodError`. To fix this, always make sure that your project has a class with a `main` method, and always choose Build⇨Execute Project to run your code.

Defining a Method within a Class (Displaying an Account)

Imagine a table containing the information about two accounts. (If you have trouble imagining such a thing, just look at Table 7-1.)

Table 7-1	Without Object-Oriented Programming	
Name	*Address*	*Balance*
Barry Burd	222 Cyberspace Lane	24.02
Jane Q. Public	111 Consumer Street	55.63

In Table 7-1, each account has three things — a name, an address, and a balance. That's the way things were done before object-oriented programming came along. But object-oriented programming involved a big shift in thinking. With object-oriented programming, each account can have a name, an address, a balance, and a way of being displayed.

In object-oriented programming, each object has its own built-in functionality. An account knows how to display itself. A string can tell you whether it has the same characters inside it as another string has. A PrintStream instance, such as System.out, knows how to do println. In object-oriented programming, each object has its own methods. These methods are little subprograms that you can call to have an object do things to (or for) itself.

And why is this a good idea? It's good because you're making pieces of data take responsibility for themselves. With object-oriented programming, all the functionality that's associated with an account is collected inside the code for the Account class. Everything you have to know about a string is located in the file String.java. Anything having to do with year numbers (whether they have two or four digits, for instance) is handled right inside the Year class. So, if anybody has problems with your Account class or your Year class, he or she knows just where to look for all the code. That's great!

So imagine an enhanced account table. In this new table, each object has built-in functionality. Each account knows how to display itself on the screen. Each row of the table has its own copy of a display method. Of course, you don't need much imagination to picture this table. I just happen to have a table you can look at. It's Table 7-2.

Table 7-2	The Object-Oriented Way		
Name	*Address*	*Balance*	*Display*
Barry Burd	222 Cyberspace Lane	24.02	out.print. . . .
Jane Q. Public	111 Consumer Street	55.63	out.print. . . .

An account that displays itself

In Table 7-2, each account object has four things — a name, an address, a balance, and a way of displaying itself on the screen. After you make the jump to object-oriented thinking, you'll never turn back. A program that implements the ideas in Table 7-2 is shown in Listings 7-3 and 7-4.

Listing 7-3:   An Account Displays Itself

```
import static java.lang.System.out;

class Account {
    String name;
    String address;
    double balance;

    void display() {
        out.print(name);
        out.print(" (");
        out.print(address);
        out.print(") has $");
        out.print(balance);
    }
}
```

Listing 7-4:   Using the Improved Account Class

```
class UseAccount {

    public static void main(String args[]) {
        Account myAccount = new Account();
        Account yourAccount = new Account();

        myAccount.name = "Barry Burd";
        myAccount.address = "222 Cyberspace Lane";
        myAccount.balance = 24.02;

        yourAccount.name = "Jane Q. Public";
        yourAccount.address = "111 Consumer Street";
        yourAccount.balance = 55.63;

        myAccount.display();
        System.out.println();
        yourAccount.display();
    }
}
```

A run of the code in Listings 7-3 and 7-4 looks just like a run for Listings 7-1 and 7-2. You can see the action back in Figure 7-3.

In Listing 7-3, the Account class has four things in it — a name, an address, a balance, and a display method. These things match up with the four columns in Table 7-2. So each instance of the Account class has a name, an address, a balance, and a way of displaying itself. The way you call these things is nice and uniform. To refer to the name stored in `myAccount`, you write

```
myAccount.name
```

To get `myAccount` to display itself on the screen, you write

```
myAccount.display()
```

The only difference is the parentheses.

When you call a method, you put parentheses after the method's name.

The display method's header

Look again at Listings 7-3 and 7-4. A call to the `display` method is inside the `UseAccount` class's `main` method. But the declaration of the `display` method is up in the `Account` class. The declaration has a header and a body. (See Chapter 3.) The header has two words and some parentheses:

- ✔ **The word *void* tells the computer that when the `display` method is called, the `display` method doesn't return anything to the place that called it.** To see a method that does return something to the place that called it, see the next section.

- ✔ **The word *display* is the method's name.** Every method must have a name. Otherwise, you don't have a way to call the method.

- ✔ **The parentheses contain all the things you're going to pass to the method when you call it.** When you call a method, you can pass information to that method on the fly. The `display` method in Listing 7-3 looks strange because the parentheses in the method's header have nothing inside them. This nothingness indicates that no information is passed to the `display` method when you call it. For a meatier example, see the next section.

Sending Values to and from Methods (Calculating Interest)

Think about sending someone to the supermarket to buy bread. When you do this, you say, "Go to the supermarket and buy some bread." (Try it at home. You'll have a fresh loaf of bread in no time at all!) Of course, some other time you send that same person to the supermarket to buy bananas. You say, "Go to the supermarket and buy some bananas." And what's the point of all this? Well, you have a method, and you have some on-the-fly information that you pass to the method when you call it. The method is named *goToTheSupermarketAndBuySome.* The on-the-fly information is either *bread* or *bananas,* depending on your culinary needs. In Java, the method calls would look like this:

```
goToTheSupermarketAndBuySome(bread);
goToTheSupermarketAndBuySome(bananas);
```

The things in parentheses are called *parameters* or *parameter lists.* With parameters, your methods become much more versatile. Instead of getting the same thing each time, you can send somebody to the supermarket to buy bread one time, bananas another time, and birdseed the third time. When you call your `goToTheSupermarketAndBuySome` method, you decide right there and then what you're going to ask your pal to buy.

And what happens when your friend returns from the supermarket? "Here's the bread you asked me to buy," says your friend. As a result of carrying out your wishes, your friend returns something to you. You make a method call, and the method returns information (or a loaf of bread).

The thing returned to you is called the method's *return value.* The general type of thing that is returned to you is called the method's *return type.* These concepts are made more concrete in Listings 7-5 and 7-6.

Listing 7-5:   An Account That Calculates Its Own Interest

```
import static java.lang.System.out;

class Account {
    String name;
    String address;
    double balance;

    void display() {
        out.print(name);
        out.print(" (");
        out.print(address);
        out.print(") has $");
        out.print(balance);
    }

    double getInterest(double percentageRate) {
        return balance * percentageRate / 100.00;
    }
}
```

Listing 7-6: Calculating Interest

```
import static java.lang.System.out;

class UseAccount {

    public static void main(String args[]) {
        Account myAccount = new Account();
        Account yourAccount = new Account();

        myAccount.name = "Barry Burd";
        myAccount.address = "222 Cyberspace Lane";
        myAccount.balance = 24.02;

        yourAccount.name = "Jane Q. Public";
        yourAccount.address = "111 Consumer Street";
        yourAccount.balance = 55.63;

        myAccount.display();

        out.print(" plus $");
        out.print(myAccount.getInterest(5.00));
        out.println(" interest ");

        yourAccount.display();

        double yourInterestRate = 7.00;
        out.print(" plus $");
        double yourInterestAmount =
            yourAccount.getInterest(yourInterestRate);
        out.print(yourInterestAmount);
        out.println(" interest ");
    }
}
```

The output of the code in Listings 7-5 and 7-6 is shown in Figure 7-5. In Listing 7-5, the Account class has a getInterest method. This getInterest method is called twice from the main method in Listing 7-6. The actual account balances and interest rates are different each time.

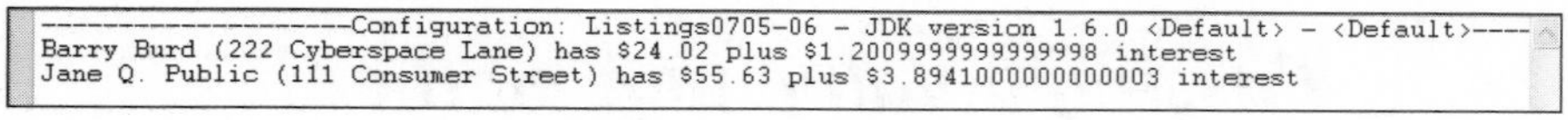

Figure 7-5:
Running the
code in
Listings 7-5
and 7-6.

```
---------------------Configuration: Listings0705-06 - JDK version 1.6.0 <Default> - <Default>----
Barry Burd (222 Cyberspace Lane) has $24.02 plus $1.2009999999999998 interest
Jane Q. Public (111 Consumer Street) has $55.63 plus $3.8941000000000003 interest
```

✔ **In the first call, the balance is 24.02, and the interest rate is 5.00.** The first call, `myAccount.getInterest(5.00)`, refers to the `myAccount` object and all the variables inside it. (See Figure 7-6.) When this call is made, the expression `balance * percentageRate / 100.00` stands for 24.02 * 5.00 / 100.00.

✔ **In the second call, the balance is 55.63, and the interest rate is 7.00.** In the `main` method, just before this second call is made, the variable `yourInterestRate` is assigned the value `7.00`. The call itself, `yourAccount.getInterest(yourInterestRate)`, refers to the `yourAccount` object and all the variables inside it. (Again, see Figure 7-6.) So, when the call is made, the expression `balance * percentageRate / 100.00` stands for 55.63 * 7.00 / 100.00.

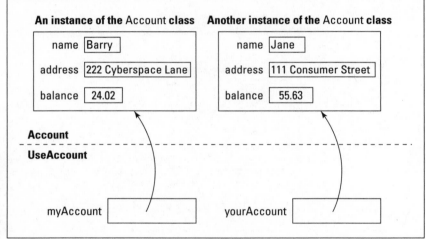

Figure 7-6:
My account
and your
account.

By the way, the `main` method in Listing 7-3 contains two calls to `getInterest`. One call has the literal `5.00` in its parameter list; the other call has the variable `yourInterestRate` in its parameter list. Why does one call use a literal and the other call use a variable? No reason. I just wanted to show you that you can do it either way.

Passing a value to a method

Take a look at the `getInterest` method's header. (As you read the explanation in the next few bullets, you can follow some of the ideas visually with the diagram in Figure 7-7.)

✔ **The word *double* tells the computer that when the `getInterest` method is called, the `getInterest` method returns a `double` value**

back to the place that called it. The statement in the `getInterest` method's body confirms this. The statement says `return balance * percentageRate / 100.00`, and the expression `balance * percentageRate / 100.00` has type `double`. (That's because all the things in the expression — `balance`, `percentageRate`, and `100.00` — have type `double`.)

When the `getInterest` method is called, the `return` statement calculates `balance * percentageRate / 100.00` and hands the calculation's result back to the code that called the method.

✔ **The word *getInterest* is the method's name.** That's the name you use to call the method when you're writing the code for the `UseAccount` class.

✔ **The parentheses contain all the things that you pass to the method when you call it.** When you call a method, you can pass information to that method on the fly. This information is the method's parameter list. The `getInterest` method's header says that the `getInterest` method takes one piece of information and that piece of information must be of type `double`.

```
double getInterest(double percentageRate)
```

Sure enough, if you look at the first call to `getInterest` (down in the `useAccount` class's `main` method), that call has the number `5.00` in it. And `5.00` is a `double` literal. When I call `getInterest`, I'm giving the method a value of type `double`.

If you don't remember what a literal is, see Chapter 4.

The same story holds true for the second call to `getInterest`. Down near the bottom of Listing 7-6, I call `getInterest` and feed the variable `yourInterestRate` to the method in its parameter list. Luckily for me, I declared `yourInterestRate` to be of type `double` just a few lines before that.

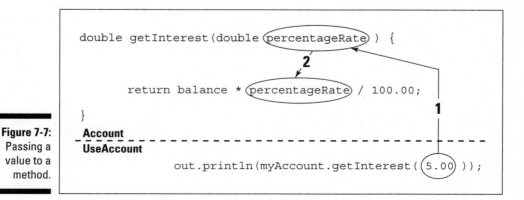

Figure 7-7: Passing a value to a method.

When you run the code in Listings 7-5 and 7-6, the flow of action isn't from top to bottom. The action goes from `main` to `getInterest`, then back to `main`, then back to `getInterest`, and finally back to `main` again. The whole business is shown in Figure 7-8.

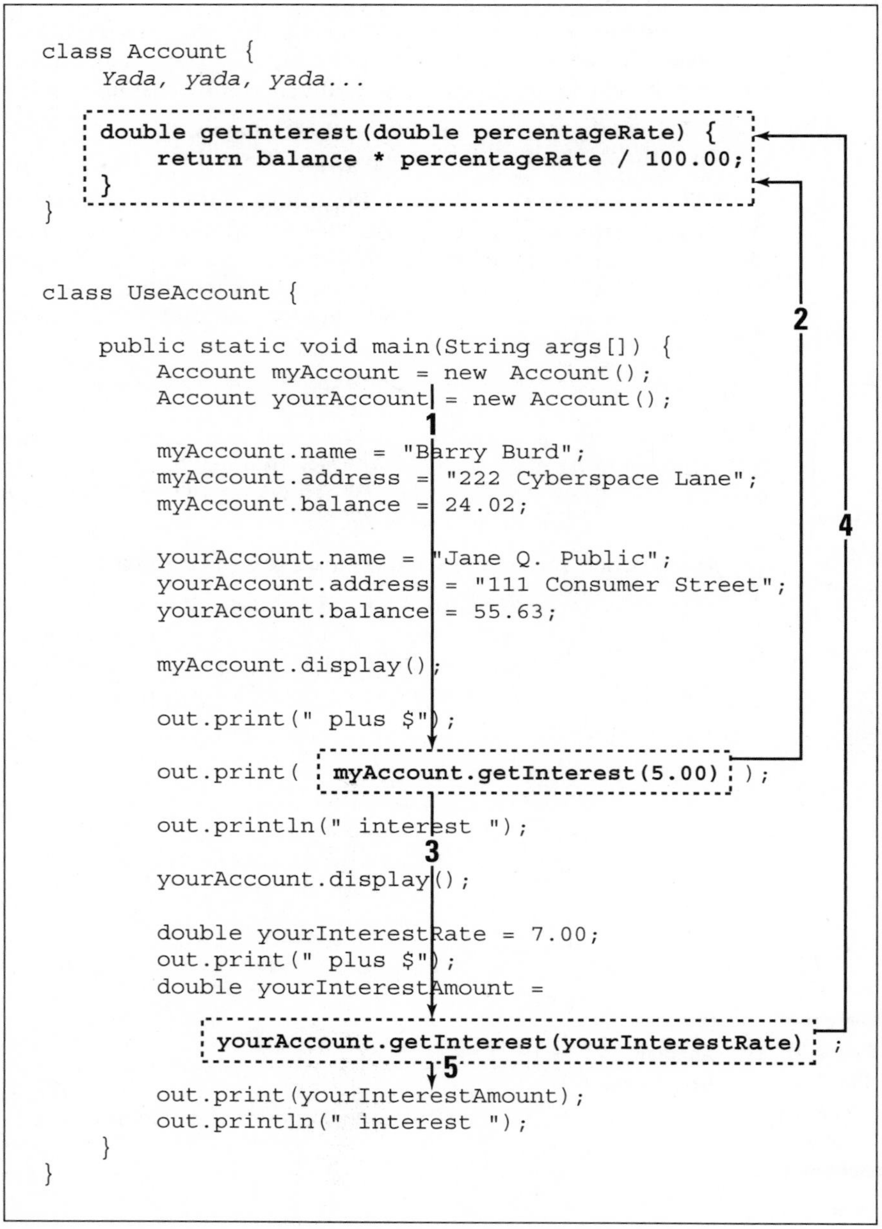

```
class Account {
    Yada, yada, yada...

    double getInterest(double percentageRate) {
        return balance * percentageRate / 100.00;
    }
}

class UseAccount {

    public static void main(String args[]) {
        Account myAccount = new Account();
        Account yourAccount = new Account();

        myAccount.name = "Barry Burd";
        myAccount.address = "222 Cyberspace Lane";
        myAccount.balance = 24.02;

        yourAccount.name = "Jane Q. Public";
        yourAccount.address = "111 Consumer Street";
        yourAccount.balance = 55.63;

        myAccount.display();

        out.print(" plus $");

        out.print( myAccount.getInterest(5.00) );

        out.println(" interest ");

        yourAccount.display();

        double yourInterestRate = 7.00;
        out.print(" plus $");
        double yourInterestAmount =

            yourAccount.getInterest(yourInterestRate) ;

        out.print(yourInterestAmount);
        out.println(" interest ");
    }
}
```

Figure 7-8:
The flow of control in Listings 7-5 and 7-6.

Returning a value from the getInterest method

When the `getInterest` method is called, the method executes the one statement that's in the method's body: a `return` statement. The `return` statement computes the value of `balance * percentageRate / 100.00`. If `balance` happens to be 24.02, and `percentageRate` is 5.00, the value of the expression is `1.201` — around $1.20. (Because the computer works exclusively with 0s and 1s, the computer gets this number wrong by an ever so tiny amount. The computer gets 1.2009999999999998. That's just something that humans have to live with.)

Anyway, after this value is calculated, the computer executes the `return`, which sends the value back to the place in `main` where `getInterest` was called. At that point in the process, the entire method call — `myAccount.getInterest(5.00)` — takes on the value 1.2009999999999998. The call itself is inside a `println`:

```
out.println(myAccount.getInterest(5.00));
```

So the `println` ends up with the following meaning:

```
out.println(1.2009999999999998);
```

The whole process, in which a value is passed back to the method call, is illustrated in Figure 7-9.

If a method returns anything, a call to the method is an expression with a value. That value can be printed, assigned to a variable, added to something else, or whatever. Anything you can do with any other kind of value, you can do with a method call.

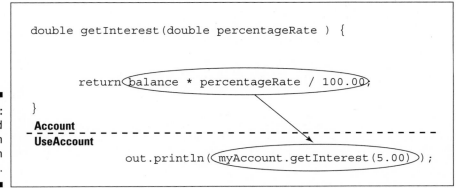

Figure 7-9: A method call is an expression with a value.

```
double getInterest(double percentageRate ) {



        return balance * percentageRate / 100.00;

}
```
Account
- -
UseAccount
```
        out.println(myAccount.getInterest(5.00));
```

Making numbers look good

Looking back at Figure 7-5, you may be concerned that the interest on my account is only $1.2009999999999998. Seemingly, the bank is cheating me out of 200-trillionths of a cent. I should go straight there and demand my fair interest. Maybe you and I should go together. We'll kick up some fur at that old bank and bust this scam right open. If my guess is correct, this is part of a big *salami scam*. In a salami scam, someone shaves little slices off millions of accounts. People don't notice their tiny little losses, but the person doing the shaving collects enough for a quick escape to Barbados (or for a whole truckload of salami).

But, wait a minute! Nothing is motivating you to come with me to the bank. Checking back at Figure 7-5, I see that you're way ahead of the game. According to my calculations, the program overpays you by 300-trillionths of a cent. Between the two of us, we're ahead by a hundred-trillionth of a cent. What gives?

Well, because computers use 0s (zeros) and 1s and don't have an infinite amount of space to do calculations, inaccuracies like the ones shown in Figure 7-5 are inevitable. The best that you can do is display numbers in a more sensible fashion. You can round the numbers and display only two digits beyond the decimal point, and some handy tools from Java's API (Application Programming Interface) can help. The code is shown in Listing 7-7, and the pleasant result is displayed in Figure 7-10.

Listing 7-7:   Making Your Numbers Look Right

```
import static java.lang.System.out;

class UseAccount {

    public static void main(String args[]) {
        Account myAccount = new Account();
        Account yourAccount = new Account();

        myAccount.balance = 24.02;
        yourAccount.balance = 55.63;

        double myInterest = myAccount.getInterest(5.00);
        double yourInterest =
          yourAccount.getInterest(7.00);

        out.printf("$%4.2f\n", myInterest);
        out.printf("$%5.2f\n", myInterest);
        out.printf("$%.2f\n", myInterest);
        out.printf("$%3.2f\n", myInterest);
        out.printf("$%.2f $%.2f", myInterest,
          yourInterest);
    }
}
```

Figure 7-10:
Numbers
that look
like dollar
amounts.

```
-------------------
$1.20
$ 1.20
$1.20
$1.20
$1.20  $3.89
Process completed.
```

Before you can run the code in Listing 7-7, you have to put two classes into your JCreator project. One class is the code in Listing 7-7; the other class is an Account class, like the one in Listing 7-5.

Listing 7-7 uses a handy method named *printf*. When you call printf, you always put at least two parameters inside the call's parentheses.

✓ **The first parameter is a *format string*.**

 The format string uses funny-looking codes to describe exactly how the other parameters are displayed.

✓ **All the other parameters (after the first) are values to be displayed.**

Look at the last printf call of Listing 7-7. The first parameter's format string has two placeholders for numbers. The first placeholder (%.2f) describes the display of myInterest. The second placeholder (another %.2f) describes the display of yourInterest. To find out exactly how these format strings work, see Figures 7-11 through 7-15.

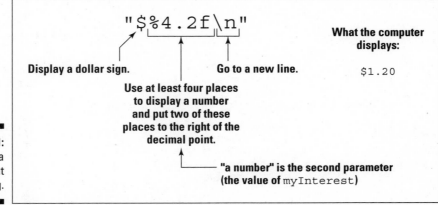

Figure 7-11:
Using a
format
string.

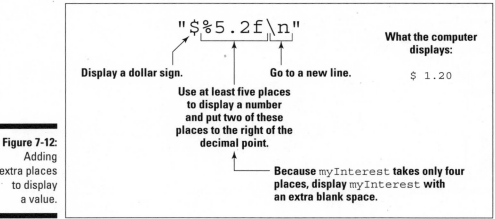

Figure 7-12:
Adding extra places to display a value.

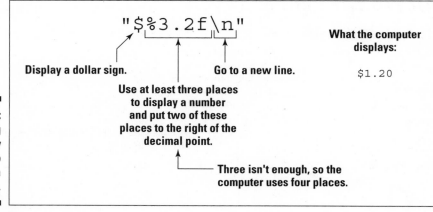

Figure 7-13:
Displaying a value without specifying the exact number of places.

Figure 7-14:
Specifying too few places to display a value.

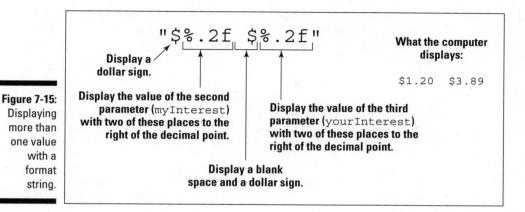

Figure 7-15:
Displaying
more than
one value
with a
format
string.

For more examples using the `printf` method and its format strings, see Chapters 8 and 9. For a complete list of options associated with the `printf` method's format string, see the `java.util.Formatter` page of Java's API documentation.

The format string in a `printf` call doesn't change the way a number is stored internally for calculations. All the format string does is create a nice-looking bunch of digit characters that can be displayed on your screen.

Hiding Details with Accessor Methods (Why You Shouldn't Micromanage a Bank Teller)

Put down this book and put on your hat. You've been such a loyal reader that I'm taking you out to lunch!

I've got just one problem. I'm a bit short on cash. Would you mind if, on the way to lunch, we stopped at an automatic teller machine and picked up a few bucks? Also, we have to use your account. My account is a little low.

Fortunately, the teller machine is easy to use. Just step right up and enter your PIN. After entering your PIN, the machine asks which of several variable names you want to use for your current balance. You have a choice of `balance324`, `myBal`, `currentBalance`, `b$`, `BALANCE`, `asj999`, or `conStanTinople`. Having selected a variable name, you're ready to select a memory location for the variable's value. You can select any number between 022FFF and 0555AA. (Those numbers are in hexadecimal format.) After you've configured the teller machine's software, you can easily get your cash. You did bring a screwdriver, didn't you?

Good programming

When it comes to good computer programming practice, one word stands out above all others — *simplicity*. When you're writing complicated code, the last thing you want is to deal with somebody else's misnamed variables; convoluted solutions to problems; or clever, last-minute kludges. You want a clean interface that makes you solve your own problems and no one else's.

In the automatic teller machine scenario that I describe earlier, the big problem is that the machine's design forces you to worry about other people's concerns. When you should be thinking about getting money for lunch, you're thinking instead about variables and storage locations. Sure, someone has to work out the teller machine's engineering problems. But the banking customer isn't the person to solve these problems.

This section is about safety, not security. Safe code keeps you from making accidental programming errors. Secure code (a completely different story) keeps malicious hackers from doing intentional damage.

So this means that everything connected with every aspect of a computer program has to be simple. Right? Well, no. That's not right. Sometimes, to make things simple in the long run, you have to do lots of preparatory work up front. The people who built the automated teller machine worked hard to make sure that the machine is consumer-proof. The machine's interface, with its screen messages and buttons, makes the machine a very complicated, but carefully designed, device.

The point is that making things look simple takes some planning. In the case of object-oriented programming, one of the ways to make things look simple is to keep code outside a class from directly using variables defined inside the class. Take a peek at the code in Listing 7-1. You're working at a company that has just spent $10 million for the code in the Account class. (That's more than a million and a half per line!) Now your job is to write the UseAccount class. You would like to write

```
myAccount.name = "Barry Burd";
```

but doing so would be getting you too far inside the guts of the Account class. After all, people who use an automatic teller machine aren't allowed to program the machine's variables. They can't use the machine's keypad to type the statement

```
balanceOnAccount29872865457 =
    balanceOnAccount29872865457 + 1000000.00;
```

Instead, they push buttons that do the job in an orderly manner. That's how a programmer achieves safety and simplicity.

So, to keep things nice and orderly, you need to change the `Account` class from Listing 7-1 by outlawing statements such as the following:

```
myAccount.name = "Barry Burd";
```

and

```
out.print(yourAccount.balance);
```

But, of course, this poses a problem. You're the person who's writing the code for the `UseAccount` class. If you can't write `myAccount.name` or `yourAccount.balance`, how are you going to accomplish anything at all? The answer lies in things called *accessor methods*. These methods are demonstrated in Listings 7-8 and 7-9.

Listing 7-8: Hide Those Variables

```
class Account {
    private String name;
    private String address;
    private double balance;

    public void setName(String n) {
        name = n;
    }

    public String getName() {
        return name;
    }

    public void setAddress(String a) {
        address = a;
    }

    public String getAddress() {
        return address;
    }

    public void setBalance(double b) {
```

(continued)

Listing 7-8 (continued)

```
        balance = b;
    }

    public double getBalance() {
        return balance;
    }
}
```

Listing 7-9:   Calling Accessor Methods

```
import static java.lang.System.out;

class UseAccount {

    public static void main(String args[]) {
        Account myAccount = new Account();
        Account yourAccount = new Account();

        myAccount.setName("Barry Burd");
        myAccount.setAddress("222 Cyberspace Lane");
        myAccount.setBalance(24.02);

        yourAccount.setName("Jane Q. Public");
        yourAccount.setAddress("111 Consumer Street");
        yourAccount.setBalance(55.63);

        out.print(myAccount.getName());
        out.print(" (");
        out.print(myAccount.getAddress());
        out.print(") has $");
        out.print(myAccount.getBalance());
        out.println();

        out.print(yourAccount.getName());
        out.print(" (");
        out.print(yourAccount.getAddress());
        out.print(") has $");
        out.print(yourAccount.getBalance());
    }
}
```

A run of the code in Listings 7-8 and 7-9 looks no different from a run of Listings 7-1 and 7-2. Either program's run is shown back in Figure 7-3. The big difference is that in Listing 7-8, the Account class enforces the carefully controlled use of its internal variables.

Public lives and private dreams: Making a variable name inaccessible

Notice the addition of the word *private* in front of each of the Account class's variable declarations. The word *private* is a Java keyword. When a variable is declared to be private, no code outside of the class can make direct reference to that variable. So if you put myAccount.name = "Barry Burd" in the UseAccount class of Listing 7-9, you get the error message name has private access in Account.

Instead of referencing myAccount.name, the UseAccount programmer must call method myAccount.setName or method myAccount.getName. These methods, setName and getName, are called *accessor* methods, because they provide access to the Account class's name variable. (Actually, the term *accessor method* isn't formally a part of the Java programming language. It's just the term that people use for methods that do this sort of thing.) To zoom in even more, setName is called a *setter* method, and getName is called a *getter* method. (I bet you won't forget that terminology!)

Another commonly used term for an accessor method is a *bean method*. The phrase *bean method* comes from the world of JavaBeans — a way of plugging Java programs into existing graphical user interface (GUI) environments. Because JavaBeans relies heavily on accessor methods, many people associate accessor methods with the JavaBeans specification.

With the Pro version of JCreator, you don't have to type your own accessor methods. First you type a variable declaration like **private String name.** Then, in JCreator Pro's menu bar, you choose Tools⇨Insert Bean Methods. After you approve the defaults in a small dialog box, JCreator creates accessor methods and adds them to your code.

Notice that all the setter and getter methods in Listing 7-8 are declared to be public. This ensures that anyone from anywhere can call these two methods. The idea here is that manipulating the actual variables from outside the Account code is impossible, but you can easily reach the approved setter and getter methods for using those variables.

To read more about the public and private keywords, see Appendix B and Chapter 15. (Chapter 15 is on the CD-ROM.)

Think again about the automatic teller machine. Someone using the ATM can't type a command that directly changes the value in his or her account's balance variable, but the procedure for depositing a million-dollar check is easy to follow. The people who build the teller machines know that if the check depositing procedure is complicated, plenty of customers will mess it up royally. So that's the story — make impossible anything that people shouldn't do and make sure that the tasks people should be doing are easy.

Nothing about having setter and getter methods is sacred. You don't have to write any setter and getter methods that you're not going to use. For instance, in Listing 7-8, I can omit the declaration of method getAddress, and everything still works. The only problem if I do this is that anyone else who wants to use my Account class and retrieve the address of an existing account is up a creek.

When you create a method to set the value in a balance variable, you don't have to name your method setBalance. You can name it tunaFish, or whatever you like. The trouble is that the set*Variablename* convention (with lowercase letters in set and an uppercase letter to start the *Variablename* part) is an established stylistic convention in the world of Java programming. If you don't follow the convention, you confuse the kumquats out of other Java programmers. If your integrated development environment has drag-and-drop GUI design capability, you may temporarily lose that capability. (For a word about drag-and-drop GUI design, see Chapter 2.)

When you call a setter method, you feed it a value of the type that's being set. That's why, in Listing 7-9, you call yourAccount.setBalance(55.63) with a parameter of type double. In contrast, when you call a getter method, you usually don't feed any values to the method. That's why, in Listing 7-9, you call yourAccount.getBalance() with an empty parameter list. Occasionally, you may want to get and set a value with a single statement. To add a dollar to your account's existing balance, you write yourAccount.setBalance (yourAccount.getBalance() + 1.00).

Enforcing rules with accessor methods

Go back to Listing 7-8 and take a quick look at the setName method. Imagine putting the method's assignment statement inside an if statement.

```
public void setName(String n) {
    if (!n.equals("")) {
        name = n;
    }
}
```

Now, if the programmer in charge of the UseAccount class writes myAccount.setName(""), the call to setName doesn't have any effect. Furthermore, because the `name` variable is private, the following statement is illegal in the `UseAccount` class:

```
myAccount.name = "";
```

Of course, a call such as `myAccount.setName("Joe Schmoe")` still works because `"Joe Schmoe"` doesn't equal the empty string `""`.

That's cool. With a private variable and an accessor method, you can prevent someone from assigning the empty string to an account's `name` variable. With more elaborate `if` statements, you can enforce any rules you want.

Chapter 8

Saving Time and Money: Reusing Existing Code

*O*nce upon a time, there was a beautiful princess. When the princess turned 25 (the optimal age for strength, good looks, and fine moral character), her kind father brought her a gift in a lovely golden box. Anxious to know what was in the box, the princess ripped off the golden wrapping paper.

When the box was finally opened, the princess was thrilled. To her surprise, her father had given her what she had always wanted — a computer program that always ran correctly. The program did everything the princess wanted and did it all exactly the way she wanted it to be done. The princess was happy, and so was her kind, old father.

As time went on, the computer program never failed. For years on end, the princess changed her needs, expected more out of life, made increasing demands, expanded her career, reached for more and more fulfillment, juggled the desires of her husband and her kids, stretched the budget, and sought peace within her soul. Through all this, the program remained her steady, faithful companion.

As the princess grew old, the program became old along with her. One evening, as she sat by the fireside, she posed a daunting question to the program. "How do you do it?" she asked. "How do you manage to keep giving the right answers, time after time, year after year?"

"Clean living," replied the program. "I swim twenty apps each day, I take C++ to Word off viruses, I avoid hogarithmic algorithms, I link Java in moderation, I say GNU to bugs, I don't smoke to backup, and I never byte off more than I can queue."

Needless to say, the princess was stunned.

Defining a Class (What It Means to Be an Employee)

Wouldn't it be nice if every piece of software did just what you wanted it to do? In an ideal world, you could just buy a program, make it work right away, plug it seamlessly into new situations, and update it easily whenever your needs change. Unfortunately, software of this kind doesn't exist. (*Nothing* of this kind exists.) The truth is, no matter what you want to do, you can find software that does some of it, but not all of it.

This is one of the reasons why object-oriented programming has been so successful. For years, companies were buying prewritten code only to discover that the code didn't do what they wanted it to do. So what did the companies do about it? They started messing with the code. Their programmers dug deep into the program files, changed variable names, moved subprograms around, reworked formulas, and generally made the code worse. The reality was that if a program didn't already do what you wanted it to do (even if it did something ever so close to what you wanted), you could never improve the situation by mucking around inside the code. The best option was always to chuck the whole program (expensive as that was) and start all over again. What a sad state of affairs!

With object-oriented programming, a big change has come about. At its heart, an object-oriented program is made to be modified. With correctly written software, you can take advantage of features that are already built-in, add new features of your own, and override features that don't suit your needs. And the best part is that the changes you make are clean. No clawing and digging into other people's brittle program code. Instead, you make nice, orderly additions and modifications without touching the existing code's internal logic. It's the ideal solution.

The last word on employees

When you write an object-oriented program, you start by thinking about the data. You're writing about accounts. So what's an account? You're writing code to handle button clicks. So what's a button? You're writing a program to send payroll checks to employees. What's an employee?

In this chapter's first example, an employee is someone with a name and a job title. Sure, employees have other characteristics, but for now I stick to the basics. The code in Listing 8-1 defines what it means to be an employee.

Listing 8-1:   What Is an Employee?

```java
import static java.lang.System.out;

class Employee {
    private String name;
    private String jobTitle;

    public void setName(String nameIn) {
        name = nameIn;
    }

    public String getName() {
        return name;
    }

    public void setJobTitle(String jobTitleIn) {
        jobTitle = jobTitleIn;
    }

    public String getJobTitle() {
        return jobTitle;
    }

    public void cutCheck(double amountPaid) {
        out.printf("Pay to the order of %s ", name);
        out.printf("(%s) ***$", jobTitle);
        out.printf("%,.2f\n", amountPaid);
    }
}
```

According to Listing 8-1, each employee has seven features. Two of these features are fairly simple. Each employee has a name and a job title.

And what else does an employee have? Each employee has four methods to handle the values of the employee's name and job title. These methods are setName, getName, setJobTitle, and getJobTitle. Methods like these (*accessor* methods) are explained in Chapter 7.

On top of all that, each employee has a cutCheck method. The idea is that the method that writes payroll checks has to belong to one class or another. Because most of the information in the payroll check is customized for a particular employee, you may as well put the cutCheck method inside the Employee class.

For details about the printf calls in the cutCheck method, see the section entitled "Cutting a check," later in this chapter.

Putting your class to good use

The Employee class in Listing 8-1 has no main method, so there's no starting point for executing code. To fix this deficiency, the programmer must write a separate program with a main method and use that program to create Employee instances. (To find out how to compile two programs separately, see Chapter 7.) Listing 8-2 shows a class with a main method — one that puts the code in Listing 8-1 to the test.

Listing 8-2:   Writing Payroll Checks

```
import java.util.Scanner;
import java.io.File;
import java.io.IOException;

class DoPayroll {

    public static void main(String args[])
                                            throws
            IOException {
        Scanner diskScanner =
            new Scanner(new File("EmployeeInfo.txt"));

        for (int empNum = 1; empNum <= 3; empNum++) {
            payOneEmployee(diskScanner);
        }
    }

    static void payOneEmployee(Scanner aScanner) {
```

```
        Employee anEmployee = new Employee();

        anEmployee.setName(aScanner.nextLine());
        anEmployee.setJobTitle(aScanner.nextLine());
        anEmployee.cutCheck(aScanner.nextDouble());
        aScanner.nextLine();
    }
}
```

The `DoPayroll` class in Listing 8-2 has two methods. One of the methods, `main`, calls the other method, `payOneEmployee`, three times. Each time around, the `payOneEmployee` method gets stuff from the `EmployeeInfo.txt` file and feeds this stuff to the `Employee` class's methods.

Here's how the variable name *anEmployee* is reused and recycled:

✔ The first time that `payOneEmployee` is called, the statement `anEmployee = new Employee()` makes `anEmployee` refer to a new object.

✔ The second time that `payOneEmployee` is called, the computer executes the same statement again. This creates a new incarnation of the `anEmployee` variable that refers to a brand-new object.

✔ The third time around, all the same stuff happens again. A new `anEmployee` variable ends up referring to a third object.

The whole story is pictured in Figure 8-1.

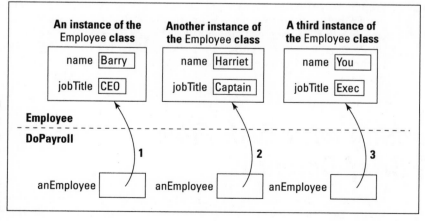

Figure 8-1:
Three calls
to the
payOne
Employee
method.

Cutting a check

Listing 8-1 has three `printf` calls. Each `printf` call has a format string (like `"(%s) ***$"`) and a variable (like `jobTitle`). Each format string has a placeholder (like `%s`) that determines where and how the variable's value is displayed.

For example, in the second `printf` call, the format string has a `%s` placeholder. This `%s` holds a place for the `jobTitle` variable's value. According to Java's rules, the notation `%s` always holds a place for a string and, sure enough, the variable `jobTitle` is declared to be of type `String` in Listing 8-1. Parentheses and some other characters surround the `%s` placeholder, so parentheses surround each job title in the program's output. (See Figure 8-2.)

Figure 8-2:
Everybody
gets paid.

```
------------------------Configuration: Listings0801-02 - JDK version 1.6.0 <Default> - <Default>----
Pay to the order of Barry Burd (CEO) ***$5,000.00
Pay to the order of Harriet Ritter (Captain) ***$7,000.00
Pay to the order of Your Name Here (Honorary Exec of the Day) ***$10,000.00
```

Back in Listing 8-1, notice the comma inside the `%,.2f` placeholder. The comma tells the program to use *grouping separators.* That's why, in Figure 8-2, you see `$5,000.00`, `$7,000.00`, and `$10,000.00` instead of `$5000.00`, `$7000.00`, and `$10000.00`.

Grouping separators vary from one country to another. For instance, in France, to write the number one thousand *(mille),* you write 1 000,00. Java can Frenchify your number automatically with a statement like `out.print(new java.util.Formatter().format(java.util.Locale.FRANCE, "%,.2f", 1000.00))`. For details, see the API (Application Programming Interface) documentation for Java's `Formatter` and `Locale` classes.

Working with Disk Files
(A Brief Detour)

In previous chapters, programs read characters from the computer's keyboard. But the code in Listing 8-2 reads characters from a specific file. The file (named *EmployeeInfo.txt*) lives on your computer's hard drive.

This `EmployeeInfo.txt` file is like a word processing document. The file can contain letters, digits, and other characters. But unlike a word processing document, the `EmployeeInfo.txt` file contains no formatting — no italics, no bold, no font sizes, nothing of that kind.

The `EmployeeInfo.txt` file contains only ordinary characters — the kinds of keystrokes that you type while you play a guessing game from Chapters 5 or 6. Of course, getting guesses from a user's keyboard and reading employee data from a disk file aren't exactly the same. In a guessing game, the program displays prompts, such as `Enter an int from 1 to 10`. The game program conducts a back-and-forth dialogue with the person sitting at the keyboard. In contrast, Listing 8-2 has no dialogue. This `DoPayroll` program reads characters from a hard drive and doesn't prompt or interact with anyone.

Most of this chapter is about code reuse. But Listing 8-2 stumbles upon an important idea — an idea that's not directly related to code reuse. Unlike the examples in previous chapters, Listing 8-2 reads data from a stored disk file. So in this section, I take a short side trip to explore disk files.

Storing data in a file

The code in Listing 8-2 doesn't run unless you have some employee data sitting in a file. Listing 8-2 says that this file is `EmployeeInfo.txt`. So before running the code of Listing 8-2, I created a small `EmployeeInfo.txt` file. The file is shown in Figure 8-3; refer to Figure 8-2 for the resulting output.

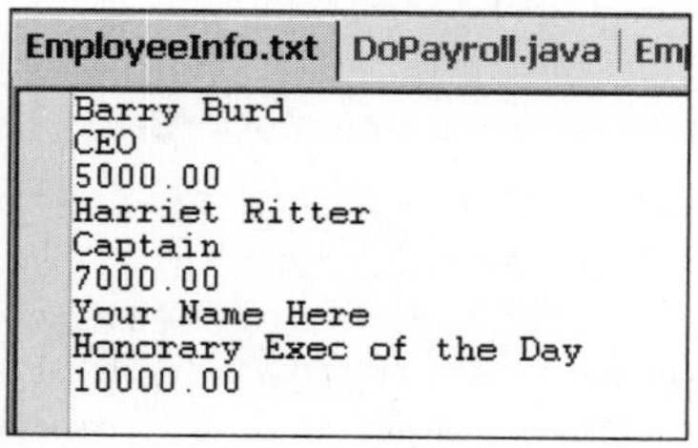

Figure 8-3:
An
Employee
Info.txt file.

```
EmployeeInfo.txt │ DoPayroll.java │ Emp
Barry Burd
CEO
5000.00
Harriet Ritter
Captain
7000.00
Your Name Here
Honorary Exec of the Day
10000.00
```

When you install JCreator from this book's CD-ROM, the computer copies my `EmployeeInfo.txt` file exactly where you need it — in the project directory for Listings 8-1 and 8-2. So you can run this section's code without worrying about the `EmployeeInfo.txt` file.

Even though you're not worried about it, you may want to see the
`EmployeeInfo.txt` file in JCreator's editor. Who knows? You may want to
change some of the data in the file. Here's how you can bring the file into the
Editor pane:

1. **With JCreator open, choose File⇨Open Workspace.**

   An Open dialog box appears.

2. **In the Open dialog box, select `Chapter08.jcw`, and click Open.**

   The Chapter08 workspace fills JCreator's File View pane.

3. **In the File View pane, right-click the `Listings0801-02` project.**

   A context menu appears.

4. **In the context menu, select Show All Files.**

   Some additional filenames appear under the `Listings0801-02` branch of
   the File View's tree. One of these other filenames is `EmployeeInfo.txt`.

5. **In the File View's tree, double-click `EmployeeInfo.txt`.**

When you write your own code, you may need to create files like my
`EmployeeInfo.txt` file. Here's how you do it:

1. **In the File View pane, right-click the name of a project. Then choose
   Add⇨New File from the context menu that appears.**

   JCreator's File Wizard opens to the File Path tab.

   Look for the File Wizard's tab names (*File Type* and *File Path*) on the left
   side of the File Wizard window. Check to make sure that the name *File
   Path* is highlighted. If not, then click the name *File Path* before moving on
   to the next step.

2. **In the Name field, type the name of your new data file.**

   You can type any name that your computer considers to be a valid file
   name. For this section's example, I used `EmployeeInfo.txt`, but
   other names, such as `EmployeeInfo.dat`, `EmployeeInfo`, or
   `Employees123.01.dataFile`, are fine. I try to avoid troublesome
   names (including short, uninformative names and names containing
   blank spaces), but the name you choose is entirely up to you (and your
   computer's operating system, and your boss's whims, and your customer's specifications).

   Always include a dot in File Path tab's Name field. If the filename has no
   extension, add a dot at the end of the name. For instance, to create a file
   named `EmployeeInfo` (not `EmployeeInfo.txt` or `EmployeeInfo.
   dat`), type **EmployeeInfo.** exactly as you see it here. If you don't type
   your own dot anywhere in the Name field, JCreator adds a default extension to the filename (turning `EmployeeInfo` into `EmployeeInfo.java`).

3. Click Finish.

The filename appears in JCreator's File View pane. A tab with the new filename appears in JCreator's Editor pane.

4. Type text in the Editor pane.

To create this section's example, I typed the text shown in Figure 8-3. To create your own example, type whatever text your program needs during its run.

This book's Web site has tips for readers who need to create data files without using JCreator. This includes instructions for Linux, Unix, and Macintosh environments.

Copying and pasting code

In almost any computer programming language, reading data from a file can be tricky. You add extra lines of code to tell the computer what to do. Sometimes you can copy and paste these lines from other peoples' code. For example, you can follow the pattern in Listing 8-2:

```java
/*
 * The pattern in Listing 8-2
 */
import java.util.Scanner;
import java.io.File;
import java.io.IOException;

class SomeClassName {

    public static void main(String args[])
                                        throws
            IOException {
        Scanner scannerName =
            new Scanner(new File("SomeFileName"));

        //Some code goes here

        scannerName.nextInt();
        scannerName.nextDouble();
        scannerName.next();
        scannerName.nextLine();

        //Some code goes here
    }
}
```

You want to read data from a file. You start by imagining that you're reading from the keyboard. Put the usual `Scanner` and `next` codes into your program. Then add some extra items from the Listing 8-2 pattern:

- ✔ Add two new import declarations — one for `java.io.File` and another for `java.io.IOException`.

- ✔ Type **throws IOException** in your method's header.

- ✔ Type **new File("")** in your call to `new Scanner`.

- ✔ Take a file that's already on your hard drive. Type that filename inside the quotation marks.

- ✔ Take the word that you use for the name of your scanner. Reuse that word in calls to `next`, `nextInt`, `nextDouble`, and so on.

Occasionally, copying and pasting code can get you into trouble. Maybe you're writing a program that doesn't fit the simple Listing 8-2 pattern. You need to tweak the pattern a bit. But in order to tweak the pattern, you need to understand some of the ideas behind the pattern.

That's how the next section comes to your rescue. It covers some of these ideas.

Reading from a file

In previous chapters, programs read characters from the computer's keyboard. These programs use things like `Scanner`, `System.in`, and `nextDouble` — things defined in Java's API. The `DoPayroll` program in Listing 8-2 puts a new spin on this story. Instead of reading characters from the keyboard, the program reads characters from the `EmployeeInfo.txt` file. The file lives on your computer's hard drive.

To read characters from a file, you use some of the same things that help you read characters from the keyboard. You use `Scanner`, `nextDouble`, and other goodies. But in addition to these goodies, you have a few extra hurdles to jump. Here's a list:

- ✔ **You need a new `File` object.** To be more precise, you need a new instance of the API's `File` class. You get this new instance with code like

  ```
  new File("EmployeeInfo.txt")
  ```

  The stuff in quotation marks is the name of a file — a file on your computer's hard drive. The file contains characters like those shown previously in Figure 8-3.

At this point, the terminology makes mountains out of molehills. Sure, I use the phrases *new* `File` *object* and *new* `File` *instance*, but all you're doing is making `new File("EmployeeInfo.txt")` stand for a file on your hard drive. After you shove `new File("EmployeeInfo.txt")` into `new Scanner`,

```
Scanner diskScanner =
               new Scanner(new File("EmployeeInfo.txt"));
```

you can forget all about the `new File` business. From that point on in the code, `diskScanner` stands for the `EmployeeInfo.txt` filename on your computer's hard drive. (The name `diskScanner` stands for a file on your hard drive just as, in previous examples, the name `myScanner` stands for the computer's keyboard.)

Creating a `new File` object in Listing 8-2 is like creating a `new Employee` object later in the same listing. It's also like creating a `new Account` object in the examples of Chapter 7. The only difference is that the `Employee` and `Account` classes are defined in this book's examples. The `File` class is defined in Java's API.

When you connect to a disk file with `new Scanner`, don't forget the `new File` part. If you write `new Scanner("EmployeeInfo.txt")` without `new File`, the compiler won't mind. (Choosing Build⇨Compile Project gives you a friendly looking `Process completed` message.) But when you run the code, you won't get anything like the results that you expect to get.

✔ **You must refer to the `File` class by its full name — `java.io.File`.** You can do this with an import declaration like the one in Listing 8-2. Alternatively, you can clutter up your code with a statement like

```
Scanner diskScanner =
    new Scanner(new java.io.File("EmployeeInfo.txt"));
```

✔ **You need a `throws IOException` clause.** Lots of things can go wrong when your program connects to `EmployeeInfo.txt`. For one thing, your hard drive may not have a file named *EmployeeInfo.txt*. For another, the file `EmployeeInfo.txt` may be in the wrong directory. To brace for this kind of calamity, the Java programming language takes certain precautions. The language insists that when a disk file is involved, you acknowledge the possible dangers of calling `new Scanner`.

You can acknowledge the hazards in several possible ways, but the simplest way is to use a `throws` clause. In Listing 8-2, the `main` method's header ends with the words *throws IOException*. By adding these two words, you appease the Java compiler. It's as if you're saying "I know that calling `new Scanner` can lead to problems. You don't have to remind me." And, sure enough, adding `throws IOException` to your `main` method keeps the compiler from complaining. (Without this `throws` clause, you get an `unreported exception` error message.)

For the full story on Java exceptions, read Chapter 12. In the meantime, add `throws IOException` to the header of any method that calls `new Scanner(new File(....`

✔ **You must refer to the `IOException` class by its full name — `java.io.IOException`.**

You can do this with an `import` declaration like the one in Listing 8-2. Alternatively, you can enlarge the `main` method's `throws` clause:

```
public static void main(String args[])
                              throws
        java.io.IOException {
```

✔ **You must pass the file scanner's name to the `payOneEmployee` method.**

In Listing 7-5 in Chapter 7, the `getInterest` method has a parameter named *percentageRate*. Whenever you call the `getInterest` method, you hand an extra, up-to-date piece of information to the method. (You hand a number — an interest rate — to the method. Figure 7-7 illustrates the idea.)

The same thing happens in Listing 8-2. The `payOneEmployee` method has a parameter named *aScanner*. Whenever you call the `payOneEmployee` method, you hand an extra, up-to-date piece of information to the method. (You hand a scanner — a reference to a disk file — to the method.)

You may wonder why the `payOneEmployee` method needs a parameter. After all, in Listing 8-2, the `payOneEmployee` method always reads data from the same file. Why bother informing this method, each time you call it, that the disk file is still the `EmployeeInfo.txt` file?

Well, there are plenty of ways to shuffle the code in Listing 8-2. Some ways don't involve a parameter. But the way that this example has arranged things, you have two separate methods — a `main` method and a `payOneEmployee` method. You create a scanner once inside the `main` method and then use the scanner three times — once inside each call to the `payOneEmployee` method.

Anything that you define inside a method is like a private joke that's known only to the code inside that method. So, the `diskScanner` that you define inside the `main` method isn't automatically known inside the `payOneEmployee` method. To make the `payOneEmployee` method aware of the disk file, you pass `diskScanner` from the `main` method to the `payOneEmployee` method.

To read more about variables that you declare inside (and outside) of methods, see Chapter 10.

Who moved my file?

If you installed JCreator from this book's CD-ROM, your MyProjects directory has a subdirectory named *Listings0801-02*. That `Listings0801-02` directory comes with files named *Employee.java* and *DoPayroll.java* — the code in Listings 8-1 and 8-2. The `Listings0801-02` directory also contains the `EmployeeInfo.txt` file. That's good, because if the `EmployeeInfo.txt` file isn't where it belongs, the whole project doesn't run properly. Instead, you get a `FileNotFoundException`.

In general, when you get a `FileNotFoundException`, some file that your program needs isn't available to it. This is an easy mistake to make. It can be frustrating because to you, a file such as `EmployeeInfo.txt` may look like it's available to your program. But remember — computers are stupid. If you make a tiny mistake, the computer can't read between the lines for you. So if your `EmployeeInfo.txt` file isn't in the right directory on your hard drive or the filename is spelled incorrectly, the computer chokes when it tries to run your code.

Sometimes you know darn well that an `EmployeeInfo.txt` (or *whatever. xyz*) file exists on your hard drive. But when you run your program, you still get a mean-looking `FileNotFoundException`. When this happens, the file is usually in the wrong directory on your hard drive. (Of course, it depends on your point of view. Maybe the file is in the right directory, but you've told your Java program to look for the file in the wrong directory.) When this happens, try copying the file to some other directories on your hard drive and rerunning your code. (Subdirectories of JCreator's `MyProjects` directory are always good places to put files.) Stare carefully at the names and locations of files on your hard drive until you figure out what's wrong.

Adding directory names to your filenames

You can specify a file's exact location in your Java code. Code like `new File("C:\\Program Files\\Xinox Software\\JCreatorV3 LE\\ MyProjects\\Listings0801-02\\EmployeeInfo.txt")` looks really ugly, but it works.

In the previous paragraph, notice the double backslashes in `"C:\\Program Files\\Xinox Software . . ."` If you're a Windows MS-DOS user, you'd be tempted to write `C:\Program Files\Xinox Software` with single backslashes. But in Java, the single backslash has its own special meaning. (For example, in Listing 7-7, `\n` means to go to the next line.) So in Java, to indicate a backslash inside a quoted string, you use a double backslash instead.

If you know where your Java program looks for files, you can worm your way from that place to the directory of your choice. For example, the code in Listing 8-2 normally looks for the `EmployeeInfo.txt` file in a directory named *Listings0801-02*. So, as an experiment, go to the `Listings0801-02` directory and create a new subdirectory named *dataFiles*. Then move my `EmployeeInfo.txt` file to the new `dataFiles` directory. To read numbers and words from the file that you moved, modify Listing 8-2 with the code `new File("dataFiles\\EmployeeInfo.txt")`.

Reading a line at a time

In Listing 8-2, the `payOneEmployee` method illustrates some useful tricks for reading data. In particular, every scanner that you create has a `nextLine` method. (You might not use this `nextLine` method, but the method is available nonetheless.) When you call a scanner's `nextLine` method, the method grabs everything up to the end of the current line of text. In Listing 8-2, a call to `nextLine` can read a whole line from the `EmployeeInfo.txt` file. (In another program, a scanner's `nextLine` call may read everything the user types on the keyboard up to the pressing of the Enter key.)

Notice my careful choice of words — `nextLine` reads everything up to the end of the current line. Unfortunately, what it means to read up to the end of the current line isn't always what you think it means. Intermingling `nextInt`, `nextDouble`, and `nextLine` calls can be messy. You have to watch what you're doing and check your program's output carefully.

To understand all this, you need to be painfully aware of a data file's line breaks. Think of a line break as an extra character, stuck between one line of text and the next. Then imagine that calling `nextLine` means to read everything up to and including the next line break.

Now take a look at Figure 8-4.

- ✔ If one call to `nextLine` reads `Barry Burd[LineBreak]`, the subsequent call to `nextLine` reads `CEO[LineBreak]`.

- ✔ If one call to `nextDouble` reads the number 5000.00, the subsequent call to `nextLine` reads the `[LineBreak]` that comes immediately after the number 5000.00. (That's all the `nextLine` reads — a `[LineBreak]` and nothing more.)

- ✔ If a call to `nextLine` reads the `[LineBreak]` after the number 5000.00, the subsequent call to `nextLine` reads `Harriet Ritter[LineBreak]`.

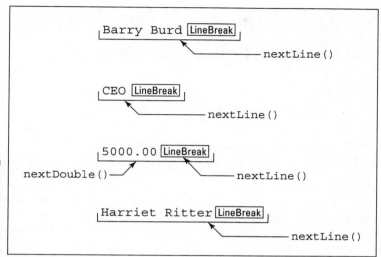

Figure 8-4:
Calling
nextDouble
and
nextLine.

So after reading the number 5000.00, you need *two* calls to `nextLine` in order to scoop up the name *Harriet Ritter*. The mistake that I usually make is to forget the first of those two calls.

Look again at the file in Figure 8-3. For this section's code to work correctly, you must have a line break after the last `10000.00`. If you don't, a final call to `nextLine` makes your program crash and burn. The error message reads `NoSuchElementException: No line found`.

I'm always surprised by the number of quirks that I find in each programming language's scanning methods. For example, the first `nextLine` that reads from the file in Figure 8-3 devours `Barry Burd[LineBreak]` from the file. But that `nextLine` call delivers `Barry Burd` (without any line break) to the running code. So `nextLine` looks for a line break, and then `nextLine` loses the line break. Yes, this is a subtle point. And no, this subtle point hardly ever causes problems for anyone.

If this business about `nextDouble` and `nextLine` confuses you, please don't put the blame on Java. Mixing input calls is delicate work in any computer programming language. And the really nasty thing is that each programming language approaches the problem a little differently. What you find out about `nextLine` in Java helps you understand the issues when you get to know C++ or Visual Basic, but it doesn't tell you all the details. Each language's details are unique to that language. (Yes, it's a big pain. But because all computer programmers become rich and famous, the pain eventually pays off.)

Defining Subclasses (What It Means to Be a Full-Time Employee or a Part-Time Employee)

This time last year, your company paid $10 million for a piece of software. That software came in the `Employee.class` file. People at Burd Brain Consulting (the company that created the software) don't want you to know about the innards of the software (otherwise, you may steal their ideas). So you don't have the Java program file that the software came from. (In other words, you don't have `Employee.java`.) You can run the bytecode in the `Employee.class` file. You can also read the documentation in a Web page named *Employee.html*. But you can't see the statements inside the `Employee.java` program, and you can't change any of the program's code.

Since this time last year, your company has grown. Unlike the old days, your company now has two kinds of employees: full-time and part-time. Each full-time employee is on a fixed, weekly salary. (If the employee works nights and weekends, then in return for this monumental effort, the employee receives a hearty handshake.) In contrast, each part-time employee works for an hourly wage. Your company deducts an amount from each full-time employee's pay-check to pay for the company's benefits package. Part-time employees, how-ever, don't get benefits.

The question is, how can the software that your company bought last year keep up with the company's growth? You invested in a great program to handle employees and their payroll, but the program doesn't differentiate between your full-time and part-time employees. You have several options:

- Call your next-door neighbor, whose 12-year-old child knows more about computer programming than anyone in your company. Get this uppity little brat to take the employee software apart, rewrite it, and hand it back to you with all the changes and additions your company requires.

  On second thought, you can't do that. No matter how smart that kid is, the complexities of the employee software will probably confuse the kid. By the time you get the software back, it'll be filled with bugs and incon-sistencies. Besides, you don't even have the `Employee.java` file to hand to the kid. All you have is the `Employee.class` file, which can't be read or modified with a text editor. (See Chapter 2.) Besides, your kid just beat up the neighbor's kid. You don't want to give your neighbor the satisfaction of seeing you beg for the whiz kid's help.

- Scrap the $10 million employee software. Get someone in your company to rewrite the software from scratch.

In other words, say goodbye to your time and money.

✔ Write a new front end for the employee software. That is, build a piece of code that does some preliminary processing on full-time employees and then hands the preliminary results to your $10 million software. Do the same for part-time employees.

This idea could be decent or spell disaster. Are you sure that the existing employee software has convenient *hooks* in it? (That is, does the employee software contain entry points that allow your front-end software to easily send preliminary data to the expensive employee software?) Remember, this plan treats the existing software as one big, monolithic lump, which can become cumbersome. Dividing the labor between your front-end code and the existing employee program is difficult. And if you add layer upon layer to existing black box code, you'll probably end up with a fairly inefficient system.

✔ Call Burd Brain Consulting, the company that sold you the employee software. Tell Dr. Burd that you want the next version of his software to differentiate between full-time and part-time employees.

"No problem," says Dr. Burd. "It'll be ready by the start of the next fiscal quarter." That evening, Dr. Burd makes a discreet phone call to his next-door neighbor. . . .

✔ Create two new Java classes named *FullTimeEmployee* and *PartTimeEmployee*. Have each new class extend the existing functionality of the expensive `Employee` class. But have each new class define its own specialized functionality for certain kinds of employees.

Way to go! Figure 8-5 shows the structure that you want to create.

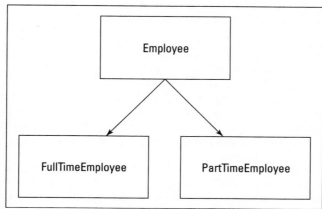

Figure 8-5:
The Employee class family tree.

Employee

FullTimeEmployee

PartTimeEmployee

Creating a subclass

In Listing 8-1, I define an Employee class. I can use what I define in Listing 8-1 and extend the definition to create new, more specialized classes. So in Listing 8-3, I define a new class — a FullTimeEmployee class.

Listing 8-3:   What Is a FullTimeEmployee?

```
class FullTimeEmployee extends Employee {
    private double weeklySalary;
    private double benefitDeduction;

    public void setWeeklySalary(double weeklySalaryIn) {
        weeklySalary = weeklySalaryIn;
    }

    public double getWeeklySalary() {
        return weeklySalary;
    }

    public void setBenefitDeduction(double benefitDedIn) {
        benefitDeduction = benefitDedIn;
    }

    public double getBenefitDeduction() {
        return benefitDeduction;
    }

    public double findPaymentAmount() {
        return weeklySalary - benefitDeduction;
    }
}
```

Looking at Listing 8-3, you can see that each instance of the FullTime Employee class has two variables: weeklySalary and benefitDeduction. But are those the only variables that each FullTimeEmployee instance has? No, they're not. The first line of Listing 8-3 says that the FullTimeEmployee class extends the existing Employee class. This means that in addition to having a weeklySalary and a benefitDeduction, each FullTimeEmployee instance also has two other variables: name and jobTitle. These two variables come from the definition of the Employee class, which you can find in Listing 8-1.

In Listing 8-3, the magic word is the word *extends*. When one class extends an existing class, the extending class automatically inherits functionality that's defined in the existing class. So, the FullTimeEmployee class *inherits* the name and jobTitle variables. The FullTimeEmployee class also inherits all the methods that are declared in the Employee class — setName, getName, setJobTitle, getJobTitle, and cutCheck. The FullTimeEmployee class is a *subclass* of the Employee class. That means the Employee class is the *superclass* of the FullTimeEmployee class. You can also talk in terms of blood relatives. The FullTimeEmployee class is the *child* of the Employee class, and the Employee class is the *parent* of the FullTimeEmployee class.

It's almost (but not quite) as if the FullTimeEmployee class were defined by the code in Listing 8-4.

Listing 8-4:   Fake (But Informative) Code

```
import static java.lang.System.out;

class FullTimeEmployee {
    private String name;
    private String jobTitle;
    private double weeklySalary;
    private double benefitDeduction;

    public void setName(String nameIn) {
        name = nameIn;
    }

    public String getName() {
        return name;
    }

    public void setJobTitle(String jobTitleIn) {
        jobTitle = jobTitleIn;
    }

    public String getJobTitle() {
        return jobTitle;
    }

    public void setWeeklySalary(double weeklySalaryIn) {
        weeklySalary = weeklySalaryIn;
    }

    public double getWeeklySalary() {
        return weeklySalary;
    }

    public void setBenefitDeduction(double benefitDedIn) {
        benefitDeduction = benefitDedIn;
    }

    public double getBenefitDeduction() {
```

(continued)

Listing 8-4 (continued)

```
        return benefitDeduction;
    }

    public double findPaymentAmount() {
        return weeklySalary - benefitDeduction;
    }

    public void cutCheck(double amountPaid) {
        out.printf("Pay to the order of %s ", name);
        out.printf("(%s) ***$", jobTitle);
        out.printf("%,.2f\n", amountPaid);
    }
}
```

Why does the title for Listing 8-4 call that code fake? (Should the code feel insulted?) Well, the main difference between Listing 8-4 and the inheritance situation in Listings 8-1 and 8-3 is this: A child class can't directly reference the private variables of its parent class. To do anything with the parent class's private variables, the child class has to call the parent class's accessor methods. Back in Listing 8-3, calling `setName("Rufus")` would be legal, but the code `name="Rufus"` wouldn't be. If you believe everything you read in Listing 8-4, you think that code in the `FullTimeEmployee` class can do `name="Rufus"`. Well, it can't. (My, what a subtle point this is!)

You don't need the `Employee.java` file on your hard drive to write code that extends the `Employee` class. All you need is the file `Employee.class`.

Creating subclasses is habit-forming

After you're accustomed to extending classes, you can get extend-happy. If you created a `FullTimeEmployee` class, you might as well create a `PartTimeEmployee` class, as shown in Listing 8-5.

Listing 8-5:   What Is a PartTimeEmployee?

```
class PartTimeEmployee extends Employee {
    private double hourlyRate;

    public void setHourlyRate(double rateIn) {
        hourlyRate = rateIn;
    }

    public double getHourlyRate() {
        return hourlyRate;
```

```
        }

        public double findPaymentAmount(int hours) {
            return hourlyRate * hours;
        }
    }
```

Unlike the `FullTimeEmployee` class, `PartTimeEmployee` has no salary or deduction. Instead `PartTimeEmployee` has an `hourlyRate` variable. (Adding a `numberOfHoursWorked` variable would also be a possibility. I chose not to do this, figuring that the number of hours a part-time employee works will change drastically from week to week.)

Using Subclasses

The previous section tells a story about creating subclasses. It's a good story, but it's incomplete. Creating subclasses is fine, but you gain nothing from these subclasses unless you write code to use them. So in this section, you explore code that uses subclasses.

Now the time has come for you to classify yourself as either a type-F person or a type-P person. A type-F person wants to see the fundamentals. (The letter *F* stands for *fundamentals.*) "Show me a program that lays out the principles in their barest, most basic form," says the type-F person. A type-F person isn't worried about bells and whistles. The bells come later, and the whistles may never come at all. If you're a type-F person, you want to see a program that uses subclasses and then moves out of your way so you can get some work done.

On the other hand, a type-P person wants practical applications. (The letter *P* stands for *practical.*) Type-P people need to see ideas in context; otherwise the ideas float away too quickly. "Show me a program that demonstrates the usefulness of subclasses," says the type-P person. "I have no use for your stinking abstractions. I want real-life examples, and I want them now!"

Because I'm always aiming to please my reader, this section has two (count 'em — two) examples that make use of the previous section's subclasses. Listing 8-6, which is for the type-F crowd, is lean and simple and makes good bedtime reading. On the other hand, Listing 8-7, which is for type-P fanatics, shows how subclasses fit into a useful context. So that's it. Choose your poison and read on.

A program for the minimalist

Listing 8-6 shows you a bare-bones program that uses the subclasses `FullTimeEmployee` and `PartTimeEmployee`. Figure 8-6 shows the program's output.

Listing 8-6:   Use Subclasses and Then Leave Me Alone

```
class DoPayrollTypeF {

    public static void main(String args[]) {

        FullTimeEmployee ftEmployee = new FullTimeEmployee();

        ftEmployee.setName("Barry Burd");
        ftEmployee.setJobTitle("CEO");
        ftEmployee.setWeeklySalary(5000.00);
        ftEmployee.setBenefitDeduction(500.00);
        ftEmployee.cutCheck(ftEmployee.findPaymentAmount());
        System.out.println();

        PartTimeEmployee ptEmployee = new PartTimeEmployee();

        ptEmployee.setName("Steve Surace");
        ptEmployee.setJobTitle("Driver");
        ptEmployee.setHourlyRate(7.53);
        ptEmployee.cutCheck(ptEmployee.findPaymentAmount(10));
    }
}
```

Figure 8-6:
The output
of the
program in
Listing 8-6.

```
----------------------Configuration: Listings0801-03-05-06 – JDK ve
Pay to the order of Barry Burd (CEO) ***$4,500.00

Pay to the order of Steve Surace (Driver) ***$75.30
```

To understand Listing 8-6, you need to keep an eye on three classes: `Employee`, `FullTimeEmployee`, and `PartTimeEmployee`. (For a look at the code that defines these classes, see Listings 8-1, 8-3, and 8-5.)

The first half of Listing 8-6 deals with a full-time employee. Notice how so many methods are available for use with the `ftEmployee` variable. For instance, you can call `ftEmployee.setWeeklySalary` because `ftEmployee` has type `FullTimeEmployee`. You can also call `ftEmployee.setName` because the `FullTimeEmployee` class extends the `Employee` class.

Because `cutCheck` is declared in the `Employee` class, you can call `ftEmployee.cutCheck`. But you can also call `ftEmployee.findPayment Amount` because a `findPaymentAmount` method is in the `FullTimeEmployee` class.

Making types match

Look again at the first half of Listing 8-6. Take special notice of that last statement — the one in which the full-time employee is actually cut a check. The statement forms a nice, long chain of values and their types. You can see this by reading the statement from the inside out.

✔ Method `ftEmployee.findPaymentAmount` is called with an empty parameter list (Listing 8-6). That's good, because the `findPaymentAmount` method takes no parameters (Listing 8-3).

✔ The `findPaymentAmount` method returns a value of type `double` (again, Listing 8-3).

✔ The `double` value that `ftEmployee.findPaymentAmount` returns is passed to method `ftEmployee.cutCheck` (Listing 8-6). That's good, because the `cutCheck` method takes one parameter of type `double` (Listing 8-1).

For a fanciful graphic illustration, see Figure 8-7.

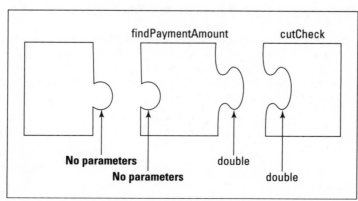

Figure 8-7: Matching parameters.

Always feed a method the value types that it wants in its parameter list.

The second half of the story

In the second half of Listing 8-6, the code creates an object of type `PartTimeEmployee`. A variable of type `PartTimeEmployee` can do some of the same things a `FullTimeEmployee` variable can do. But the `PartTimeEmployee` class doesn't have the `setWeeklySalary` and `setBenefitDeduction` methods. Instead, the `PartTimeEmployee` class has the `setHourlyRate` method. (See Listing 8-5.) So, in Listing 8-6, the next-to-last line is a call to the `setHourlyRate` method.

The last line of Listing 8-6 is by far the most interesting. On that line, the code hands the number `10` (the number of hours worked) to the `findPayment Amount` method. Compare this with the earlier call to `findPaymentAmount` — the call for the full-time employee in the first half of Listing 8-6. Between the two subclasses, `FullTimeEmployee` and `PartTimeEmployee`, are two different `findPaymentAmount` methods. The two methods have two different kinds of parameter lists:

✔ The `FullTimeEmployee` class's `findPaymentAmount` method takes no parameters (Listing 8-3).

✔ The `PartTimeEmployee` class's `findPaymentAmount` method takes one `int` parameter (Listing 8-5).

This is par for the course. Finding the payment amount for a part-time employee isn't the same as finding the payment amount for a full-time employee. A part-time employee's pay changes each week, depending on the number of hours the employee works in a week. The full-time employee's pay stays the same each week. So the `FullTimeEmployee` and `PartTimeEmployee` classes both have `findPaymentAmount` methods, but each class's method works quite differently.

A program for the maximalist

If you crave useful results and practical applications, you either skipped over the last listing or gritted your teeth while you read through it. Listing 8-7 gives you the same information with a more practical point of view. Of course, there's a price. Listing 8-7 is longer and more complicated than the listing in the previous section. Oh, well!

Listing 8-7:   Big-Time Payroll Program

```java
import static java.lang.System.out;
import java.util.Scanner;
import java.io.File;
import java.io.IOException;

class DoPayrollTypeP {

    public static void main(String args[])
                                        throws IOException {
        Scanner diskScanner =
                    new Scanner(new File("EmpInfoNew.txt"));
        Scanner kbdScanner = new Scanner(System.in);

        for (int empNum = 1; empNum <= 3; empNum++) {
            payOneFTEmployee(diskScanner);
        }

        for (int empNum = 4; empNum <= 6; empNum++) {
            payOnePTEmployee(diskScanner, kbdScanner);
        }
    }

    public static void payOneFTEmployee(Scanner diskScanner) {
        FullTimeEmployee employee = new FullTimeEmployee();

        employee.setName(diskScanner.nextLine());
        employee.setJobTitle(diskScanner.nextLine());
        employee.setWeeklySalary(diskScanner.nextDouble());
        employee.setBenefitDeduction(diskScanner.nextDouble());
        diskScanner.nextLine();
        diskScanner.nextLine(); //Reads the dashed line that
                                //  separates two employees

        employee.cutCheck(employee.findPaymentAmount());
        out.println();
    }

    public static void payOnePTEmployee
                    (Scanner diskScanner, Scanner kbdScanner) {
        PartTimeEmployee employee = new PartTimeEmployee();

        employee.setName(diskScanner.nextLine());
        employee.setJobTitle(diskScanner.nextLine());
```

(continued)

Listing 8-7 (continued)

```
        employee.setHourlyRate(diskScanner.nextDouble());
        diskScanner.nextLine();
        diskScanner.nextLine(); //Reads the dashed line that
                               //  separates two employees

        out.print("Enter ");
        out.print(employee.getName());
        out.print("'s hours worked this week: ");
        int hours = kbdScanner.nextInt();

        employee.cutCheck(employee.findPaymentAmount(hours));
        out.println();
    }
}
```

For all its complexity, the code in Listing 8-7 still isn't a full-blown payroll program. It's a toy program, but it's a bit more realistic than the program in Listing 8-6. The code in Listing 8-7 writes checks for six employees — three full-time employees and three part-time employees. Calls to payOneFTEmployee and payOnePTEmployee make sure that each employee receives a check. Each of these payOneEmployee methods reads data from a file and uses the data to fill the employee object's variables with values. Figure 8-8 shows the file that I used to test Listing 8-7, and the resulting run is shown in Figure 8-9.

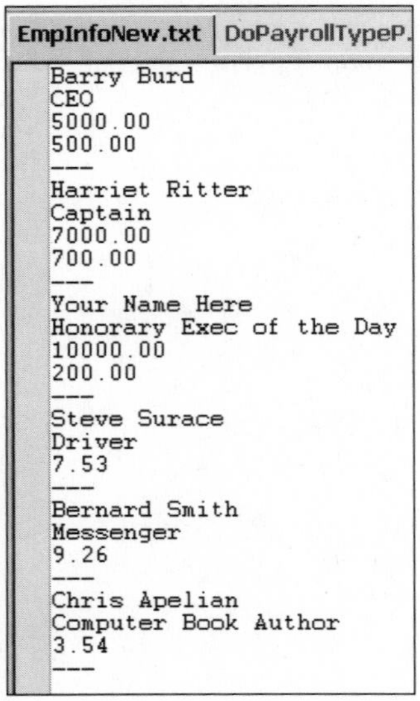

Figure 8-8:
Input for the
big-time
payroll
program.

```
EmpInfoNew.txt | DoPayrollTypeP.
Barry Burd
CEO
5000.00
500.00
----
Harriet Ritter
Captain
7000.00
700.00
----
Your Name Here
Honorary Exec of the Day
10000.00
200.00
----
Steve Surace
Driver
7.53
----
Bernard Smith
Messenger
9.26
----
Chris Apelian
Computer Book Author
3.54
----
```

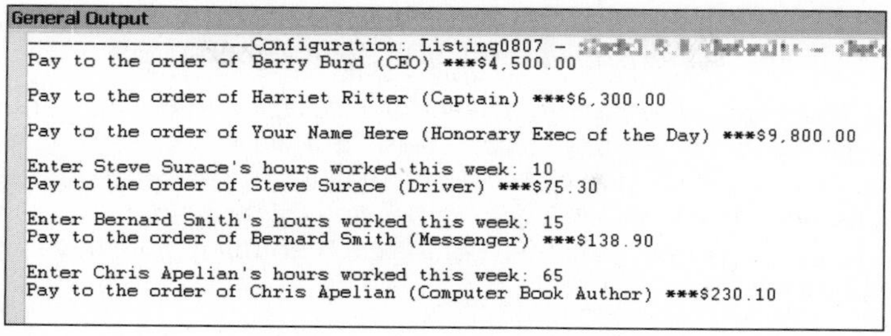

```
General Output
─────────────────Configuration: Listing0807 ─ ▓▓▓▒.▓.▓ ◄▒▒▒▒▒▒▒ ─ ▒▒▓
Pay to the order of Barry Burd (CEO) ***$4,500.00

Pay to the order of Harriet Ritter (Captain) ***$6,300.00

Pay to the order of Your Name Here (Honorary Exec of the Day) ***$9,800.00

Enter Steve Surace's hours worked this week: 10
Pay to the order of Steve Surace (Driver) ***$75.30

Enter Bernard Smith's hours worked this week: 15
Pay to the order of Bernard Smith (Messenger) ***$138.90

Enter Chris Apelian's hours worked this week: 65
Pay to the order of Chris Apelian (Computer Book Author) ***$230.10
```

Figure 8-9:
Paying your
employees.

Compared with its full-time cousin, the payOnePTEmployee method pulls one extra idea out of its bag of tricks. When the time comes to get the number of hours the employee worked, the payOnePTEmployee method doesn't consult a disk file. Instead, the method asks the user for live keyboard input. The thought here is that the disk file is where all the long-term information about employees lives. Because the number of hours an employee worked this week isn't long-term information, the payOnePTEmployee method gets the user to enter this information on the fly.

The payOnePTEmployee method reads a name, a job title, and an hourly rate from the disk file. Then the method reads a number of hours from the keyboard. Because the payOnePTEmployee method reads data from two different sources, you pass two different scanners to the method. In the method's parameter list, you separate the two items with a comma.

Overriding Existing Methods (Changing the Payments for Some of Your Employees)

Wouldn't you know it! Some knucklehead in the human resources department offered double pay for overtime to one of your part-time employees. Now word is getting around, and some of the other part-timers want double pay for their overtime work. If this keeps up, you'll end up in the poorhouse, so you need to send out a memo to all the part-time employees, explaining why earning more money is not to their benefit.

In the meantime, you have two kinds of part-time employees — the ones who receive double pay for overtime hours and the ones who don't — so you need to modify your payroll software. What are your options?

✔ Well, you can dig right into the `PartTimeEmployee` class code, make a few changes, and hope for the best. (Not a good idea!)

✔ You can follow the previous section's advice and create a subclass of the existing `PartTimeEmployee` class. "But wait," you say. "The existing `PartTimeEmployee` class already has a `findPaymentAmount` method. Do I need some tricky way of bypassing this existing `findPaymentAmount` method for each double-pay-for-overtime employee?"

At this point, you can thank your lucky stars that you're doing object-oriented programming in Java. With object-oriented programming, you can create a subclass that overrides the functionality of its parent class. Listing 8-8 has just such a subclass.

Listing 8-8:   Yet Another Subclass

```
class PartTimeWithOver extends PartTimeEmployee {

    public double findPaymentAmount(int hours) {

        if(hours <= 40) {
            return getHourlyRate() * hours;
        } else {
            return getHourlyRate() * 40 +
                        getHourlyRate() * 2 * (hours -
            40);
        }
    }
}
```

Figure 8-10 shows the relationship between the code in Listing 8-8 and other pieces of code in this chapter. In particular, `PartTimeWithOver` is a subclass of a subclass. In object-oriented programming, a chain of this kind is not the least bit unusual. In fact, as subclasses go, this chain is rather short.

The `PartTimeWithOver` class extends the `PartTimeEmployee` class, but `PartTimeWithOver` picks and chooses what it wants to inherit from the `PartTimeEmployee` class. Because `PartTimeWithOver` has its own declaration for the `findPaymentAmount` method, the `PartTimeWithOver` class doesn't inherit a `findPaymentAmount` method from its parent. (See Figure 8-11.)

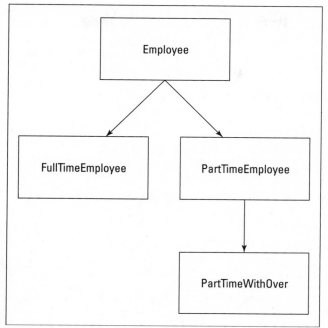

Figure 8-10:
A tree of
classes.

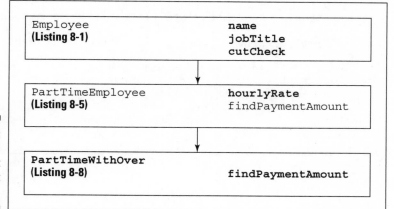

Figure 8-11:
Method
findPayment
Amount isn't
inherited.

According to the official terminology, the PartTimeWithOver class *overrides* its parent class's findPaymentAmount method. If you create an object from the PartTimeWithOver class, that object has the name, jobTitle, hourlyRate, and cutCheck of the PartTimeEmployee class, but the object has the findPaymentAmount method that's defined in Listing 8-8.

If you need clarification on the stuff that you just read, look at the code in Listing 8-9. A run of that code is shown in Figure 8-12.

Listing 8-9:   Testing the Code from Listing 8-8

```
class DoPayrollTypeF {

    public static void main(String args[]) {

        FullTimeEmployee ftEmployee = new FullTimeEmployee();

        ftEmployee.setName("Barry Burd");
        ftEmployee.setJobTitle("CEO");
        ftEmployee.setWeeklySalary(5000.00);
        ftEmployee.setBenefitDeduction(500.00);
        ftEmployee.cutCheck(ftEmployee.findPaymentAmount());

        PartTimeEmployee ptEmployee = new PartTimeEmployee();

        ptEmployee.setName("Chris Apelian");
        ptEmployee.setJobTitle("Computer Book Author");
        ptEmployee.setHourlyRate(7.53);
        ptEmployee.cutCheck(ptEmployee.findPaymentAmount(50));

        PartTimeWithOver ptoEmployee = new PartTimeWithOver();

        ptoEmployee.setName("Steve Surace");
        ptoEmployee.setJobTitle("Driver");
        ptoEmployee.setHourlyRate(7.53);
        ptoEmployee.cutCheck
                        (ptoEmployee.findPaymentAmount(50));
    }
}
```

Figure 8-12:
Running the
code of
Listing 8-9.

```
-----------------------Configuration: Listings0801-03-05-08-09 - JDK version 1.6.0 <
Pay to the order of Barry Burd (CEO) ***$4,500.00
Pay to the order of Chris Apelian (Computer Book Author) ***$376.50
Pay to the order of Steve Surace (Driver) ***$451.80
```

The code in Listing 8-9 writes checks to three employees. The first employee is a full-timer. The second is one of those part-time employees who hasn't yet gotten wind of the overtime payment scheme. The third employee knows about the overtime payment scheme and demands a fair wage.

With the subclasses, all three of these employees coexist in Listing 8-9. Sure, one subclass comes from the old PartTimeEmployee class, but that doesn't mean you can't create an object from the PartTimeEmployee class. In fact, Java is very smart about this. Listing 8-9 has three calls to the findPaymentAmount method, and each call reaches out to a different version of the method.

✔ In the first call, ftEmployee.findPaymentAmount, the ftEmployee variable is an instance of the FullTimeEmployee class. So the method that's called is the one in Listing 8-3.

✔ In the second call, ptEmployee.findPaymentAmount, the ptEmployee variable is an instance of the PartTimeEmployee class. So the method that's called is the one in Listing 8-5.

✔ In the third call, ptoEmployee.findPaymentAmount, the ptoEmployee variable is an instance of the PartTimeWithOver class. So the method that's called is the one in Listing 8-8.

This code is fantastic. It's clean, elegant, and efficient. With all the money that you save on software, you can afford to pay everyone double for overtime hours. (Whether you do that or keep the money for yourself is another story.)

Chapter 9

Constructing New Objects

. . . .

In This Chapter

▶ Defining constructors

▶ Using constructors in subclasses

▶ Using Java's default constructor features

▶ Constructing a simple GUI

. . . .

Ms. Jennie Rebekah Burd
121 Schoolhouse Lane
Anywhere, Kansas

Dear Ms. Burd,

In response to your letter of June 21, I believe I can say with complete assurance that objects are not created spontaneously from nothing. Although I have never actually seen an object being created (and no one else in this office can claim to have seen an object in its moment of creation), I have every confidence that some process or other is responsible for the building of these interesting and useful thingamajigs. We here at ClassesAndObjects.com support the unanimous opinions of both the scientific community and the private sector on matters of this nature. Furthermore, we agree with the recent finding of a Blue Ribbon Presidential Panel, which concludes beyond any doubt that spontaneous object creation would impede the present economic outlook.

Please be assured that I have taken all steps necessary to ensure the safety and well being of you, our loyal customer. If you have any further questions, please do not hesitate to contact our complaint department. The department's manager is Mr. Blake Wholl. You can contact him by visiting our company's Web site.

Once again, let me thank you for your concern, and I hope you continue to patronize ClassesAndObjects.com.

Yours truly,

Mr. Scott Brickenchicker
The one who couldn't get on the elevator in Chapter 4

Defining Constructors (What It Means to Be a Temperature)

Here's a statement that creates an object:

```
Account myAccount = new Account();
```

I know this works — I got it from one of my own examples in Chapter 7. Anyway, in Chapter 7, I say, "when the computer executes `new Account()`, you're creating an object by calling the `Account` class's constructor." What does this mean?

Well, when you ask the computer to create a new object, the computer responds by performing certain actions. For starters, the computer finds a place in its memory to store information about the new object. If the object has variables, the variables should eventually have meaningful values.

So one question is, when you ask the computer to create a new object, can you control what's placed in the object's variables? And what if you're interested in doing more than filling variables? Perhaps, when the computer creates a new object, you have a whole list of jobs for the computer to carry out. For instance, when the computer creates a new window object, you want the computer to realign the sizes of all the buttons in that window.

Creating a new object can involve all kinds of tasks, so in this chapter, you create constructors. A constructor tells the computer to perform a new object's startup tasks.

What is a temperature?

"Good morning, and welcome to Object News. The local temperature in your area is a pleasant 73 degrees Fahrenheit."

Each temperature consists of two things — a number and a temperature scale. The code in Listing 9-1 makes this fact abundantly clear.

Listing 9-1:   The Temperature Class

```
class Temperature {
    private double number;
    private ScaleName scale;

    public Temperature() {
        number = 0.0;
        scale = ScaleName.fahrenheit;
    }

    public Temperature(double number) {
        this.number = number;
        scale = ScaleName.fahrenheit;
    }

    public Temperature(ScaleName scale) {
        number = 0.0;
        this.scale = scale;
    }

    public Temperature(double number, ScaleName scale) {
        this.number = number;
        this.scale = scale;
    }

    public void setNumber(double number) {
        this.number = number;
    }

    public double getNumber() {
        return number;
    }

    public void setScale(ScaleName scale) {
        this.scale = scale;
    }

    public ScaleName getScale() {
        return scale;
    }
}
```

At the top of the code in Listing 9-1 are two variables: `number` and `scale`. A number is just a `double` value, such as `32.0` or `70.52`. A scale is an `enum` value. I define the `enum` type `ScaleName` in Listing 9-2.

For an introduction to enum types, see Chapter 6.

Listing 9-2:   The ScaleName enum Type

```
enum ScaleName {celsius, fahrenheit, kelvin, rankine};
```

The code in Listing 9-1 also has the usual setter and getter methods (accessor methods for the number and scale variables).

For some good reading on setter and getter methods (also known as accessor methods) see Chapter 7.

On top of all that, Listing 9-1 has four other method-like looking things. Each of these method-like things has the name *Temperature,* which happens to be the same as the name of the class. None of these Temperature method-like things has a return type of any kind — not even void, which is the copout return type.

Each of these method-like things is called a *constructor.* A constructor is like a method, except that a constructor has a very special purpose — creating new objects.

Whenever the computer creates a new object, the computer executes the statements inside a constructor.

What you can do with a temperature

Listing 9-3 gives form to some of the ideas that I describe above. In Listing 9-3, you call the constructors that are declared back in Listing 9-1. Figure 9-1 shows what happens when you run all this code.

Listing 9-3:   Using the Temperature Class

```
import static java.lang.System.out;

class UseTemperature {

    public static void main(String args[]) {
        final String format = "%5.2f degrees %s\n";

        Temperature temp = new Temperature();
        temp.setNumber(70.0);
        temp.setScale(ScaleName.fahrenheit);
```

```
        out.printf(format, temp.getNumber(),
            temp.getScale());

        temp = new Temperature(32.0);
        out.printf(format, temp.getNumber(),
            temp.getScale());

        temp = new Temperature(ScaleName.celsius);
        out.printf(format, temp.getNumber(),
            temp.getScale());

        temp = new Temperature(2.73, ScaleName.kelvin);
        out.printf(format, temp.getNumber(),
            temp.getScale());
    }
}
```

In Listing 9-3, each statement of the kind

```
temp = new Temperature(blah,blah,blah);
```

calls one of the constructors from Listing 9-1. So, by the time the code in Listing 9-3 is done running, it creates four instances of the `Temperature` class. Each instance is created by calling a different constructor from Listing 9-1.

Figure 9-1:
Running the
code from
Listing 9-3.

```
-----------------------Confi
70.00 degrees fahrenheit
32.00 degrees fahrenheit
 0.00 degrees celsius
 2.73 degrees kelvin
```

Calling new Temperature (32.0): A case study

When the computer executes one of the `new Temperature` statements in Listing 9-3, the computer has to decide which of the constructors in Listing 9-1 to use. The computer decides by looking at the *parameter list* (the stuff in parentheses) after the words `new Temperature`. For instance, when the computer executes

```
temp = new Temperature(32.0);
```

from Listing 9-3, the computer says to itself, "The number 32.0 in parentheses is a `double` value. One of the `Temperature` constructors in Listing 9-1 has just one parameter with type `double`. The constructor's header looks like this.

```
public Temperature(double number)
```

"So, I guess I'll execute the statements inside that particular constructor." The computer goes on to execute the following statements:

```
this.number = number;
scale = ScaleName.fahrenheit;
```

As a result, you get a brand-new object, whose number variable has the value 32.0, and whose `scale` variable has the value `fahrenheit`.

In the two lines of code, you have two statements that set values for the variables `number` and `scale`. Take a look at the second of these statements, which is a bit easier to understand. The second statement sets the new object's `scale` variable to `fahrenheit`. You see, the constructor's parameter list is `(double number)`, and that list doesn't include a `scale` value. So whoever programmed this code had to make a decision about what value to use for the `scale` variable. The programmer could have chosen `fahrenheit` or `celsius`, but she could also have chosen `kelvin` or `rankine`. (This programmer happens to live in New Jersey, in the United States, where people commonly use the old Fahrenheit temperature scale.)

Marching back to the first of the two statements, this first statement assigns a value to the new object's `number` variable. The statement uses a cute trick that you can see in many constructors (and in other methods that assign values to objects' variables). To understand the trick, take a look at Listing 9-4. The listing shows you two ways that I could have written the same constructor code.

Listing 9-4: Two Ways to Accomplish the Same Thing

```
//Use this constructor ...

    public Temperature(double whatever) {
        number = whatever;
        scale = ScaleName.fahrenheit;
    }

//... or use this constructor ...

    public Temperature(double number) {
```

```
        this.number = number;
        scale = ScaleName.fahrenheit;
    }

//... but don't put both constructors in your code.
```

Listing 9-4 has two constructors in it. In the first constructor, I use two different names — number and whatever. In the second constructor, I don't need two names. Instead of making up a new name for the constructor's parameter, I reuse an existing name by writing this.number.

So here's what's going on in Listing 9-1:

✔ In the statement this.number = number, the name *this.number* refers to the new object's number variable — the variable that's declared near the very top of Listing 9-1. (See Figure 9-2.)

✔ In the statement this.number = number, the word *number* (on its own, without this) refers to the constructor's parameter. (Again, see Figure 9-2.)

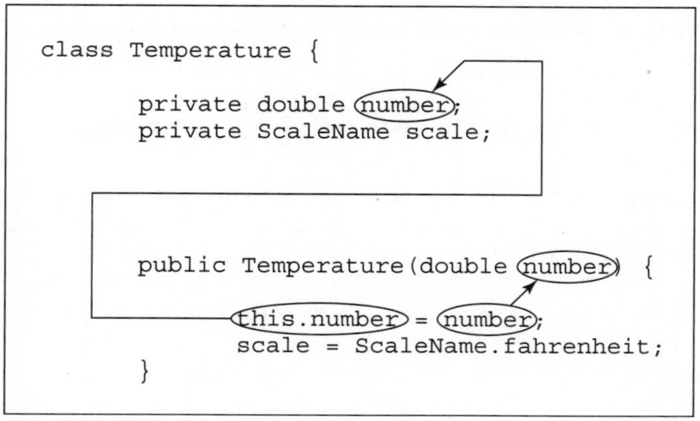

Figure 9-2:
What
this.number
and number
mean.

In general, this.*someName* refers to a variable belonging to the object that contains the code. In contrast, plain old *someName* refers to the closest place where *someName* happens to be declared. In the statement this.number = number (Listing 9-1), that closest place happens to be the Temperature constructor's parameter list.

What's this all about?

Suppose your code contains a constructor — the first of the two constructors in Listing 9-4. The whatever parameter is passed a number like 32.0, for instance. Then the first statement in the constructor's body assigns that value, 32.0, to the new object's number variable. The code works. But in writing this code, you had to make up a new name for a parameter — the name *whatever*. And the only purpose for this new name is to hand a value to the object's number variable. What a waste! To distinguish between the parameter and the number variable, you gave a name to something that was just momentary storage for the number value.

Making up names is an art, not a science. I've gone through plenty of naming phases. Years ago, whenever I needed a new name for a parameter,

I picked a confusing misspelling of the original variable name. (I'd name the parameter something like numbr or nuhmber.) I've also tried changing a variable name's capitalization to come up with a parameter name. (I'd use parameter names like Number or nUMBER.) In Chapter 8, I name all my parameters by adding the suffix *In* to their corresponding variable names. (The jobTitle variable matched up with the jobTitleIn parameter.) None of these naming schemes works very well. I can never remember the quirky new names that I've created. The good news is that this parameter naming effort isn't necessary. You can give the parameter the same name as the variable. To distinguish between the two, you use the Java keyword this.

enum types as first-class citizens

A peek at the code from this book's CD-ROM tells an interesting story. The project for this section's example contains three Java files: Temperature.java (Listing 9-1), ScaleName.java (Listing 9-2), and UseTemperature.java (Listing 9-3). The big news in this trio is ScaleName.java. Why does this wimpy little one-line enum type deserve to be in its own separate Java file?

Well, two issues exist here, and both are important:

 ✔ **An enum type is a class in disguise.** When the Java compiler gets hold of your enum declaration, the compiler immediately turns the enum type into a class:

```
class ScaleName extends Enum {
    //There's code here that I'm not showing to you

    celsius = new ScaleName("celsius", 0);
    fahrenheit = new ScaleName("fahrenheit", 1);
    kelvin = new ScaleName("kelvin", 2);
    rankine = new ScaleName("rankine", 3);

    //There's code here that I'm not showing to you
}
```

This normally happens behind the scenes. So in previous examples (Listing 6-5, for instance), you don't have to think about it. But in most of this book's examples (and according to standard Java programming practice), each Java class lives in a `.java` file all its own. Because `ScaleName` is a class, having a separate `ScaleName.java` file makes perfect sense.

Back in Listing 6-5, I stuffed three `enum` type declarations inside another class — a class named *Clue*. In Chapter 6, this doesn't seem unusual, but now you may be thinking, "A class can be nestled inside another class." Well, stop thinking that way. It's true that Java supports a feature called *inner classes* — classes defined within other classes. It's also true that this inner class feature allows you to define a `Suspect` enum type inside a `Clue` class. What's not true is that novice Java programmers should use inner classes, except in the narrowly defined context of `enum` types. So in general, when you're tempted to put one class inside another, don't do it.

✔ **The `ScaleName` enum type must be available to both the `Temperature` and the `UseTemperature` classes.** In the first draft of this section's code, I put the `ScaleName` enum type declaration inside Listing 9-1. That was fine until I wrote the `UseTemperature` class (Listing 9-3). The `UseTemperature` class refers to `ScaleName`. So in order to get at this `ScaleName` thing that I'd tucked inside Listing 9-1, I had to put some long, cumbersome statements in Listing 9-3:

```
temp.setScale(Temperature.ScaleName.fahrenheit);
...
temp = new Temperature(Temperature.ScaleName.celsius);
...
temp = new Temperature
              (2.73, Temperature.ScaleName.kelvin);
```

At this point, a little voice told me that it was easier to put the `ScaleName` enum declaration in a file all its own. That way, both the `Temperature` and `UseTemperature` classes could refer to `ScaleName` without any extra chains full of names and dots.

Some things never change

Chapter 7 introduces the `printf` method, and explains that each `printf` call starts with a format string. The format string describes the way the other parameters are to be displayed.

In previous examples, this format string is always a quoted literal. For instance, the first `printf` call in Listing 7-7 is

```
out.printf("$%4.2f\n", myInterest);
```

In Listing 9-3, I break with tradition and begin the `printf` call with a variable that I name *format*.

```
out.printf(format, temp.getNumber(), temp.getScale());
```

That's okay as long as my `format` variable is of type `String`. And indeed, in Listing 9-3, the first variable declaration is

```
final String format = "%5.2f degrees %s\n";
```

In this declaration of the `format` variable, take special note of the word *final*. This Java keyword indicates that the value of `format` can't be changed. If I add an additional assignment statement to Listing 9-3

```
format = "%6.2f (%s)\n";
```

then the compiler barks back at me with a `cannot assign a value to final variable` message.

When I write the code in Listing 9-3, the use of the `final` keyword isn't absolutely necessary. But the `final` keyword provides some extra protection. When I initialize `format` to `"%5.2f degrees %s\n"`, I intend to use this same `format` just as it is, over and over again. I know darn well that I don't intend to change the `format` variable's value. Of course, in a 10,000-line program, I can become confused and try to assign a new value to `format` somewhere deep down in the code. So to prevent me from accidentally changing the format string, I declare the `format` variable to be final. It's just good, safe programming practice.

More Subclasses (Doing Something about the Weather)

In Chapter 8, I make a big fuss over the notion of subclasses. That's the right thing to do. Subclasses make code reusable, and reusable code is good code. With that in mind, it's time to create a subclass of the `Temperature` class (which I develop in this chapter's first section).

Building better temperatures

After perusing the code in Listing 9-3, you decide that the responsibility for displaying temperatures has been seriously misplaced. Listing 9-3 has several tedious repetitions of the lines to print temperature values. A 1970s programmer would tell you to collect those lines into one place and turn them into a method. (The 1970s programmer wouldn't have used the word *method*, but that's not important right now.) Collecting lines into methods is fine, but with today's object-oriented programming methodology, you think in broader terms. Why not get each `temperature` object to take responsibility for displaying itself? After all, if you develop a `display` method, you probably want to share the method with other people who use temperatures. So put the method right inside the declaration of a `temperature` object. That way, anyone who uses the code for temperatures has easy access to your `display` method.

Now replay the tape from Chapter 8. "Blah, blah, blah . . . don't want to modify existing code . . . blah, blah, blah . . . too costly to start again from scratch . . . blah, blah, blah . . . extend existing functionality." It all adds up to one thing:

> Don't abuse it. Instead, reuse it.

So you decide to create a subclass of the `Temperature` class, which is defined in Listing 9-1. Your new subclass complements the `Temperature` class's functionality by having methods to display values in a nice, uniform fashion. The new class, `TemperatureNice`, is shown in Listing 9-5.

Listing 9-5: The TemperatureNice Class

```java
import static java.lang.System.out;

class TemperatureNice extends Temperature {

    public TemperatureNice() {
        super();
    }

    public TemperatureNice(double number) {
        super(number);
    }

    public TemperatureNice(ScaleName scale) {
        super(scale);
    }

    public TemperatureNice(double number, ScaleName scale)
            {
        super(number, scale);
    }

    public void display() {
        out.printf("%5.2f degrees %s\n",
                            getNumber(), getScale());
    }
}
```

In the `display` method of Listing 9-5, notice the calls to the `Temperature` class's `getNumber` and `getScale` methods. Why do I do this? Well, inside the `TemperatureNice` class's code, any direct references to the `number` and `scale` variables would generate error messages. It's true that every `TemperatureNice` object has its own `number` and `scale` variables. (After all, `TemperatureNice` is a subclass of the `Temperature` class, and the code for the `Temperature` class defines the `number` and `scale` variables.) But because `number` and `scale` are declared to be private inside the `Temperature` class, only code that's right inside the `Temperature` class can directly use these variables.

Don't put additional declarations of the `number` and `scale` variables inside the `TemperatureNice` class's code. If you do, you inadvertently create four different variables (two called *number,* and another two called *scale*). You'll assign values to one pair of variables. Then you'll be shocked that, when you display the other pair of variables, those values seem to have disappeared.

When an object's code contains a call to one of the object's own methods, you don't need to preface the call with a dot. For instance, in the last statement of Listing 9-5, the object calls its own methods with `getNumber()` and `getScale()`, not with *someObject*`.getNumber()` and *something OrOther*`.getScale()`. If going dotless makes you queasy, you can compensate by taking advantage of yet another use for the `this` keyword. Just write `this.getNumber()` and `this.getScale()` in the last line of Listing 9-5.

Constructors for subclasses

By far, the biggest news in Listing 9-5 is the way the code declares constructors. The `TemperatureNice` class has four of its own constructors. If you've gotten in gear thinking about subclass inheritance, you may wonder why these constructor declarations are necessary. Doesn't `TemperatureNice` inherit the parent `Temperature` class's constructors? No, subclasses don't inherit constructors.

Subclasses don't inherit constructors.

That's right. Subclasses don't inherit constructors. In one oddball case, a constructor may look like it's being inherited, but that oddball situation is a fluke, not the norm. In general, when you define a subclass, you declare new constructors to go with the subclass.

I describe the oddball case (in which a constructor looks like it's being inherited) later in this chapter, in the section "The default constructor."

So the code in Listing 9-5 has four constructors. Each constructor has the name *TemperatureNice,* and each constructor has its own, uniquely identifiable parameter list. That's the boring part. The interesting part is that each constructor makes a call to something named *super,* which is a Java keyword.

In Listing 9-5, `super` stands for a constructor in the parent class.

- The statement `super()` in Listing 9-5 calls the parameterless `Temperature()` constructor that's in Listing 9-1. That parameterless constructor assigns `0.0` to the `number` variable and `ScaleName.fahrenheit` to the `scale` variable.

- The statement `super(number, scale)` in Listing 9-5 calls the constructor `Temperature(double number, ScaleName scale)` that's in Listing 9-1. In turn, the constructor assigns values to the `number` and `scale` variables.

- In a similar way, the statements `super(number)` and `super(scale)` in Listing 9-5 call constructors from Listing 9-1.

The computer decides which of the `Temperature` class's constructors is being called by looking at the parameter list after the word *super.* For instance, when the computer executes

```
super(number, scale);
```

from Listing 9-5, the computer says to itself, "The `number` and `scale` variables in parentheses have types `double` and `ScaleName`. But only one of the `Temperature` constructors in Listing 9-1 has two parameters with types `double` and `ScaleName`. The constructor's header looks like this:

```
public Temperature(double number, ScaleName scale)
```

So, I guess I'll execute the statements inside that particular constructor."

Using all this stuff

In Listing 9-5, I define what it means to be in the `TemperatureNice` class. Now it's time to put this `TemperatureNice` class to good use. Listing 9-6 has code that uses `TemperatureNice`.

Listing 9-6:   Using the TemperatureNice Class

```
class UseTemperatureNice {

    public static void main(String args[]) {

        TemperatureNice temp = new TemperatureNice();
        temp.setNumber(70.0);
        temp.setScale(ScaleName.fahrenheit);
        temp.display();

        temp = new TemperatureNice(32.0);
        temp.display();

        temp = new TemperatureNice(ScaleName.celsius);
        temp.display();

        temp = new TemperatureNice(2.73,
            ScaleName.kelvin);
        temp.display();
    }
}
```

The code in Listing 9-6 is very much like its cousin code in Listing 9-3. The big differences are as follows:

- Listing 9-6 creates instances of the TemperatureNice class. That is, Listing 9-6 calls constructors from the TemperatureNice class, not the Temperature class.

- Listing 9-6 takes advantage of the display method in the Temperature Nice class. So the code in Listing 9-6 is much tidier than its counterpart in Listing 9-3.

A run of Listing 9-6 looks exactly like a run of the code in Listing 9-3. The run is shown previously in Figure 9-1.

The default constructor

The main message in the previous section is that subclasses don't inherit constructors. So what gives with all the listings back in Chapter 8? In Listing 8-6, a statement says

```
FullTimeEmployee ftEmployee = new FullTimeEmployee();
```

But, here's the problem: The code defining `FullTimeEmployee` (Listing 8-3) doesn't seem to have any constructors declared inside it. So, in Listing 8-6, how can you possibly call the `FullTimeEmployee` constructor?

Here's what's going on. When you create a subclass and don't put any explicit constructor declarations in your code, then Java creates one constructor for you. It's called a *default constructor.* If you're creating the `public` `FullTimeEmployee` subclass, the default constructor looks like the one in Listing 9-7.

Listing 9-7:   A Default Constructor

```
public FullTimeEmployee() {
    super();
}
```

The constructor in Listing 9-7 takes no parameters, and its one statement calls the constructor of whatever class you're extending. (Woe be to you if the class that you're extending doesn't have a parameterless constructor.)

You've just read about default constructors, but watch out! Notice one thing that this talk about default constructors *doesn't* say: It doesn't say that you always get a default constructor. In particular, if you create a subclass and define any constructors yourself, Java doesn't add a default constructor for the subclass (and the subclass doesn't inherit any constructors, either).

So how can this trip you up? Listing 9-8 has a copy of the code from Listing 8-3, but with one constructor added to it. Take a look at this modified version of the `FullTimeEmployee` code.

Listing 9-8:   Look, I Have a Constructor!

```
class FullTimeEmployee extends Employee {
    private double weeklySalary;
    private double benefitDeduction;

    public FullTimeEmployee(double weeklySalary) {
        this.weeklySalary=weeklySalary;
    }

    public void setWeeklySalary(double weeklySalaryIn) {
        weeklySalary = weeklySalaryIn;
    }

    public double getWeeklySalary() {
```

(continued)

Listing 9-8 (continued)

```
        return weeklySalary;
    }

    public void setBenefitDeduction(double benefitDedIn) {
        benefitDeduction = benefitDedIn;
    }

    public double getBenefitDeduction() {
        return benefitDeduction;
    }

    public double findPaymentAmount() {
        return weeklySalary - benefitDeduction;
    }
}
```

If you use the `FullTimeEmployee` code in Listing 9-8, a line like the following doesn't work:

```
FullTimeEmployee ftEmployee = new FullTimeEmployee();
```

It doesn't work because, having declared a `FullTimeEmployee` constructor that takes one `double` parameter, you no longer get a default parameterless constructor for free.

So what do you do about this? If you declare any constructors, declare all the constructors that you're possibly going to need. Take the constructor in Listing 9-7 and add it to the code in Listing 9-8. Then the call `new FullTimeEmployee()` starts working again.

An invisible constructor call

Here's a program that I like to yank out and show people at Java parties. (Believe me, it surprises some of the veteran Java programmers.) The program is shown in Listings 9-9, 9-10, and 9-11.

Listing 9-9:   First Class Accomodations

```
class MyClass {

    MyClass() {
        System.out.println
                ("MyClass constructor being called.");
    }
}
```

Listing 9-10: Second Class Accomodations

```
class MySubclass extends MyClass {

    MySubclass() {
        System.out.println
                    ("MySubclass constructor being
        called.");
    }
}
```

Listing 9-11: What's My Output?

```
class UseMyClasses {

    public static void main(String args[]) {
        new MySubclass();
    }
}
```

So what's the output when you run the code in Listing 9-11? Huh? You think you get just one line of output? Sorry, that's not the way it works. The output that you get is shown in Figure 9-3.

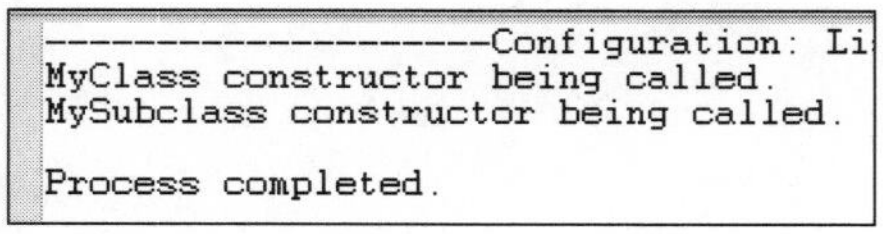

Figure 9-3:
Surprise!

```
--------------------Configuration: Li
MyClass constructor being called.
MySubclass constructor being called.

Process completed.
```

Under certain circumstances, Java automatically adds an invisible call to super, which is at the top of a constructor body. It's as if the MySubclass constructor in Listing 9-10 really looks like this:

```
MySubclass() {
    super();
    System.out.println
                ("MySubclass constructor being called.");
}
```

In Listing 9-10, the invisible super call fires up the MyClass constructor, which prints the message MyClass constructor being called. This automatic addition of a super call is a tricky bit of business that doesn't appear often, so when it does appear, it may seem quite mysterious.

A Constructor That Does More

Here's a quote from someplace near the start of this chapter: "And what if you're interested in doing more than filling variables? Perhaps, when the computer creates a new object, you have a whole list of jobs for the computer to carry out." Okay, what if?

This section's example has a constructor that does more than just assign values to variables. The example is in Listings 9-12 and 9-13. The result of running the example's code is shown in Figure 9-4.

Listing 9-12: Defining a Frame

```
import java.awt.FlowLayout;
import javax.swing.JFrame;
import javax.swing.JButton;

class SimpleFrame extends JFrame {

    public SimpleFrame() {
        setTitle("Don't click the button!");
        setLayout(new FlowLayout());
        setDefaultCloseOperation(EXIT_ON_CLOSE);
        add(new JButton("Panic"));
        setSize(300,100);
        setVisible(true);
    }
}
```

Listing 9-13: Displaying a Frame

```
class ShowAFrame {

    public static void main(String args[]) {
        new SimpleFrame();
    }
}
```

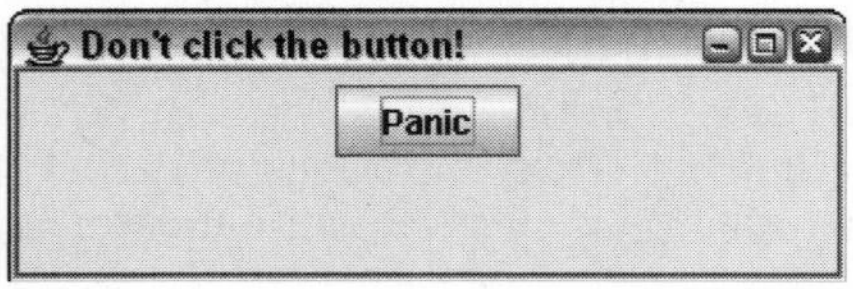

Figure 9-4:
Don't panic.

The code in Listing 9-12 is made up mostly of calls to Java API (Application Programming Interface) methods. What this means to you is that the code contains lots of names that are probably unfamiliar to you. When I was first becoming acquainted with Java, I foolishly believed that knowing Java meant knowing all these names. Quite the contrary: These names are just carry-on baggage. The real Java is the way the language implements object-oriented concepts.

Packages and import declarations

Java has a feature that lets you lump classes into groups of classes. Each lump of classes is called a *package.* In the Java world, programmers customarily give these packages long, dot-filled names. For instance, because I've registered the domain name *burdbrain.com,* I may name a package com.burdbrain.utils. textUtils. The Java API is actually a big collection of packages. The API has packages with names like java.lang, java.util, java.awt, javax.swing, and so on.

With this information about packages, I can clear up some of the confusion about import declarations. Any import declaration that doesn't use the word static must start with the name of a package and must end with either of the following:

✔ The name of a class within that package

✔ An asterisk (indicating all classes within that package)

For example, the declaration

    import java.util.Scanner;

is valid because java.util is the name of a package in the Java API, and Scanner is the name of a class in the java.util package. The dotted name java.util.Scanner is the *fully qualified name* of the Scanner class. A class's fully qualified name includes the name of the package in which the class is defined. (You can find out all this stuff about java. util and Scanner by reading Java's API documentation. For tips on reading the documentation, see Chapter 3 and this book's Web site.)

Here's another example. The declaration

    import javax.swing.*;

is valid because javax.swing is the name of a package in the Java API, and the asterisk refers to all classes in the javax.swing package. With this import declaration at the top of your Java code, you can use abbreviated names for classes in the javax.swing package — names like JFrame, JButton, JMenuBar, JCheckBox, and many others.

Here's one more example. A line like

    import javax.*;   //Bad!!

is *not* a valid import declaration. The Java API has no package with the one-word name javax. You may think that this line allows you to abbreviate all names beginning with javax (names like javax.swing.JFrame and javax.sound.midi), but that's not the way the import declaration works. Because javax isn't the name of a package, the line import javax.* just angers the Java compiler.

Anyway, the code's anorexic main method has only one statement — a call to the constructor in the SimpleFrame class. Notice how the object that this call creates isn't even assigned to a variable. That's okay, because the code doesn't need to refer to the object anywhere else.

Up in the SimpleFrame class is only one constructor declaration. Far from just setting variables' values, this constructor calls method after method from the Java API.

All the methods called in the SimpleFrame class's constructor come from the parent class, JFrame. The JFrame class lives in the javax.swing package. This package and another package, java.awt, have classes that help you put windows, images, drawings, and other gizmos on a computer screen. (In the java.awt package, the letters *awt* stand for *abstract windowing toolkit*.)

For a little gossip about the notion of a Java package, see the sidebar entitled "Packages and import declarations." For lots of gossip about the notion of a Java package, see Appendix B and (on the CD-ROM) Chapter 15.

In the Java API, what people normally call a *window* is an instance of the javax.swing.JFrame class.

Looking at Figure 9-4, you can probably tell that an instance of the SimpleFrame class doesn't do much. The frame has only one button and, when you click the button, nothing happens. I made the frame this way to keep the example from becoming too complicated. Even so, the code in Listing 9-12 uses several API classes and methods. The setTitle, setLayout, setDefaultCloseOperation, add, setSize, and setVisible methods all belong to the javax.swing.JFrame class. Here's a list of names used in the code:

- **setTitle:** Calling setTitle puts words in the frame's title bar. (The new SimpleFrame object is calling its own setTitle method.)

- **FlowLayout:** An instance of the FlowLayout class positions objects on the frame in centered, typewriter fashion. Because the frame in Figure 9-4 has only one button on it, that button is centered near the top of the frame. If the frame had eight buttons, five of them may be lined up in a row across the top of the frame and the remaining three would be centered along a second row.

- **setLayout:** Calling setLayout puts the new FlowLayout object in charge of arranging components, such as buttons, on the frame. (The new SimpleFrame object is calling its own setLayout method.)

✔ **setDefaultCloseOperation:** Calling setDefaultCloseOperation tells Java what to do when you click the little × in the frame's upper-right corner. Without this method call, the frame itself disappears, but the Java Virtual Machine (JVM) keeps running. If you use JCreator, you have to halt the JVM by choosing Tools➪Stop Tool.

Calling setDefaultCloseOperation(EXIT_ON_CLOSE) tells Java to shut itself down when you click the × in the frame's upper-right corner. The alternatives to EXIT_ON_CLOSE are HIDE_ON_CLOSE, DISPOSE_ON_CLOSE, and my personal favorite, DO_NOTHING_ON_CLOSE.

✔ **JButton:** The JButton class lives in the javax.swing package. One of the class's constructors takes a String instance (such as "Panic") for its parameter. Calling this constructor makes that String instance into the label on the face of the new button.

✔ **add:** The new SimpleFrame object calls its add method. Calling the add method places the button on the object's surface (in this case, the surface of the frame).

✔ **setSize:** The frame becomes 300 pixels wide and 100 pixels tall. (In the javax.swing package, whenever you specify two dimension numbers, the width number always comes before the height number.)

✔ **setVisible:** When it's first created, a new frame is invisible. But when the new frame calls setVisible(true), the frame appears on your computer screen.

Part IV
Savvy Java Techniques

The 5th Wave   By Rich Tennant

"I've been in hardware all of my life, and all of a sudden it's software that'll make me rich."

In this part . . .

*H*ere's where I start sharing some big-time Java concepts. This part of the book describes the tricky
things, the little nooks and crannies, the special rules, and
the not-so-special exceptions. As usual, you shouldn't feel
intimidated. I take you one step at a time and keep the
whole thing light, interesting, and manageable.

Chapter 10

Putting Variables and Methods Where They Belong

*H*ello, again. You're listening to radio station WWW, and I'm your host, Sam Burd. It's the start again of the big baseball season, and today station WWW brought you live coverage of the Hankees versus Socks game. At this moment, I'm awaiting news of the game's final score.

If you remember from earlier this afternoon, the Socks looked like they were going to take those Hankees to the cleaners. Then, the Hankees were belting ball after ball, giving the Socks a run for their money. Those Socks! I'm glad I wasn't in their shoes.

Anyway, as the game went on, the Socks pulled themselves up. Now the Socks are nose to nose with the Hankees. We'll get the final score in a minute, but first, a few reminders. Stay tuned after this broadcast for the big Jersey's game. And don't forget to tune in next week when the Cleveland Gowns play the Bermuda Shorts.

Okay, here's the final score. Which team has the upper hand? Which team will come out a head? And the winner is . . . oh, no! It's a tie!

Defining a Class (What It Means to Be a Baseball Player)

As far as I'm concerned, a baseball player has a name and a batting average. Listing 10-1 puts my feeling about this into Java program form.

Listing 10-1:   The Player Class

```java
import java.text.DecimalFormat;

class Player {
    private String name;
    private double average;

    public Player(String name, double average) {
        this.name=name;
        this.average=average;
    }

    public String getName() {
        return name;
    }

    public double getAverage() {
        return average;
    }

    public String getAverageString() {
        DecimalFormat decFormat =
                            new DecimalFormat("
        .000");
        return decFormat.format(average);
    }
}
```

So here I go, picking apart the code in Listing 10-1. Luckily, earlier chapters cover lots of stuff in this code. The code defines what it means to be an instance of the Player class. Here's what's in the code:

✔ **Declarations of the variables name and average.** For bedtime reading about variable declarations, see Chapter 4.

✔ **A constructor to make new instances of the Player class.** For the lowdown on constructors, see Chapter 9.

✔ **Getter methods for the variables name and average.** For chitchat about accessor methods (that is, setter and getter methods), see Chapter 7.

✔ **A method that returns the player's batting average in String form.** For the good word about methods, see Chapter 7.

Another way to beautify your numbers

The last method in Listing 10-1 takes the value from the `average` variable (a player's batting average), converts that value (normally of type `double`) into a `String`, and then sends that `String` value right back to the method caller. The use of `DecimalFormat`, which comes right from the Java API (Application Programming Interface), makes sure that the `String` value looks like a baseball player's batting average. That is, the `String` value starts with lots of blank spaces, has no digits to the left of the decimal point, and has exactly three digits to the right of the decimal point. (The blank spaces ensure that a gap exists between the batting average and whatever text appears before it.)

Java's `DecimalFormat` class can be quite handy. For example, to display the values `345` and `-345` with an accounting-friendly format, you can use the following code:

```
DecimalFormat decFormat =
    new DecimalFormat("$###0.00;($###0.00)");

System.out.println(decFormat.format(345));
System.out.println(decFormat.format(-345));
```

In this little example's format string, everything before the semicolon dictates the way positive numbers are displayed, and everything after the semicolon determines the way negative numbers are displayed. So with this format, the numbers 345 and -345 appear as follows:

```
$345.00
($345.00)
```

To discover some other tricks with numbers, visit the `DecimalFormat` page of Java's API documentation.

Using the Player class

Listings 10-2 and 10-3 have code that uses the `Player` class — the class that's defined way back in Listing 10-1.

Listing 10-2:   Using the Player Class

```
import java.util.Scanner;
import java.io.File;
import java.io.IOException;
import javax.swing.JFrame;
import javax.swing.JLabel;
```

(continued)

Listing 10-2 (continued)

```java
import java.awt.GridLayout;

class TeamFrame extends JFrame {

    public TeamFrame() throws IOException {
        Player player;
        Scanner myScanner =
                    new Scanner(new File("Hankees.txt"));

        for (int num = 1; num <= 9; num++) {
            player =
                new Player(myScanner.nextLine(),
                                myScanner.nextDouble());
            myScanner.nextLine();

            addPlayerInfo(player);
        }

        setTitle("The Hankees");
        setLayout(new GridLayout(9,2));
        setDefaultCloseOperation(EXIT_ON_CLOSE);
        pack();
        setVisible(true);
    }

    void addPlayerInfo(Player player) {
        add(new JLabel(player.getName()));
        add(new JLabel(player.getAverageString()));
    }
}
```

Listing 10-3:   Displaying a Frame

```java
import java.io.IOException;

class ShowTeamFrame {

    public static void main(String args[])
                                            throws
            IOException {
        new TeamFrame();
    }
}
```

For a run of the code in Listings 10-1, 10-2, and 10-3, see Figure 10-1. To run this program yourself, you need the Hankees.txt file. (The file is loaded automatically onto your hard drive when you install JCreator from this book's CD-ROM.) This file contains data on your favorite baseball players. (See Figure 10-2.)

Figure 10-1:
Would you
bet money
on these
people?

The Hankees	
Barry Burd	.101
Harriet Ritter	.200
Weelie J. Katz	.030
Harry "The Crazyman" Spoonswagler	.124
Felicia "Fishy" Katz	.075
Mia, Just "Mia"	.111
Jeremy Flooflong Jones	.102
I. M. D'Arthur	.001
Hugh R. DaReader	.212

Figure 10-2:
What a
team!

```
Hankees.txt | ShowTeamFrame.java | Player.java

Barry Burd
.101
Harriet Ritter
.200
Weelie J. Katz
.030
Harry "The Crazyman" Spoonswagler
.124
Felicia "Fishy" Katz
.075
Mia, Just "Mia"
.111
Jeremy Flooflong Jones
.102
I. M. D'Arthur
.001
Hugh R. DaReader
.212
```

For this section's code to work correctly, you must have a line break after the last .212 in Figure 10-2. For details about line breaks, see Chapter 8.

Nine, count 'em, nine

The code in Listing 10-2 calls the Player constructor nine times. This means that the code creates nine instances of the Player class. The first time through the loop, the code creates an instance with the name Barry Burd. The second time through the loop, the code abandons the Barry Burd instance and creates another instance with name Harriet Ritter. The third time through, the code abandons poor Harriet Ritter and creates an instance for Weelie J. Katz. The code has only one instance at a time but, all in all, the code creates nine instances.

Each Player instance has its own name and average variables. Each instance also has its own Player constructor and its own getName, getAverage, and getAverageString methods. Look at Figure 10-3 and think of the Player class with its nine incarnations.

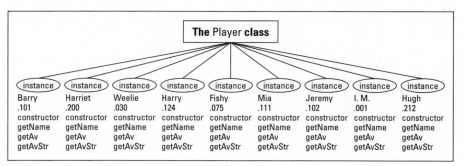

Figure 10-3:
A class and
its objects.

Don't get all GUI on me

The code in Listing 10-2 uses several names from the Java API. Some of these names are explained in Chapter 9. Others are explained right here:

✔ **JLabel:** A JLabel is an object with some text in it. One of the ways to display text inside the frame is to add an instance of the JLabel class to the frame.

In Listing 10-2, the addPlayerInfo method is called nine times, once for each player on the team. Each time addPlayerInfo is called, the method adds two new JLabel objects to the frame. The text for each JLabel object comes from a player object's getter method.

✔ **GridLayout:** A GridLayout arranges things in evenly spaced rows and columns. This constructor for the GridLayout class takes two parameters — the number of rows and the number of columns.

In Listing 10-2, the call to the GridLayout constructor takes parameters (9,2). So in Figure 10-1, the display has nine rows (one for each player) and two columns (one for a name and another for an average).

✔ **pack:** When you pack a frame, you set the frame's size. That's the size the frame has when it appears on your computer screen. Packing a frame shrink-wraps the frame around whatever objects you've added inside the frame.

In Listing 10-2, by the time you've reached the call to pack, you've already called addPlayerInfo nine times and added 18 labels to the frame. In executing the pack method, the computer picks a nice size for each label, given whatever text you've put inside the label. Then, the computer picks a nice size for the whole frame, given that the frame has these 18 labels inside it.

When you plop stuff onto frames, you have quite a bit of leeway with the order in which you do things. For instance, you can set the layout before or after you've added labels and other stuff to the frame. If you call `setLayout` and then add labels, the labels appear in nice, orderly positions on the frame. If you reverse this order (add labels and then call `setLayout`), the calling of `setLayout` rearranges the labels in a nice, orderly fashion. It works fine either way.

In setting up a frame, the one thing that you shouldn't do is violate the following sequence:

```
Add things to the frame, then
pack();
setVisible(true);
```

If you call `pack` and then add more things to the frame, the `pack` method doesn't take the more recent things that you've added into consideration. If you call `setVisible` before you add things or call `pack`, the user sees the frame as it's being constructed. Finally, if you forget to set the frame's size (by calling `pack` or some other sizing method), the frame that you see looks like the one in Figure 10-4. (Normally, I wouldn't show you an anomalous run like the one in Figure 10-4, but I've made the mistake so many times that I feel as if this puny frame is an old friend of mine.)

Figure 10-4:
An under-
nourished
frame.

Tossing an exception from method to method

Chapter 8 introduces input from a disk file, and along with that topic comes the notion of an exception. When you tinker with a disk file, you need to acknowledge the possibility of raising an `IOException`. That's the lesson from Chapter 8, and that's why the constructor in Listing 10-2 has a `throws IOException` clause.

But what about the `main` method in Listing 10-3? With no apparent reference to disk files in this `main` method, why does the method need its own `throws IOException` clause? Well, an exception is a hot potato. If you have one, you either have to eat it (as you can see in Chapter 12) or use a `throws` clause to toss it to someone else. If you toss an exception with a `throws` clause, someone else is stuck with the exception just the way you were.

The constructor in Listing 10-2 throws an `IOException`, but to whom is this exception thrown? Who in this chain of code becomes the bearer of responsibility for the problematic `IOException`? Well, who called the constructor in Listing 10-2? It was the `main` method in Listing 10-3 — that's who called the `TeamFrame` constructor. Because the `TeamFrame` constructor throws its hot potato to the `main` method in Listing 10-3, the `main` method has to deal with it. As shown in Listing 10-3, the `main` method deals with it by tossing the `IOException` again (by having a `throws IOException` clause of its own). That's how the `throws` clause works in Java programs.

If a method calls another method, and the called method has a `throws` clause, the calling method must contain code that deals with the exception. To find out more about dealing with exceptions, read Chapter 12.

At this point in the book, the astute *For Dummies* reader may pose a follow-up question or two. "When a `main` method has a `throws` clause, someone else has to deal with the exception in that `throws` clause. But who called the `main` method? Who deals with the `IOException` in the `throws` clause of Listing 10-3?" The answer is that the Java Virtual Machine (or JVM, the thing that runs all your Java code) called the `main` method. So the JVM takes care of the `IOException` in Listing 10-3. If the program has any trouble reading the `Hankees.txt` file, the responsibility ultimately falls on the JVM. The JVM takes care of things by displaying an error message and then ending the run of your program. How convenient!

Making Static (Finding the Team Average)

Thinking about the code in Listings 10-1 through 10-3, you decide that you'd like to find the team's overall batting average. Not a bad idea! The Hankees in Figure 10-1 have an average of about .106, so the team needs some intensive training. While the players are out practicing on the ball field, you have a philosophical hurdle to overcome.

In Listings 10-1 through 10-3, you have three classes: a `Player` class and two other classes that help display data from the `Player` class. So in this class morass, where do the variables storing your overall, team-average tally go?

✔ It makes no sense to put tally variables in either of the displaying classes (TeamFrame and ShowTeamFrame). After all, the tally has something or other to do with players, teams, and baseball. The displaying classes are about creating windows, not about playing baseball.

✔ You're uncomfortable putting an overall team average in an instance of the Player class because an instance of the Player class represents just one player on the team. What business does a single player have storing overall team data? Sure, you could make the code work, but it wouldn't be an elegant solution to the problem.

Finally, you discover the keyword static. Anything that's declared to be static belongs to the whole class, not to any particular instance of the class. When you create the static variable, totalOfAverages, you create just one copy of the variable. This copy stays with the entire Players class. No matter how many instances of the Player class you create — one, nine, or none — you have just one totalOfAverages variable. And, while you're at it, you create other static variables (playerCount and decFormat) and static methods (findTeamAverage and findTeamAverageString). To see what I mean, look at Figure 10-5.

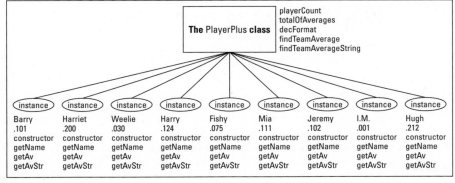

Figure 10-5: Some static and nonstatic variables and methods.

Going along with your passion for subclasses, you put code for team-wide tallies in a subclass of the Player class. The code is shown in Listing 10-4.

Listing 10-4:   Creating a Team Batting Average

```
import java.text.DecimalFormat;

class PlayerPlus extends Player {
    private static int playerCount = 0;
    private static double totalOfAverages = .000;
```

(continued)

Listing 10-4 (continued)

```
    private static DecimalFormat decFormat =
                             new DecimalFormat("
        .000");

    public PlayerPlus(String name, double average) {
        super(name, average);
        playerCount++;
        totalOfAverages += average;
    }

    public static double findTeamAverage() {
        return totalOfAverages / playerCount;
    }

    public static String findTeamAverageString() {
        return decFormat.format
                          (totalOfAverages /
            playerCount);
    }
}
```

Why is there so much static?

Maybe you've noticed — the code in Listing 10-4 is overflowing with the word
static. That's because nearly everything in this code belongs to the entire
PlayerPlus class and not to individual instances of the class. That's good
because something like playerCount (the number of players on the team)
shouldn't belong to individual players, and having each PlayerPlus object
keep track of its own count would be silly. ("I know how many players I am.
I'm just one player!") If you had nine individual playerCount variables, either
each variable would store the number 1 (which is useless) or you would have
nine different copies of the count, which is wasteful and prone to error. So by
making playerCount static, you're keeping the playerCount in just one
place, where it belongs.

The same kind of reasoning holds for the totalOfAverages. Eventually, the
totalOfAverages variable will store the sum of the players' batting aver-
ages. For all nine members of the Hankees, this adds up to .956. It's not until
someone calls the findTeamAverage or findTeamAverageString method
that the computer actually finds the overall Hankee team batting average.

You also want the methods `findTeamAverage` and `findTeamAverageString` to be static. Without the word *static*, there would be nine `findTeamAverage` methods — one for each instance of the `PlayerPlus` class. This wouldn't make much sense. Each instance would have the code to calculate `totalOf Averages/playerCount` on its own, and each of the nine calculations would yield the very same answer.

In general, any task that all the instances have in common (and that yields the same result for each instance) should be coded as a `static` method.

Constructors are never static.

In Listing 10-4, the `decFormat` variable is static. This makes sense, because `decFormat` makes `totalOfAverages / playerCount` look nice, and both variables in the expression `totalOfAverages / playerCount` are static. Thinking more directly, the code needs only one thing for formatting numbers. If you have several numbers to format, the same `decFormat` thing that belongs to the entire class can format each number. Creating a `decFormat` for each player is not only inelegant, but also wasteful.

In this book, my first serious use of the word *static* is way back in Listing 3-1. I use the `static` keyword as part of every `main` method (and lots of `main` methods are in this book's listings). So why does `main` have to be static? Well, remember that non-static things belong to objects, not classes. If the `main` method isn't static, you can't have a `main` method until you create an object. But, when you start up a Java program, no objects have been created yet. The statements that are executed in the `main` method start creating objects. So, if the `main` method isn't static, you have a big chicken-and-egg problem.

Displaying the overall team average

You may be noticing a pattern. When you create code for a class, you generally write two pieces of code. One piece of code defines the class, and the other piece of code uses the class. (The ways to use a class include calling the class's constructor, referencing the class's nonprivate variables, calling the class's methods, and so on.) Listing 10-4, shown previously, contains code that defines the `PlayerPlus` class, and Listing 10-5 contains code that uses this `PlayerPlus` class.

Listing 10-5:   Using the Code from Listing 10-4

```java
import java.util.Scanner;
import java.io.File;
import java.io.IOException;
import javax.swing.JFrame;
import javax.swing.JLabel;
import java.awt.GridLayout;

class TeamFrame extends JFrame {

    public TeamFrame() throws IOException {
        PlayerPlus player;
        Scanner myScanner =
                    new Scanner(new File("Hankees.txt"));

        for (int num = 1; num <= 9; num++) {
            player =
                new PlayerPlus(myScanner.nextLine(),
                                myScanner.nextDouble());
            myScanner.nextLine();

            addPlayerInfo(player);
        }

        add(new JLabel());
        add(new JLabel("     ------"));
        add(new JLabel("Team Batting Average:"));
        add(new
            JLabel(PlayerPlus.findTeamAverageString()));

        setTitle("The Hankees");
        setLayout(new GridLayout(11,2));
        setDefaultCloseOperation(EXIT_ON_CLOSE);
        pack();
        setVisible(true);
    }

    void addPlayerInfo(PlayerPlus player) {
        add(new JLabel(player.getName()));
        add(new JLabel(player.getAverageString()));
    }
}
```

To run the code in Listing 10-5, you need a class with a main method. The ShowTeamFrame class in Listing 10-3 works just fine. (If you run JCreator from this book's CD-ROM, you're all set because the ShowTeamFrame.java file is already in a project along with Listing 10-5.)

Figure 10-6 shows a run of the code from Listing 10-5. This run depends on the availability of the `Hankees.txt` file from Figure 10-2. The code in Listing 10-5 is almost an exact copy of the code from Listing 10-2. (So close is the copy that if I could afford it, I'd sue myself for theft of intellectual property.) The only thing new in Listing 10-5 is the stuff shown in bold.

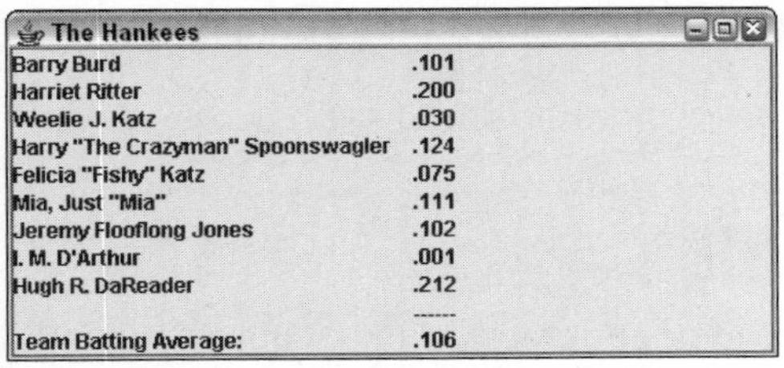

Figure 10-6:
A run of the
code in
Listing 10-5.

The Hankees	
Barry Burd	.101
Harriet Ritter	.200
Weelie J. Katz	.030
Harry "The Crazyman" Spoonswagler	.124
Felicia "Fishy" Katz	.075
Mia, Just "Mia"	.111
Jeremy Flooflong Jones	.102
I. M. D'Arthur	.001
Hugh R. DaReader	.212

Team Batting Average:	.106

In Listing 10-5, the `GridLayout` has two extra rows: one row for spacing and another row for the Hankee team's average. Each of these rows has two `Label` objects in it.

- **The spacing row has a blank label and a label with a dashed line.** The blank label is a placeholder. When you add components to a `GridLayout`, the components are added row by row, starting at the left end of a row and working toward the right end of the row. Without this blank label, the dashed line label would appear at the left end of the row, under Hugh R. DaReader's name.

- **The other row has a label displaying the words *Team Batting Average*, and another label displaying the number *.106*.** The method call that gets the number .106 is interesting. The call looks like this:

```
PlayerPlus.findTeamAverageString()
```

Take a look at that method call. That call has the following form:

```
ClassName.methodName()
```

That's new and different. In earlier chapters, I say that you normally preface a method call with an object's name, not a class's name. So why do I use a class name here? The answer: When you call a `static` method, you preface the method's name with the name of the class that contains the method. The same holds true whenever you reference another class's `static` variable. This makes sense. Remember, the whole class that defines a `static` variable or method owns that variable or method. So, to refer to a `static` variable or method, you preface the variable or method's name with the class's name.

When you're referring to a `static` variable or method, you can cheat and use an object's name in place of the class name. For instance, in Listing 10-5, with judicious rearranging of some other statements, you can use the expression `player.findTeamAverageString()`.

Java has a neat feature called the *static initializer*. Using this feature, you can execute statements involving `static` variables before calling any of the class's methods. To find out more about `static` initializers, visit this book's Web site.

Static is old hat

This section makes a big noise about `static` variables and methods, but `static` things have been part of the picture since early in this book. For example, Chapter 3 introduces `System.out.println`. The name *System* refers to a class, and *out* is a `static` variable in that class. That's why, in Chapter 4 and beyond, I use the `static` keyword to import the `out` variable:

```
import static java.lang.System.out;
```

In Java, `static` variables and methods show up all over the place. When they're declared in someone else's code, and you're making use of them in your code, you hardly ever have to worry about them. But when you're declaring your own variables and methods and must decide whether to make them static, you have to think a little harder.

Could cause static; handle with care

When I first started writing Java, I had recurring dreams about getting a certain error message. The message was `non-static variable or method cannot be referenced from a static context`. So often did I see this message, so thoroughly was I perplexed, that the memory of this message became burned into my subconscious existence.

These days, I know why I got that error message so often. I can even make the message occur if I want. But I still feel a little shiver whenever I see this message on my screen.

Before you can understand why the message occurs and how to fix the problem, you need to get some terminology under your belt. If a variable or method isn't static, it's called *non-static*. (Real surprising, hey?) Given that terminology, there are at least two ways to make the dreaded message appear:

   ✔ Put *Class.nonstaticThing* somewhere in your program.

   ✔ Put *nonstaticThing* somewhere inside a `static` method.

In either case, you're getting yourself into trouble. You're taking something that belongs to an object (the non-static thing) and putting it in a place where no objects are in sight.

Take, for instance, the first of the two situations I just described. To see this calamity in action, go back to Listing 10-5. Toward the end of the listing, change `player.getName()` to `Player.getName()`. That does the trick. What could `Player.getName` possibly mean? If anything, the expression `Player.getName` means "call the `getName` method that belongs to the entire `Player` class." But look back at Listing 10-1. The `getName` method isn't static. Each instance of the `Player` (or `PlayerPlus`) class has a `getName` method. None of the `getName` methods belong to the entire class. So the call `Player.getName` doesn't make any sense. (Maybe the computer is pulling punches when it displays the inoffensive `cannot be referenced . . .` message. Perhaps a harsh `nonsensical expression` message would be more fitting.)

For a taste of the second situation (in the bullet list that I give earlier in this section), go back to Listing 10-4. While no one's looking, quietly remove the word *static* from the declaration of the `decFormat` variable (near the top of the listing). This turns `decFormat` into a non-static variable. Suddenly, each player on the team has a separate `decFormat` variable.

Well, things are just hunky-dory until the computer reaches the `findTeamAverageString` method. That `static` method has four `decFormat.SuchAndSuch` statements in it. Once again, you're forced to ask what a statement of this kind could possibly mean. Method `findTeamAverageString` belongs to no instance in particular. (The method is static, so the entire `PlayerPlus` class has one `findTeamAverageString` method.) But with the way you've just butchered the code, plain old `decFormat` without reference to a particular object has no meaning. So again, you're referencing the non-static variable, `decFormat`, from inside a `static` method's context. Shame!

Experiments with Variables

One summer during my college days, I was sitting on the front porch, loafing around, talking with someone I'd just met. I think her name was Janine. "Where are you from?" I asked. "Mars," she answered. She paused to see whether I'd ask a follow-up question.

As it turned out, Janine was from Mars, Pennsylvania, a small town about 20 miles north of Pittsburgh. Okay, so what's my point? The point is that the meaning of a name depends on the context. If you're just north of Pittsburgh and ask, "How do I get to Mars from here?" you may get a sensible, nonchalant answer. But if you ask the same question standing on a street corner in Manhattan, you'll probably arouse some suspicion. (Okay, knowing Manhattan, people would probably just ignore you.)

Of course, the people who live in Mars, Pennsylvania, are very much aware that their town has an oddball name. Fond memories of teenage years at Mars High School don't prevent a person from knowing about the big red planet. On a clear evening in August, you can still have the following conversation with one of the local residents:

> *You:* How do I get to Mars?
>
> *Local resident:* You're in Mars, pal. What particular part of Mars are you looking for?
>
> *You:* No, I don't mean Mars, Pennsylvania. I mean the planet Mars.
>
> *Local resident:* Oh, the planet! Well, then, catch the 8:19 train leaving for Cape Canaveral . . . No, wait, that's the local train. That'd take you through West Virginia. . . .

So the meaning of a name depends on where you're using the name. Although most English-speaking people think of Mars as a place with a carbon dioxide atmosphere, some folks in Pennsylvania think about all the shopping they can do in Mars. And those folks in Pennsylvania really have two meanings for the name *Mars*. In Java, those names may look like this: `Mars` and `planets.Mars`.

Putting a variable in its place

Your first experiment is shown in Listings 10-6 and 10-7. The listings' code highlights the difference between variables that are declared inside and outside methods.

Listing 10-6:   Two Meanings for Mars

```
import static java.lang.System.out;

class EnglishSpeakingWorld {
    String mars = "    red planet";

    void visitPennsylvania() {
```

```
        out.println("visitPA is running:");

        String mars = "   Janine's home town";

        out.println(mars);
        out.println(this.mars);
    }
}
```

Listing 10-7: Calling the Code of Listing 10-6

```
import static java.lang.System.out;

class GetGoing {

    public static void main(String args[]) {

        out.println("main is running:");

        EnglishSpeakingWorld e = new
            EnglishSpeakingWorld();

        //out.println(mars);    cannot resolve symbol
        out.println(e.mars);
        e.visitPennsylvania();
    }
}
```

Figure 10-7 shows a run of the code in Listings 10-6 and 10-7. Figure 10-8 shows a diagram of the code's structure. In the GetGoing class, the main method creates an instance of the EnglishSpeakingWorld class. The variable e refers to the new instance. The new instance is an object with a variable named *mars* inside it. That mars variable has value "red planet". The mars variable is called an *instance variable,* because the variable belongs to an object — an instance of the EnglishSpeakingWorld class.

Now look at the main method in Listing 10-7. Inside the GetGoing class's main method, you aren't permitted to write out.println(mars). In other words, a bare-faced reference to any mars variable is a definite no-no. The mars variable that I mention in the previous paragraph belongs to the EnglishSpeakingWorld object, not the GetGoing class.

However, inside the GetGoing class's main method, you can certainly write e.mas because the e variable refers to your EnglishSpeakingWorld object. That's nice.

Near the bottom of the code, the visitPennsylvania method is called. When you're inside visitPennsylvania, you have another declaration of a mars variable, whose value is "Janine's home town". This particular mars variable is called a *method-local variable* because it belongs to just one method — the visitPennsylvania method.

Figure 10-7:
A run of the
code in
Listings 10-6
and 10-7.

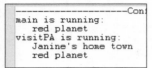

```
---------------------Con:
main is running:
    red planet
visitPA is running:
    Janine's home town
    red planet
```

```
┌─────────────────────────────────────┐
│  EnglishSpeakingWorld                │
│    ┌───────────────────────────────┐ │
│    │   mars (instance variable)    │ │
│    │   ┌───────────────────────┐   │ │
│    │   │     red planet        │   │ │
│    │   └───────────────────────┘   │ │
│    │  visitPennsylvania            │ │
│    │   ┌───────────────────────────┐│ │
│    │   │  mars (method-local       ││ │
│    │   │         variable)         ││ │
│    │   │  ┌─────────────────────┐  ││ │
│    │   │  │ Janine's home town  │  ││ │
│    │   │  └─────────────────────┘  ││ │
│    │   └───────────────────────────┘│ │
│    └───────────────────────────────┘ │
│  GetGoing                            │
│    ┌───────────────────────────────┐ │
│    │     e                         │ │
│    │     ┌────┐                    │ │
│    │     │    │                    │ │
│    │     └────┘                    │ │
│    └───────────────────────────────┘ │
└─────────────────────────────────────┘
```

Figure 10-8:
The
structure of
the code in
Listings 10-6
and 10-7.

So now you have two variables, both with the name *mars.* One mars variable, an instance variable, has the value "red planet". The other mars variable, a method-local variable, has the value "Janine's home town". In the code, when you use the word *mars,* to which of the two variables are you referring?

The answer is, when you're visiting Pennsylvania, the variable with value "Janine's home town" wins. When in Pennsylvania, think the way the Pennsylvanians think. When you're executing code inside the visit Pennsylvania method, resolve any variable name conflicts by going with variables that are declared right inside the visitPennsylvania method.

So what if you're in Pennsylvania and need to refer to that two-mooned celestial object? More precisely, how does code inside the `visitPennsylvania` method refer to the variable with value `"red planet"`? The answer is, use `this.mars`. The word *this* points to whatever object contains all this code (and not to any methods inside the code). That object, an instance of the `EnglishSpeakingWorld` class, has a big, fat `mars` variable, and that variable's value is `"red planet"`. So that's how you can force code to see outside the method it's in — you use the Java keyword `this`.

For more information on the keyword `this`, see Chapter 9.

Telling a variable where to go

Years ago, when I lived in Milwaukee, Wisconsin, I made frequent use of the local bank's automatic teller machines. Machines of this kind were just beginning to become standardized. The local teller machine system was named *TYME*, which stood for *Take Your Money Everywhere*.

I remember traveling by car out to California. At one point, I got hungry and stopped for a meal, but I was out of cash. So I asked a gas station attendant, "Do you know where there's a TYME machine around here?"

So you see, a name that works well in one place could work terribly, or not at all, in another place. In Listings 10-8 and 10-9, I illustrate this point (with more than just an anecdote about teller machines).

Listing 10-8:   Tale of Atomic City

```
import static java.lang.System.out;

class EnglishSpeakingWorld2 {
    String mars;

    void visitIdaho() {
        out.println("visitID is running:");

        mars = "    red planet";
        String atomicCity = "    Population: 25";

        out.println(mars);
        out.println(atomicCity);
    }

    void visitNewJersey() {
        out.println("visitNJ is running:");

        out.println(mars);
```

(continued)

Listing 10-8 (continued)

```
            //out.println(atomicCity);
            //   cannot resolve symbol
    }
}
```

Listing 10-9: Calling the Code of Listing 10-8

```
class GetGoing2 {

    public static void main(String args[]) {
        EnglishSpeakingWorld2 e = new
            EnglishSpeakingWorld2();

        e.visitIdaho();
        e.visitNewJersey();
    }
}
```

Figure 10-9 shows a run of the code in Listings 10-8 and 10-9. Figure 10-10 shows a diagram of the code's structure. The code for EnglishSpeaking World2 has two variables. The mars variable, which isn't declared inside a method, is an instance variable. The other variable, atomicCity, is a method-local variable and is declared inside the visitIdaho method.

In Listing 10-8, notice where each variable can and can't be used. When you try to use the atomicCity variable inside the visitNewJersey method, you get an error message. Literally, the message says cannot resolve symbol. Figuratively, the message says, "Hey, buddy, Atomic City is in Idaho, not New Jersey." Technically, the message says that the method-local variable atomicCity is available only in the visitIdaho method because that's where the variable was declared.

So back inside the visitIdaho method, you're free to use the atomicCity variable as much as you want. After all, the atomicCity variable is declared inside the visitIdaho method.

Figure 10-9:
A run of the code in Listings 10-8 and 10-9.

```
-------------------------
visitID is running:
    red planet
    Population: 25
visitNJ is running:
    red planet
```

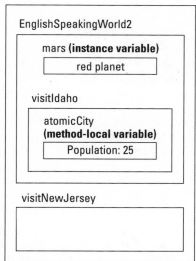

EnglishSpeakingWorld2

mars **(instance variable)**

red planet

visitIdaho

atomicCity
(method-local variable)
Population: 25

Figure 10-10:
The
structure of
the code in
Listings 10-8
and 10-9.

visitNewJersey

And what about Mars? Have you forgotten about your old friend, that lovely eighty-degrees-below-zero planet? Well, both the `visitIdaho` and `visitNewJersey` methods can access the `mars` variable. That's because the `mars` variable is an instance variable. The `mars` variable is declared in the code for the `EnglishSpeakingWorld2` class but not inside any particular method. (In my stories about the names for things, remember that people who live in both states, Idaho and New Jersey, have heard of the planet Mars.)

The lifecycle of the mars variable has three separate steps:

✔ When the `EnglishSpeakingWorld2` class first flashes into existence, the computer sees `String mars` and creates space for the variable.

✔ When the `visitIdaho` method is executed, the method assigns the value `"red planet"` to the `mars` variable. (The `visitIdaho` method also prints the value of the `mars` variable.)

✔ When the `visitNewJersey` method is executed, the method prints the `mars` value once again.

In this way, the `mars` variable's value is passed from one method to another.

Passing Parameters

A method can communicate with another part of your Java program in several ways. One of the ways is through the method's parameter list. Using a parameter list, you pass on-the-fly information to a method as the method is being called.

So imagine that the information you pass to the method is stored in one of your program's variables. What, if anything, does the method actually do with that variable? This section presents a few interesting case studies.

Pass by value

According to my Web research, the town of Smackover, Arkansas, has 2,232 people in it. But my research isn't current. Just yesterday, Dora Kermongoos celebrated a joyous occasion over at Smackover General Hospital — the birth of her healthy, blue-eyed baby girl. (The girl weighs 7 pounds, 4 ounces, and is 21 inches tall.) Now the town's population has risen to 2,233.

Listing 10-10 has a very bad program in it. The program is supposed to add 1 to a variable that stores Smackover's population, but the program doesn't work. Take a look at Listing 10-10 and see why.

Listing 10-10:   This Program Doesn't Work

```
class TrackPopulation {

    public static void main(String args[]) {
        int smackoverARpop = 2232;

        birth(smackoverARpop);
        System.out.println(smackoverARpop);
    }

    static void birth(int cityPop) {
        cityPop++;
    }
}
```

When you run the program in Listing 10-10, the program displays the number 2,232 on-screen. After nine months of planning and anticipation and Dora's whopping seven hours in labor, the Kermongoos family's baby girl wasn't registered in the system. What a shame!

The improper use of parameter passing caused the problem. In Java, when you pass a parameter that has one of the eight primitive types to a method, that parameter is *passed by value*.

For a review of Java's eight primitive types, see Chapter 4.

Here's what this means in plain English: Any changes that the method makes to the value of its parameter don't affect the values of variables back in the calling code. In Listing 10-10, the `birth` method can apply the ++ operator to `cityPop` all it wants — the application of ++ to the `cityPop` parameter has absolutely no effect on the value of the `smackoverARpop` variable back in the `main` method.

Technically, what's happening is the copying of a value. (See Figure 10-11.) When the `main` method calls the `birth` method, the value stored in `smackoverARpop` is copied to another memory location — a location reserved for the `cityPop` parameter's value. During the `birth` method's execution, 1 is added to the `cityPop` parameter. But the place where the original `2232` value was stored — the memory location for the `smackoverARpop` variable — remains unaffected.

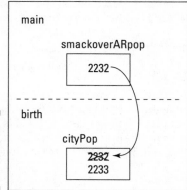

Figure 10-11:
Pass by
value, under
the hood.

When you do parameter passing with any of the eight primitive types, the computer uses pass by value. The value stored in the calling code's variable remains unchanged. This happens even if the calling code's variable and the called method's parameter happen to have the exact same name.

Returning a result

You must fix the problem that the code in Listing 10-10 poses. After all, a young baby Kermongoos can't go through life untracked. To record this baby's existence, you have to add 1 to the value of the smackoverARpop variable. You can do this in plenty of ways, and the way presented in Listing 10-11 isn't the simplest. Even so, the way shown in Listing 10-11 illustrates a point: Returning a value from a method call can be an acceptable alternative to parameter passing. Look at Listing 10-11 to see what I mean.

Listing 10-11:   This Program Works

```
class TrackPopulation2 {

    public static void main(String args[]) {
        int smackoverARpop = 2232;

        smackoverARpop = birth(smackoverARpop);
        System.out.println(smackoverARpop);
    }

    static int birth(int cityPop) {
        return cityPop + 1;
    }
}
```

After running the code in Listing 10-11, the number you see on your computer screen is the correct number, 2,233.

The code in Listing 10-11 has no new features in it (unless you call *working correctly* a new feature). The most important idea in Listing 10-11 is the return statement, which also appears in Chapter 7. Even so, Listing 10-11 presents a nice contrast to the approach in Listing 10-10, which had to be discarded.

Pass by reference

In the previous section or two, I take great pains to emphasize a certain point — that when a parameter has one of the eight primitive types, the parameter is passed by value. If you read this, you probably missed the emphasis on the parameter's having one of the eight primitive types. The emphasis is needed because passing objects (reference types) doesn't quite work the same way.

When you pass an object to a method, the object is *passed by reference*. What this means to you is that statements in the called method *can* change any values that are stored in the object's variables. Those changes *do* affect the values that are seen by whatever code called the method. Listings 10-12 and 10-13 illustrate the point.

Listing 10-12:   What Is a City?

```
class City {
    int population;
}
```

Listing 10-13:   Passing an Object to a Method

```
class TrackPopulation3 {

    public static void main(String args[]) {
        City smackoverAR = new City();
        smackoverAR.population = 2232;
        birth(smackoverAR);
        System.out.println(smackoverAR.population);
    }

    static void birth(City aCity) {
        aCity.population++;
    }
}
```

When you run the code in Listings 10-12 and 10-13, the output that you get is the number 2,233. That's good because the code has things like ++ and the word *birth* in it. The deal is, adding 1 to aCity.population inside the birth method actually changes the value of smackoverAR.population as it's known in the main method.

To see how the birth method changes the value of smackoverAR.population, look at Figure 10-12. When you pass an object to a method, the computer doesn't make a copy of the entire object. Instead, the computer makes a copy of a reference to that object. (Think of it the way it's shown in Figure 10-12. The computer makes a copy of an arrow that points to the object.)

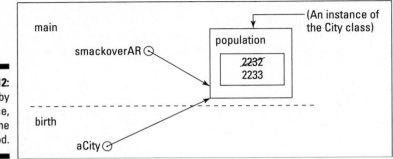

Figure 10-12:
Pass by
reference,
under the
hood.

In Figure 10-12, you see just one instance of the `City` class, with a population variable inside it. Now keep your eye on that object as you read the following steps:

1. Just before the `birth` method is called, the `smackoverAR` variable refers to that object — the instance of the `City` class.

2. When the `birth` method is called and `smackoverAR` is passed to the birth method's `aCity` parameter, the computer copies the reference from `smackoverAR` to `aCity`. Now `aCity` refers to that same object — the instance of the `City` class.

3. When the statement `aCity.population++` is executed inside the `birth` method, the computer adds 1 to the object's population variable. Now the program's one and only `City` instance has `2233` stored in its population variable.

4. The flow of execution goes back to the `main` method. The value of `smackoverAR.population` is printed. But `smackoverAR` refers to that one instance of the `City` class. So `smackoverAR.population` has the value `2233`. The Kermongoos family is so proud.

Returning an object from a method

Believe it or not, the previous sections on parameter passing left one nook and cranny of Java methods unexplored. When you call a method, the method can return something right back to the calling code. In previous chapters and sections, I return primitive values, such as `int` values, or nothing (otherwise known as *void*). In this section, I return a whole object. It's an object of type `City` from Listing 10-12. The code that makes this happen is in Listing 10-14.

Listing 10-14:   Here, Have a City

```
class TrackPopulation4 {

    public static void main(String args[]) {
        City smackoverAR = new City();
        smackoverAR.population = 2232;
        smackoverAR = doBirth(smackoverAR);
        System.out.println(smackoverAR.population);
    }

    static City doBirth(City aCity) {
        City myCity = new City();
        myCity.population = aCity.population + 1;
        return myCity;
    }
}
```

If you run the code in Listing 10-14, you get the number 2,233. That's good. The code works by telling the doBirth method to create another City instance. In the new instance, the value of population is 2333 (Figure 10-13).

Figure 10-13: The doBirth method creates a City instance.

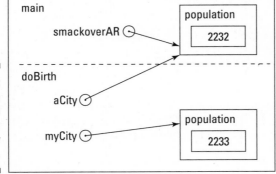

After the doBirth method is executed, that City instance is returned to the main method. Then, back in the main method, that instance (the one that doBirth returns) is assigned to the smackoverAR variable. (See Figure 10-14.) Now smackoverAR refers to a brand-new City instance — an instance whose population is 2,233.

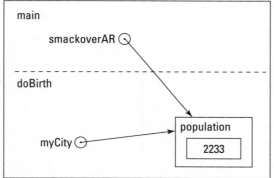

Figure 10-14:
The new
City
instance is
assigned to
the
smackover-
AR variable.

In Listing 10-14, notice the type consistency in the calling and returning of the doBirth method:

- The smackoverAR variable has type City. The smackoverAR variable is passed to the aCity parameter, which is also of type City.

- The myCity variable is of type City. The myCity variable is sent back in the doBirth method's return statement. That's consistent, because the doBirth method's header begins with the promise public static City — the promise to return an object of type City.

- The doBirth method returns an object of type City. Back in the main method, the object that the call to doBirth returns is assigned to the smackoverAR variable, and (you guessed it) the smackoverAR variable is of type City.

Aside from being very harmonious, all this type agreement is absolutely necessary. If you write a program in which your types don't agree with one another, the compiler spits out an unsympathetic incompatible types message.

Epilogue

Dora Kermongoos and her newborn baby daughter are safe, healthy, and resting happily in their Smackover, Arkansas, home.

Chapter 11

Using Arrays and Collections to Juggle Values

In This Chapter

▶ Dealing with several values at once
▶ Creating values as you get a program running
▶ Impressing other programmers with fancy generic types

*W*elcome to the Java Motel! No haughty bellhops, no overpriced room service, none of the usual silly puns. Just a clean double room that's a darn good value!

Getting Your Ducks All in a Row

The Java Motel, with its ten comfortable rooms, sits in a quiet place off the main highway. Aside from a small, separate office, the motel is just one long row of ground floor rooms. Each room is easily accessible from the spacious front parking lot.

Oddly enough, the motel's rooms are numbered 0 through 9. I could say that the numbering is a fluke — something to do with the builder's original design plan. But the truth is that starting with 0 makes the examples in this chapter easier to write.

Anyway, you're trying to keep track of the number of guests in each room. Because you have ten rooms, you may think about declaring ten variables:

```
int guestsInRoomNum0, guestsInRoomNum1, guestsInRoomNum2,
    guestsInRoomNum3, guestsInRoomNum4, guestsInRoomNum5,
    guestsInRoomNum6, guestsInRoomNum7, guestsInRoomNum8,
    guestsInRoomNum9;
```

Doing it this way may seem a bit inefficient. But inefficiency isn't the only thing wrong with this code. Even more problematic is the fact that you can't loop through these variables. To read a value for each variable, you have to copy the `nextInt` method ten times.

```
guestsInRoomNum0 = diskScanner.nextInt();
guestsInRoomNum1 = diskScanner.nextInt();
guestsInRoomNum2 = diskScanner.nextInt();
... and so on.
```

Surely a better way exists.

That better way involves an array. An *array* is a row of values, like the row of rooms in a one-floor motel. To picture the array, just picture the Java Motel:

✔ First, picture the rooms, lined up next to one another.

✔ Next, picture the same rooms with their front walls missing. Inside each room you can see a certain number of guests.

✔ If you can, forget that the two guests in Room 9 are putting piles of bills into a big briefcase. Ignore the fact that the guests in Room 6 haven't moved away from the TV set in a day and a half. Instead of all these details, just see numbers. In each room, see a number representing the count of guests in that room. (If freeform visualization isn't your strong point, look at Figure 11-1.)

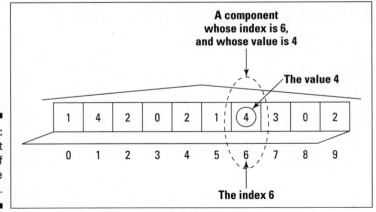

Figure 11-1: An abstract snapshot of rooms in the Java Motel.

In the lingo of this chapter, the entire row of rooms is called an *array*. Each room in the array is called a *component* of the array (also known as an array *element*). Each component has two numbers associated with it:

- The room number (a number from 0 to 9), which is called an *index* of the array
- A number of guests, which is a *value* stored in a component of the array

Using an array saves you from all the repetitive nonsense in the sample code shown at the beginning of this section. For instance, to declare an array with ten values in it, you can write one fairly short statement:

```
int guests[] = new int[10];
```

If you're especially verbose, you can expand this statement so that it becomes two separate statements:

```
int guests[];
guests = new int[10];
```

In either of these code snippets, notice the use of the number 10. This number tells the computer to make the `guests` array have ten components. Each component of the array has a name of its own. The starting component is named *guests[0]*, the next is named *guests[1]*, and so on. The last of the ten components is named *guests[9]*.

In creating an array, you always specify the number of components. The array's indices start with 0 and end with the number that's one less than the total number of components.

The snippets that I show you give you two ways to create an array. The first way uses one line. The second way uses two lines. If you take the single line route, you can put that line inside or outside a method. The choice is yours. On the other hand, if you use two separate lines, the second line, `guests = new int[10]`, should be inside a method.

In an array declaration, you can put the square brackets before or after the variable name. In other words, you can write **int guests[]** or **int[] guests**. The computer creates the same `guests` variable no matter which form you use.

Creating an array in two easy steps

Look once again at the two lines that you can use to create an array:

```
int guests[];
guests = new int[10];
```

Each line serves its own distinct purpose:

- ✔ **int guests[]:** This first line is a declaration. The declaration reserves the array name (a name like *guests*) for use in the rest of the program. In the Java Motel metaphor, this line says, "I plan to build a motel here and put a certain number of guests in each room." (See Figure 11-2.)

  Never mind what the declaration int guests[] does. It's more important to notice what the declaration int guests[] *doesn't* do. The declaration doesn't reserve ten memory locations. Indeed, a declaration like int guests[] doesn't really create an array. All the declaration does is set up the guests variable. At that point in the code, the guests variable still doesn't refer to a real array. (In other words, the motel hasn't been built yet.)

- ✔ **guests = new int[10]:** This second line is an assignment statement. The assignment statement reserves space in the computer's memory for ten int values. In terms of real estate, this line says, "I've finally built the motel. Go ahead and put guests in each room." (Again, see Figure 11-2.)

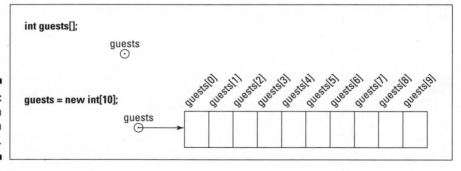

Figure 11-2:
Two steps in creating an array.

Storing values

After you've created an array, you can put values into the array's components. For instance, you would like to store the fact that Room 6 contains 4 guests. To put the value 4 in the component with index 6, you write **guests[6] = 4**.

Now business starts to pick up. A big bus pulls up to the motel. On the side of the bus is a sign that says "Noah's Ark." Out of the bus come 25 couples, each walking, stomping, flying, hopping, or slithering to the motel's small office. Only 10 of the couples can stay at the Java Motel, but that's okay because you can send the other 15 couples down the road to the old C-Side Resort and Motor Lodge.

Anyway, to register 10 couples into the Java Motel, you put a couple (2 guests) in each of your 10 rooms. Having created an array, you can take advantage of the array's indexing and write a `for` loop, like this:

```
for (int roomNum = 0; roomNum < 10; roomNum++) {
    guests[roomNum] = 2;
}
```

This loop takes the place of ten assignment statements. Notice how the loop's counter goes from 0 to 9. Compare this with Figure 11-2, and remember that the indices of an array go from 0 to one less than the number of components in the array.

However, given the way the world works, your guests won't always arrive in neat pairs, and you'll have to fill each room with a different number of guests. You probably store information about rooms and guests in a database. If you do, you can still loop through an array, gathering numbers of guests as you go. The code to perform such a task may look like this:

```
resultset =
    statement.executeQuery("select GUESTS from RoomData");
for (int roomNum = 0; roomNum < 10; roomNum++) {
    resultset.next();
    guests[roomNum] = resultset.getInt("GUESTS");
}
```

But because this book doesn't cover databases until Chapter 18 (on the CD-ROM), you may be better off reading numbers of guests from a plain text file. A sample file is shown in Figure 11-3. After you've made a file, you can call on the `Scanner` class to get values from the file. The code is shown in Listing 11-1, and the resulting output is in Figure 11-4.

For instructions on creating your own file like the one in Figure 11-3, see Chapter 8.

Figure 11-3:
The GuestList.txt file.

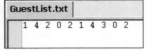

GuestList.txt

1 4 2 0 2 1 4 3 0 2

Listing 11-1:   Filling an Array with Values

```java
import static java.lang.System.out;
import java.util.Scanner;
import java.io.File;
import java.io.IOException;

class ShowGuests {

    public static void main(String args[])
                                        throws
         IOException {
        int guests[] = new int[10];
        Scanner diskScanner =
                new Scanner(new File("GuestList.txt"));

        for(int roomNum = 0; roomNum < 10; roomNum++) {
            guests[roomNum] = diskScanner.nextInt();
        }

        out.println("Room\tGuests");

        for(int roomNum = 0; roomNum < 10; roomNum++) {
            out.print(roomNum);
            out.print("\t");
            out.println(guests[roomNum]);
        }
    }
}
```

The code in Listing 11-1 has two `for` loops. The first loop reads numbers of guests, and the second loop writes numbers of guests.

```
General Output

------------------------
Room     Guests
0        1
1        4
2        2
3        0
4        2
5        1
6        4
7        3
8        0
9        2
```

Figure 11-4:
Running the
code from
Listing 11-1.

Every array has a built-in length field. An array's *length* is the number of components in the array. So, in Listing 11-1, if you print the value of `guests.length`, you get 10.

Tab stops and other special things

In Listing 11-1, some calls to `print` and `println` use the `\t` escape sequence. It's called an *escape sequence* because you escape from displaying the letter `t` on the screen. Instead, the characters `\t` stand for a tab. The computer moves forward to the next tab stop before printing any more characters. Java has a few of these handy escape sequences. Some of them are shown in Table 11-1.

Table 11-1	Escape Sequences
Sequence	*Meaning*
\b	backspace
\t	horizontal tab
\n	line feed
\f	form feed
\r	carriage return
\"	double quote "
\'	single quote '
\\	backslash \

Using an array initializer

Besides what you see in Listing 11-1, you have another way to fill an array in Java — with an *array initializer*. When you use an array initializer, you don't even have to tell the computer how many components the array has. The computer figures this out for you.

Listing 11-2 shows a new version of the code to fill an array. The program's output is the same as the output of Listing 11-1. (It's the stuff shown in Figure 11-4.) The only difference between Listings 11-1 and 11-2 is the bold text in Listing 11-2. That bold doodad is an array initializer.

Listing 11-2:   Using an Array Initializer

```java
import static java.lang.System.out;

class ShowGuests {

    public static void main(String args[]) {

        int guests[] = {1, 4, 2, 0, 2, 1, 4, 3, 0, 2};

        out.println("Room\tGuests");

        for (int roomNum = 0; roomNum < 10; roomNum++) {
            out.print(roomNum);
            out.print("\t");
            out.println(guests[roomNum]);
        }
    }
}
```

An array initializer can contain expressions as well as literals. In plain English, this means that you can put all kinds of things between the commas in the initializer. For instance, an initializer like {1 + 3, myScanner.nextInt(), 2, 0, 2, 1, 4, 3, 0, 2} works just fine.

Stepping through an array with the enhanced for loop

Java has an enhanced for loop — a for loop that doesn't use counters or indices.

Listing 6-5 in Chapter 6 uses enhanced for loops to step through enum types. Loosely speaking, an enum type is just a bunch of values. But think about this chapter's arrays. An array is a bunch of values, too. So it may come as no surprise that an enhanced `for` loop can step through an array's values. Listing 11-3 shows you how to do it.

The material in this section applies to Java 5.0, Java 6, or whatever higher version number comes along in the next few years. But this section's material doesn't work with older versions of Java — versions such as 1.3, 1.4, and so on. For a bit more about Java's version numbers, see Chapter 2.

Listing 11-3: Get a load o' that for loop!

```
import static java.lang.System.out;

class ShowGuests {

    public static void main(String args[]) {
        int guests[] = {1, 4, 2, 0, 2, 1, 4, 3, 0, 2};
        int roomNum = 0;

        out.println("Room\tGuests");
        for (int numGuests : guests) {
            out.print(roomNum++);
            out.print("\t");
            out.println(numGuests);
        }
    }
}
```

Listings 11-1 and 11-3 have the same output. It's in Figure 11-4.

If you look at the loop in Listing 11-3, you see the same old pattern. Just like the loops in Listing 6-5, this example's loop has three parts:

```
for (variable-type variable-name : range-of-values)
```

The first two parts are *variable-type* and *variable-name*. The loop in Listing 11-3 defines a variable named `numGuests`, and `numGuests` has type `int`. During each loop iteration, the variable `numGuests` takes on a new value. Look at Figure 11-4 to see these values. The initial value is 1. The next value is 4. After that comes 2. And so on.

Where is the loop finding all these numbers? The answer lies in the loop's *range-of-values*. In Listing 11-3, the loop's *range-of-values* is `guests`. So, during the initial loop iteration, the value of `numGuests` is `guests[0]` (which is 1). During the next iteration, the value of `numGuests` is `guests[1]` (which is 4). After that comes `guests[2]` (which is 2). And so on.

Searching

You're sitting behind the desk at the Java Motel. Look! Here comes a party of five. These people want a room, so you need software that checks whether a room is vacant. If one is, the software modifies the GuestList.txt file (refer to Figure 11-3) by replacing the number 0 with the number 5. As luck would have it, the software is right on your hard drive. The software is shown in Listing 11-4.

Listing 11-4:   Do You Have a Room?

```java
import static java.lang.System.out;
import java.util.Scanner;
import java.io.File;
import java.io.IOException;
import java.io.PrintStream;

public class FindVacancy {

    public static void main(String args[])
                                        throws
        IOException {
        Scanner kbdScanner = new Scanner(System.in);
        Scanner diskScanner =
            new Scanner(new File("GuestList.txt"));
        int guests[] = new int[10];
        int roomNum;

        for (roomNum = 0; roomNum < 10; roomNum++) {
            guests[roomNum] = diskScanner.nextInt();
        }

        roomNum = 0;
        while (roomNum < 10 && guests[roomNum] != 0) {
            roomNum++;
        }

        if (roomNum == 10) {
            out.println("Sorry, no v cancy");
        } else {
            out.print("How many people for room ");
            out.print(roomNum);
            out.print("? ");
            guests[roomNum] = kbdScanner.nextInt();

            PrintStream listOut =
                new PrintStream("GuestList.txt");

            for (roomNum = 0; roomNum < 10; roomNum++) {
```

```
                        listOut.print(guests[roomNum]);
                        listOut.print(" ");
                }
        }
    }
}
```

Figures 11-5 through 11-7 show the running of the code in Listing 11-4. Back in Figure 11-3, the motel starts with two vacant rooms — Rooms 3 and 8. (Remember, the rooms start with Room 0.) The first time that you run the code in Listing 11-4, the program tells you that Room 3 is vacant and puts five people into the room. The second time you run the code, the program finds the remaining vacant room (Room 8) and puts a party of ten in the room. (What a party!) The third time you run the code, you don't have any more vacant rooms. When the program discovers this, it displays the message Sorry, no v cancy, omitting at least one letter in the tradition of all motel neon signs.

Figure 11-5: Filling a vacancy.

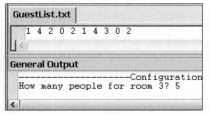

Figure 11-6: Filling the last vacant room.

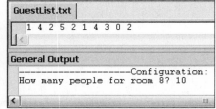

Figure 11-7: Sorry, Bud. No rooms.

Each run of Listing 11-4's code writes a brand-new GuestList.txt file. If you use JCreator, you can easily monitor the changes to GuestList.txt. Keep GuestList.txt showing in JCreator's Editor pane. After running the code in Listing 11-4, switch to some other window on your screen (your Web browser, for instance) or to some other document in JCreator's Editor pane. Then return to the display of GuestList.txt in JCreator. Upon your return, JCreator tells you that GuestList.txt has been modified. "Do you want to reload it?" asks JCreator. "Yes," you click. Then JCreator displays the updated version of GuestList.txt.

The code in Listing 11-4 uses tricks from other chapters and sections of this book. The code's only brand-new feature is the use of PrintStream to write to a disk file. Think about any example in this book that calls System.out.print, out.println, or their variants. What's really going on when you call one of these methods?

The thing called System.out is an object. The object is defined in the Java API. In fact, System.out is an instance of a class named java.io.Print Stream (or just PrintStream to its close friends). Now each object created from the PrintStream class has methods named print and println. Just as each Account object in Listing 7-3 has a display method, and just as the DecimalFormat object in Listing 10-1 has a format method, so the Print Stream object named out has print and println methods. When you call System.out.println, you're calling a method that belongs to a Print Stream instance.

Okay, so what of it? Well, System.out always stands for some text area on your computer screen. If you create your own PrintStream object and you make that object refer to a disk file, then that PrintStream object refers to the disk file. When you call that object's print method, you write text to a file on your hard drive.

So in Listing 11-4, when you say

```
PrintStream listOut =
            new PrintStream("GuestList.txt");

listOut.print(guests[roomNum]);
listOut.print(" ");
```

you're telling Java to write text to a file on your hard drive — the GuestList.txt file.

That's how you update the count of guests staying in the hotel. When you call listOut.print for the number of guests in Room 3, you may print the number 5. So, between Figures 11-5 and 11-6, a number in the GuestList.txt file changes from 0 to 5. Then in Figure 11-6, you run the program a second time. When the program gets data from the newly written GuestList.txt file, Room 3 is no longer vacant. So this time, the program suggests Room 8.

Like many other methods and constructors of its kind, the PrintStream constructor doesn't pussyfoot around with files. If it can't find a GuestList.txt file, the constructor creates one and prepares to write values into it. But, if a GuestList.txt file already exists, the constructor clobbers the existing file and prepares to write to a new, empty GuestList.txt file. If you don't like it when files are clobbered, take precautions before calling the PrintStream constructor.

This is more an observation than a tip. Say that you want to *read* data from a file named Employees.txt. To do this, you make a scanner. You call new Scanner(new File("Employees.txt")). If you accidentally call new Scanner("Employees.txt") without the new File part, the call doesn't connect to your Employees.txt file. But notice how you prepare to *write* data to a file. You make a PrintStream instance by calling new PrintStream ("GuestList.txt"). You don't use new File anywhere in the call. If you goof and accidentally include new File, the Java compiler becomes angry, jumps out, and bites you.

In Listing 11-4, the condition roomNum < 10 && guests[roomNum] != 0 can be really tricky. If you move things around, and write **guests[roomNum] != 0 && roomNum < 10**, you can get yourself into lots of trouble. For details, see this book's Web site.

Arrays of Objects

The Java Motel is open for business, now with improved guest registration software! The people who brought you this chapter's first section are always scratching their heads, looking for the best ways to improve their services. Now, with some ideas from object-oriented programming, they've started thinking in terms of a Room class.

"And what," you ask, "is a Room instance?" That's easy. A Room instance has three properties — the number of guests in the room, the room rate, and a smoking/nonsmoking stamp. Figure 11-8 illustrates the situation.

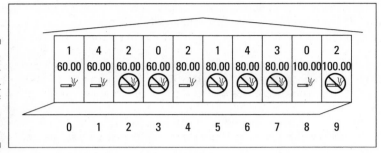

Listing 11-5 shows the code that describes the Room class. As promised, each instance of the Room class has three variables: the guests, rate, and smoking variables. (A false value for the boolean variable, smoking, indicates a non-smoking room.) In addition, the entire Room class has a static variable named currency. This currency object makes room rates look like dollar amounts.

To find out what static means, see Chapter 10.

Listing 11-5:   So This is What a Room Looks Like!

```java
import static java.lang.System.out;
import java.util.Scanner;
import java.text.NumberFormat;

class Room {
    private int guests;
    private double rate;
    private boolean smoking;
    private static NumberFormat currency =
        NumberFormat.getCurrencyInstance();

    public void readRoom(Scanner diskScanner) {
        guests = diskScanner.nextInt();
        rate = diskScanner.nextDouble();
        smoking = diskScanner.nextBoolean();
    }

    public void writeRoom() {
        out.print(guests);
        out.print("\t");
        out.print(currency.format(rate));
        out.print("\t");
        out.println(smoking ? "yes" : "no");
    }
}
```

Listing 11-5 has a few interesting quirks, but I'd rather not describe them until after you see all the code in action. That's why, at this point, I move right on to the code that calls the Listing 11-5 code. After you read about arrays of rooms (shown in Listing 11-6), check out my description of the Listing 11-5 quirks.

Using the Room class

So now you need an array of rooms. The code to create such a thing is in Listing 11-6. The code reads data from the RoomList.txt file. (Figure 11-9 shows the contents of the RoomList.txt file.)

Figure 11-10 shows a run of the code in Listing 11-6.

Listing 11-6:   Would You Like to See a Room?

```
import static java.lang.System.out;
import java.util.Scanner;
import java.io.File;
import java.io.IOException;

class ShowRooms {

    public static void main(String args[])
                                             throws
        IOException {
        Room rooms[];
        rooms = new Room[10];

        Scanner diskScanner =
            new Scanner(new File("RoomList.txt"));

        for (int roomNum = 0; roomNum < 10; roomNum++) {
            rooms[roomNum] = new Room();
            rooms[roomNum].readRoom(diskScanner);
        }

        out.println("Room\tGuests\tRate\tSmoking?");
        for (int roomNum = 0; roomNum < 10; roomNum++) {
            out.print(roomNum);
            out.print("\t");
            rooms[roomNum].writeRoom();
        }
    }
}
```

Say what you want about the code in Listing 11-6. As far as I'm concerned, only one issue in the whole listing should concern you. And what, you ask, is that issue? Well, to create an array of objects, you have to do three things: make the array variable, make the array itself, and then construct each individual object in the array. This is different from creating an array of `int` values or an array containing any other primitive type values. When you create an array of primitive type values, you do only the first two of these three things.

To help make sense of all this, follow along in Listing 11-6 and Figure 11-11 as you read the following points.

- ✔ **`Room rooms[];`:** This declaration creates a `rooms` variable. This variable is destined to refer to an array (but doesn't yet refer to anything at all).

- ✔ **`rooms = new Room[10];`:** This statement reserves ten slots of storage in the computer's memory. The statement also makes the `rooms` variable refer to the group of storage slots. Each slot is destined to refer to an object (but doesn't yet refer to anything at all).

- ✔ **`rooms[roomNum] = new Room();`:** This statement is inside a `for` loop. The statement is executed once for each of the ten room numbers. For example, the first time through the loop, this statement says `rooms[0] = new Room()`. That first time around, the statement makes the slot `rooms[0]` refer to an actual object (an instance of the `Room` class).

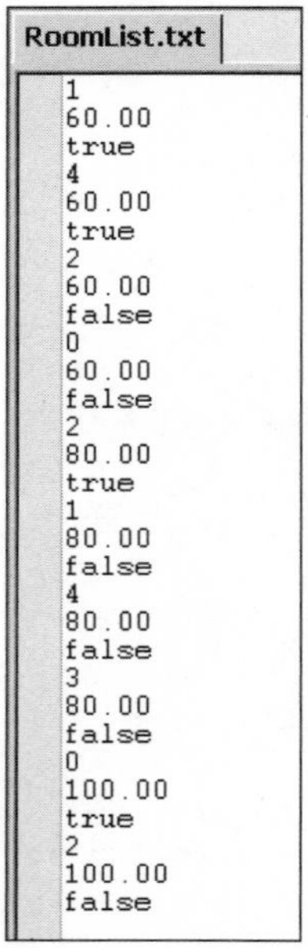

Figure 11-9:
A file of
Room data.

```
RoomList.txt

1
60.00
true
4
60.00
true
2
60.00
false
0
60.00
false
2
80.00
true
1
80.00
false
4
80.00
false
3
80.00
false
0
100.00
true
2
100.00
false
```

```
General Output
----------------------Configuration:
Room    Guests   Rate      Smoking?
0       1        $60.00    yes
1       4        $60.00    yes
2       2        $60.00    no
3       0        $60.00    no
4       2        $80.00    yes
5       1        $80.00    no
6       4        $80.00    no
7       3        $80.00    no
8       0        $100.00   yes
9       2        $100.00   no
```

Figure 11-10:
A run of the code in Listing 11-6.

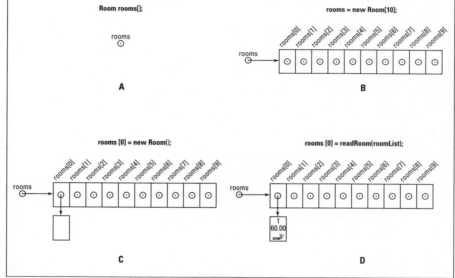

Figure 11-11:
Steps in creating an array of objects.

Although it's technically not considered a step in array making, you still have to fill each object's variables with values. For instance, the first time through the loop, the `readRoom` call says `rooms[1].readRoom(diskScanner)`, which means, "Read data from the `RoomList.txt` file into the `rooms[1]` object's variables." Each time through the loop, the program creates a new object and reads data into that new object's variables.

You can squeeze the steps together just as you do when creating arrays of primitive values. For instance, you can do the first two steps in one fell swoop, like this:

```
Room rooms[] = new Room[10];
```

You can also use an array initializer. (For an introduction to array initializers, see the section, "Using an array initializer," earlier in this chapter.)

Yet another way to beautify your numbers

You can make numbers look nice in plenty of ways. For instance, Listing 7-7 uses `printf` and Listing 10-1 uses a `DecimalFormat`. But in Listing 11-5, I display a currency amount. I use the `NumberFormat` class with its `getCurrencyInstance` method.

If you compare the formatting statements in Listings 10-1 and 11-5, you don't see much difference.

✔ **One listing uses a constructor; the other listing calls `getCurrency Instance`.**

  The `getCurrencyInstance` method is a good example of what's called a *factory method*. A factory method is a convenient tool for creating commonly used objects. People always need code that displays dollar amounts. So the `getCurrencyInstance` method creates a dollar format without forcing you to write `new DecimalFormat ("$###0.00;($###0.00)")`.

  Like a constructor, a factory method returns a brand-new object. But unlike a constructor, a factory method has no special status. When you create a factory method, you can name it anything you want. When you call a factory method, you don't use the keyword `new`.

✔ **One listing uses `DecimalFormat`; the other listing uses `NumberFormat`.**

  A decimal number is a certain kind of number. (In fact, a decimal number is a number written in the base-10 system.) Accordingly, the `DecimalFormat` class is a subclass of the `NumberFormat` class. The `DecimalFormat` methods are more specific, so for most purposes, I use `DecimalFormat`. But it's harder to use the `DecimalFormat` class's `getCurrencyInstance` method. So for programs that involve money, I tend to use `NumberFormat`.

✔ **Both listings use `format` methods.**

  In the end, you just write something like `currency.format(rate)` or `decFormat.format(average)`. After that, Java does the work for you.

The conditional operator

Listing 11-5 uses an interesting doodad called the *conditional operator.* This conditional operator takes three expressions and returns the value of just one of them. It's like a mini `if` statement. When you use the conditional operator, it looks something like this:

```
conditionToBeTested ? expression1 : expression2
```

The computer evaluates the `conditionToBeTested` condition. If the condition is true, the computer returns the value of *expression1*. But, if the condition is false, the computer returns the value of *expression2*.

So, in the code

```
smoking ? "yes" : "no"
```

the computer checks whether `smoking` has the value `true`. If so, the whole three-part expression stands for the first string, `"yes"`. If not, the whole expression stands for the second string, `"no"`.

In Listing 11-5, the call to `out.println` causes either `"yes"` or `"no"` to display. Which string gets displayed depends on whether `smoking` has the value `true` or `false`.

Command Line Arguments

Since you first started working with Java, you've been seeing this `String args[]` business in the header of every `main` method. Well, it's high time you found out what that's all about.

When you want to run a Java program, you can get the program going by choosing Build⇨Execute Project or by clicking somewhere else within your particular development environment.

In plenty of situations, clicking is all you need to do. But sometimes, you want to add a little extra information as you get the program going. Say, for instance, that the program puts a new file on your computer's hard drive. Maybe, when you start the program, you want to tell the program what it should name that new file. Hey, maybe you give the program even more information. Imagine that this file of yours has random numbers in it. (It's a list of numbers to be read aloud at your motel's weekly Bingo game.) When you get the program running, you tell the program the name of the new file and how many numbers you want the new file to contain.

All this leads to one big question. How do you give the program some extra information each time the program starts running?

That's where this `String args[]` business enters the picture. The parameter `args[]` is an array of `String` values. These `String` values are called *command line arguments*.

Using command line arguments in a Java program

Listing 11-7 shows you how to use command line arguments in your code.

Listing 11-7: Generate a File of Numbers

```java
import java.util.Random;
import java.io.File;
import java.io.PrintStream;
import java.io.IOException;

class MakeRandomNumsFile {

    public static void main(String args[])
                                            throws
        IOException {
        Random generator = new Random();

        if (args.length < 2) {
            System.out.println
                ("Usage: MakeRandomNumsFile filename
            number");
            System.exit(1);
        }

        PrintStream printOut = new PrintStream(args[0]);
        int numLines = Integer.parseInt(args[1]);

        for (int count = 1; count <= numLines; count++) {
            printOut.println(generator.nextInt(10) + 1);
        }
    }
}
```

In preparing the code for this book's CD-ROM, I tweaked some settings for this section's JCreator project. As a result, choosing Build⇨Execute Project gets you the window shown in Figure 11-12. Before executing the code, JCreator prompts the user for extra information. In Figure 11-12, I type two extra pieces of information — the MyNumberedFile.txt file and the value 5. After clicking OK, the code in Listing 11-7 begins running.

Figure 11-12:
JCreator
prompts the
user for
command
line
arguments.

When the code begins running, the args array gets its values. In the main method of Listing 11-7, the array component args[0] automatically takes on the value "MyNumberedFile.txt", and args[1] automatically becomes "5". So the program's assignment statements end up having the following meaning:

```
PrintStream printOut = new
        PrintStream("MyNumberedFile.txt");
int numLines = Integer.parseInt("5");
```

The program creates a file named *MyNumberedFile.txt* and sets numLines to 5. So later in the code, the program randomly generates five values and puts those values into MyNumberedFile.txt. One run of the program gives me the file shown in Figure 11-13.

Notice how each command line argument is a String value. When you look at args[1], you don't see the number 5 — you see the string "5" with a digit character in it. Unfortunately, you can't use that "5" to do any counting. To get an int value from "5", you have to apply the parseInt method.

Figure 11-13:
A file from a
run of the
code in
Listing 11-7.

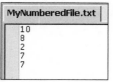

The parseInt method lives inside a class named *Integer*. So, to call parseInt, you preface the name *parseInt* with the word *Integer*. The Integer class has all kinds of handy methods for doing things with int values.

In Java, *Integer* is the name of a class, and *int* is the name of a primitive (simple) type. The two things are related, but they're not the same. The Integer class has methods and other tools for dealing with int values.

Checking for the right number of command line arguments

What happens if the user makes a mistake? What if the dialog box in Figure 11-12 (shown previously) pops up and the user forgets to type the number 5. The user types **MyNumberedFile.txt**, and nothing else.

Then the computer assigns "MyNumberedFile.txt" to args[0], but it doesn't assign anything to args[1]. This is bad. If the computer ever reaches the statement

```
int numLines = Integer.parseInt(args[1]);
```

the program crashes with an unfriendly ArrayIndexOutOfBoundsException.

So, what do you do about this? In Listing 11-7, you check the length of the args array. You compare args.length with 2. If the args array has fewer than two components, you display a message on the screen and you exit from the program. Figure 11-14 shows the resulting output.

Figure 11-14:
The code in
Listing 11-7
tells you
how to run it.

General Output
```
-------------------Configuration: Listing11
Usage: MakeRandomNumsFile filename number

Process completed.
```

Despite the checking of `args.length` in Listing 11-7, the code still isn't crash-proof. If you type **five** instead of **5**, the program takes a nosedive with a `NumberFormatException`. The second command line argument can't be a word. The argument has to be a number (and a whole number at that). I can add statements to Listing 11-7 to make the code more bulletproof, but checking for the `NumberFormatException` is better done in Chapter 12.

When you're working with command line arguments, you can enter a `String` value with a blank space in it. Just enclose the value in double quote marks. For instance, you can run the code of Listing 11-7 with arguments `"My File.txt"` 7.

Setting up JCreator for command line arguments

Normally, when you choose Build⇨Execute Project, the computer starts running your code. The computer doesn't wait for you to enter any extra pieces of information, so things like an extra filename and the number of values in the file can get lost in the dust. To use command line arguments, the computer has to pause for a moment. During this pause, the computer prompts the user to type in a few more bits of information.

For the code on the CD-ROM, I rigged JCreator to display the dialog box in Figure 11-12. But if you're creating a program on your own, how do you tell JCreator to pause and prompt the user for information? To find out, follow these steps:

1. **In JCreator's File View pane, find the project whose main program uses command line arguments.**

   If you're using this book's sample code, pick the `Listing1107` project.

2. **Right-click the project's branch in the File View tree. In the resulting context menu, choose Sets As Active Project.**

   This makes the appropriate project active.

   It's easy to forget Step 2. Don't forget Step 2!

3. **In JCreator's menu bar, choose Project⇨Project Settings.**

   A Project Settings window appears.

4. **In the Project Settings window, select the JDK Tools tab. (See Figure 11-15.)**

5. **Make sure that Run Application appears in the Select Tool Type drop-down list.**

6. **Beneath the Select Tool Type list, select the Default configuration.**

7. **Click the Copy button.**

   A window titled Tool Configuration : Run Application appears.

8. **In the Tool Configuration window's Name text box, type anything that reminds you what this example is all about.**

   In Figure 11-16, I typed **GetCommandLineArguments**.

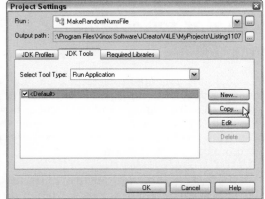

Figure 11-15:
Preparing to copy the default Run Application configuration.

Figure 11-16:
The Tool Configuration window.

9. **In the Tool Configuration window, select the Parameters tab.**

10. **Select the Prompt For main Method Arguments check box.**

11. **Click OK.**

   The Tool Configuration window disappears. Now you're staring at the Project Settings window again.

12. **In the Project Settings window, select the check box next to your newly created configuration.**

   In Figure 11-17, I selected my new `GetCommandLineArguments` configuration.

13. **Click OK.**

   Isn't that the way these lists of instructions always seem to end?

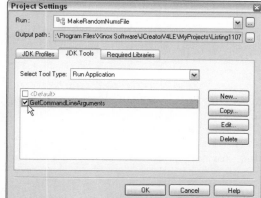

Figure 11-17:
Selecting your new configuration.

After following Steps 1 through 13, your project is changed. Whenever that project is the active project, choosing Build⇨Execute Project gives you a dialog box like the one shown previously in Figure 11-12.

For hints on the use of command line arguments in environments other than JCreator, see this book's Web site.

The sun is about to set on this book's discussion of arrays. The next section deals with something slightly different. But before you leave the subject of arrays, think about this: An array is a row of things, and not every kind of thing fits into just one row. Take the first few examples in this chapter involving the motel. The motel rooms, numbered 0 through 9, are in one big line.

But what if you move up in the world? You buy a big hotel with 50 floors and with 100 rooms on each floor. Then the data is square shaped. We have 50 rows, and each row contains 100 items. Sure, you can think of the rooms as if they're all in one big row, but why should you have to do that? How about having a `two-dimensional array`? It's a square-shaped array in which each component has two indices — a row number and a column number. Alas, I have no space in this book to show you a two-dimensional array (and I can't afford a big hotel's prices anyway). But if you visit this book's Web site, you can read all about it.

Using Java Collections

Arrays are nice, but arrays have some serious limitations. Imagine that you store customer names in some predetermined order. Your code contains an array, and the array has space for 100 names.

```
String name[] = new String[100];
for (int i = 0; i < 100; i++) {
    name[i] = new String();
}
```

All is well until, one day, customer number 101 shows up. As your program runs, you enter data for customer 101, hoping desperately that the array with 100 components can expand to fit your growing needs.

No such luck. Arrays don't expand. Your program crashes with an `ArrayIndexOutOfBoundsException`.

"In my next life, I'll create arrays of length 1,000," you say to yourself. And when your next life rolls around, you do just that.

```
String name[] = new String[1000];
for (int i = 0; i < 1000; i++) {
    name[i] = new String();
}
```

But during your next life, an economic recession occurs. Instead of having 101 customers, you have only 3 customers. Now you're wasting space for 1,000 names when space for 3 names would do.

And what if no economic recession occurs? You're sailing along with your array of size 1,000, using a tidy 825 spaces in the array. The components with indices 0 through 824 are being used, and the components with indices 825 through 999 are waiting quietly to be filled.

One day, a brand-new customer shows up. Because your customers are stored in order (alphabetically by last name, numerically by Social Security number, whatever), you want to squeeze this customer into the correct component of your array. The trouble is that this customer belongs very early on in the array, at the component with index 7. What happens then?

You take the name in component number 824 and move it to component 825. Then you take the name in component 823 and move it to component 824. Take the name in component 822 and move it to component 823. You keep doing this until you've moved the name in component 7. Then you put the new customer's name into component 7. What a pain! Sure, the computer doesn't complain. (If the computer has feelings, it probably likes this kind of busy work.) But as you move around all these names, you waste processing time, you waste power, and you waste all kinds of resources.

"In my next life, I'll leave three empty components between every two names." And of course, your business expands. Eventually you find that three aren't enough.

Collection classes to the rescue

The issues in the previous few paragraphs aren't new. Computer scientists have been working on these issues for a long time. They haven't discovered any magic one-size-fits-all solution, but they've discovered some clever tricks.

The Java API has a bunch of classes known as *collection* classes. Each collection class has methods for storing bunches of values. And each collection class's methods use some clever tricks. For you, the bottom line is as follows: Certain collection classes deal as efficiently as possible with the issues raised in the previous few paragraphs. If you're writing code, and you know that you have to deal with such issues, you can use these collection classes and call the classes' methods. Instead of fretting about a customer whose name belongs in position 7, you can just call a class's add method. The method inserts the name at a position of your choice, and deals reasonably with whatever ripple effects have to take place. In the best circumstances, the insertion is very efficient. In the worst circumstances, you can rest assured that the code does everything the best way it can.

Using an ArrayList

The most useful of Java's collection classes is the ArrayList. Listing 11-8 shows you how it works.

Listing 11-8: Working with a Java Collection

```
import static java.lang.System.out;
import java.util.Scanner;
import java.io.File;
import java.io.IOException;
import java.util.ArrayList;

class ShowNames {

    public static void main(String args[])
                                        throws
        IOException {
        ArrayList<String> people = new
            ArrayList<String>();
        Scanner diskScanner =
            new Scanner(new File("names.txt"));

        while (diskScanner.hasNext()) {
            people.add(diskScanner.nextLine());
        }

        people.remove(0);
        people.add(2, "Jim Newton");

        for (String name : people) {
            out.println(name);
        }
    }
}
```

Figure 11-18 shows you a sample `names.txt` file. The code in Listing 11-8 reads that `names.txt` file, and prints the stuff in Figure 11-19.

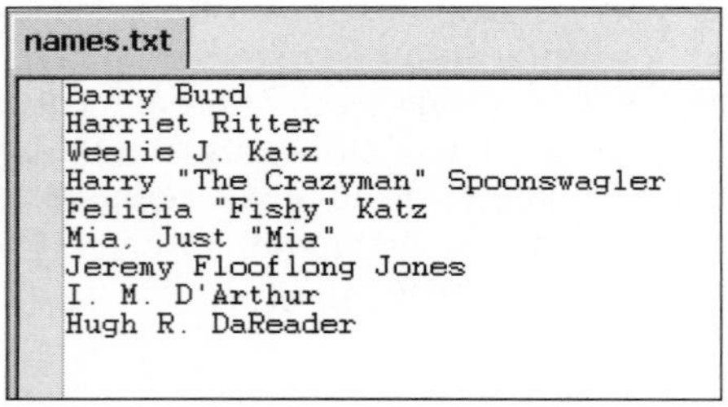

Figure 11-18:
Several
names in a
file.

```
names.txt
Barry Burd
Harriet Ritter
Weelie J. Katz
Harry "The Crazyman" Spoonswagler
Felicia "Fishy" Katz
Mia, Just "Mia"
Jeremy Flooflong Jones
I. M. D'Arthur
Hugh R. DaReader
```

Figure 11-19:
The code in
Listing 11-8
changes
some of the
names.

```
General Output
----------------------Configuration:
Harriet Ritter
Weelie J. Katz
Jim Newton
Harry "The Crazyman" Spoonswagler
Felicia "Fishy" Katz
Mia, Just "Mia"
Jeremy Flooflong Jones
I. M. D'Arthur
Hugh R. DaReader
```

All the interesting things happen when you execute the remove and add methods. The variable named people refers to an ArrayList object. When you call that object's remove method

```
people.remove(0);
```

you eliminate a value from the list. In this case, you eliminate whatever value is in the list's initial position (the position numbered 0). So in Listing 11-8, the call to remove takes the name Barry Burd out of the list.

That leaves only eight names in the list, but then the next statement,

```
people.add(2, "Jim Newton");
```

inserts a name into position number 2. (After Barry is removed, position number 2 is the position occupied by Harry Spoonswagler, so Harry moves to position 3, and Jim Newton becomes the number 2 man.)

Notice that an ArrayList object has two different add methods. The method that adds Jim Newton has two parameters — a position number and a value to be added. Another add method

```
people.add(diskScanner.nextLine());
```

takes only one parameter. This statement takes whatever name it finds on a line of the input file and appends that name to the end of the list. (The add method with only one parameter always appends its value to what's currently the end of the ArrayList object.)

Using generics (hot stuff!)

Look again at Listing 11-8, and notice the funky `ArrayList` declaration:

```
ArrayList<String> people = new ArrayList<String>();
```

Starting with Java 5.0, each collection class is *generified*. That ugly-sounding word means that every declaration should contain *<SomeTypeName>*. The thing that's sandwiched between < and > tells Java what kinds of values the new collection may contain.

The material in this section applies to Java 5.0, Java 6, or whatever higher version number comes along in the next few years. For more about Java's version numbers, see Chapter 2.

For example, in Listing 11-8 the words `ArrayList<String> people` say that the `people` variable can refer only to a collection of `String` values. So from that point on, any reference to an item from the `people` collection is treated exclusively as a `String`. If you write

```
people.add(new Room());
```

then the compiler coughs up your code and spits it out because a `Room` isn't the same as a `String`. (This coughing and spitting happens even if the compiler has access to the `Room` class's code — the code in Listing 11-5.) But the statement

```
people.add("George Gow");
```

is just fine. Because `"George Gow"` has type `String`, the compiler smiles happily.

Testing for the presence of more data

Here's a pleasant surprise. When you write a program like the one shown previously in Listing 11-8, you don't have to know how many names are in the input file. Having to know the number of names may defeat the purpose of using the easily expandable `ArrayList` class. Instead of looping until you read exactly nine names, you can loop until you run out of data.

The `Scanner` class has several nice methods like `hasNextInt`, `hasNextDouble`, and plain old `hasNext`. Each of these methods checks for more input data. If there's more data, the method returns `true`. Otherwise, the method returns `false`.

Listing 11-8 uses the general purpose `hasNext` method. This `hasNext` method returns `true` as long as there's anything more to read from the program's input. So after the program scoops up that last `Hugh R. DaReader` line in Figure 11-18, the subsequent `hasNext` call returns `false`. This `false` condition ends execution of the `while` loop and plummets the computer toward the remainder of the Listing 11-8 code.

All about generics

One of Java's original design goals was to keep the language as simple as possible. The language's developer took some unnecessarily complicated features of C++ and tossed them out the window. The result was a language that was elegant and sleek. Some people said the language was too sleek. So after several years of discussion and squabbling, Java became a bit more complicated. By the year 2004, Java had `enum` types, enhanced `for` loops, static import, and some other interesting new features. But the most talked-about new feature was the introduction of generics.

```
ArrayList<String> people =
    new ArrayList<String>();
```

The use of anything like `<String>` was new in Java 5.0. In old-style Java, you'd write

```
ArrayList people = new
    ArrayList();
```

In those days, an `ArrayList` could store almost anything you wanted to put in it — a number, an `Account`, a `Room`, a `String` — anything. The `ArrayList` class was very versatile, but with this versatility came some headaches. If you could put anything into an `ArrayList`, you couldn't easily predict what you would get out of an `ArrayList`. In particular, you couldn't easily write code that assumed you had stored certain types of values in the `ArrayList`. Here's an example:

```
ArrayList things = new
    ArrayList();
```

```
things.add(new Account());
Account myAccount =
    things.get(0);
//DON'T USE THIS. IT'S BAD
    CODE.
```

In the third line, the call to `get(0)` grabs the earliest value in the `things` collection. The call to `get(0)` is okay, but then the compiler chokes on the attempted assignment to `myAccount`. You get a message on the third line saying that whatever you get from the `things` list can't be stuffed into the `myAccount` variable. You get this message because, by the time the compiler reaches the third line, it has forgotten that the item added on the second line was of type `Account`!

The introduction of generics fixes this problem:

```
ArrayList<Account> things =
    new ArrayList<Account>();
things.add(new Account());
Account myAccount =
    things.get(0);
//USE THIS CODE INSTEAD. IT'S
    GOOD CODE.
```

Adding `<Account>` in two places tells the compiler that `things` stores `Account` instances — nothing else. So, in the third line in the preceding code, you get a value from the `things` collection. Then, because `things` stores only `Account` objects, you can make `myAccount` refer to that new value. It works!

Chapter 12

Looking Good When Things Take Unexpected Turns

• •

In This Chapter

▶ Recovering from bad input and other nasty situations

▶ Making your code (more or less) crash proof

▶ Defining your own exception class

• •

*S*eptember 9, 1945: A moth flies into one of the relays of the Harvard Mark II computer and gums up the works. This becomes the first recorded case of a real computer bug.

April 19, 1957: Herbert Bright, manager of the data processing center at Westinghouse in Pittsburgh, receives an unmarked deck of computer punch cards in the mail (which is like getting an unlabeled CD-ROM in the mail today). Mr. Bright guesses that this deck comes from the development team for FORTRAN — the first computer programming language. He's been waiting a few years for this software. (No Web downloads were available at the time.)

Armed with nothing but this good guess, Bright writes a small FORTRAN program and tries to compile it on his IBM 704. (The IBM 704 lives in its own specially built, 2,000-square-foot room. With vacuum tubes instead of transistors, the machine has a whopping 32K of RAM. The operating system has to be loaded from tape before the running of each program, and a typical program takes between two and four hours to run.) After the usual waiting time, Bright's attempt to compile a FORTRAN program comes back with a single error — a missing comma in one of the statements. Bright corrects the error, and the program runs like a charm.

July 22, 1962: Mariner I, the first U.S. spacecraft aimed at another planet, is destroyed when it behaves badly four minutes after launch. The bad behavior is attributed to a missing bar (like a hyphen) in the formula for the rocket's velocity.

Around the same time, orbit computation software at NASA is found to contain the incorrect statement DO 10 I=1.10 (instead of the correct DO 10 I=1,10). In modern notation, this is like writing do10i = 1.10 in place of for (int i=1; i<=10; i++). The change from a comma to a period turns a loop into an assignment statement.

January 1, 2000: The Year 2000 Problem wreaks havoc on the modern world.

Any historically accurate facts in these notes were borrowed from the following sources: the Computer Folklore newsgroup (alt.folklore.computers, which you can access through groups.google.com), the Free On-line Dictionary of Computing (www.foldoc.org), the "Looking Back" column in *Computer* magazine (www.computer.org/computer), and the Web pages of the IEEE (www.computer.org/history).

Handling Exceptions

You're taking inventory. This means counting item after item, box after box, and marking the numbers of such things on log sheets, in little handheld gizmos, and into forms on computer keyboards. A particular part of the project involves entering the number of boxes that you find on the Big Dusty Boxes That Haven't Been Opened Since Year One shelf. Rather than break the company's decades-old habit, you decide not to open any of these boxes. You arbitrarily assign the value $3.25 to each box.

Listing 12-1 shows the software to handle this bit of inventory. The software has a flaw, which is revealed in Figure 12-1. When the user enters a whole number value, things are okay. But when the user enters something else (like the number 3.5), the program comes crashing to the ground. Surely something can be done about this. Computers are stupid, but they're not so stupid that they should fail royally when a user enters an improper value.

Listing 12-1:   Counting Boxes

```
import static java.lang.System.out;
import java.util.Scanner;
import java.text.NumberFormat;

class InventoryA {

    public static void main(String args[]) {
        final double boxPrice = 3.25;
        Scanner myScanner = new Scanner(System.in);
        NumberFormat currency =
```

```
                    NumberFormat.getCurrencyInstance();

            out.print("How many boxes do we have? ");
            String numBoxesIn = myScanner.next();
            int numBoxes = Integer.parseInt(numBoxesIn);

            out.print("The value is ");
            out.println(currency.format(numBoxes * boxPrice));
        }
    }
```

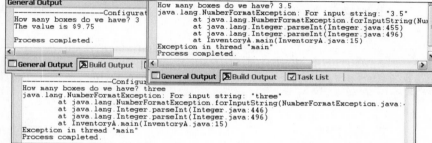

Figure 12-1:
Oops! That's
not a
number.

The key to fixing a program bug is examining the message that appears when the program crashes. The inventory program's message says `java.lang.NumberFormatException`. That means a class named *NumberFormatException* is in the `java.lang` API package. Somehow, the call to `Integer.parseInt` brought this `NumberFormatException` class out of hiding.

For a brief explanation of the `Integer.parseInt` method, see Chapter 11.

Well, here's what's going on. The Java programming language has a mechanism called *exception handling*. With exception handling, a program can detect that things are about to go wrong and respond by creating a brand-new object. In the official terminology, the program is said to be *throwing* an exception. That new object, an instance of the `Exception` class, is passed like a hot potato from one piece of code to another until some piece of code decides to *catch* the exception. When the exception is caught, the program executes some recovery code, buries the exception, and moves on to the next normal statement as if nothing had ever happened. The process is illustrated in Figure 12-2.

The whole thing is done with the aid of several Java keywords. These keywords are as follows:

✔ **throw:** Creates a new exception object.

✔ **throws:** Passes the buck from a method up to whatever code called the method.

✔ **try:** Encloses code that has the potential to create a new exception object. In the usual scenario, the code inside a `try` clause contains calls to methods whose code can create one or more exceptions.

✔ **catch:** Deals with the exception, buries it, and then moves on.

So, the truth is out. Through some chain of events like the one shown in Figure 12-2, the method `Integer.parseInt` can throw a `NumberFormatException`. When you call `Integer.parseInt`, this `NumberFormatException` is passed on to you.

 The Java API (Application Programming Interface) documentation for the `parseInt` method says, "Throws: `NumberFormatException` — if the string does not contain a parsable integer." Once in a while, reading the documentation actually pays.

```
void method1() {
    try {
        method2();
    } catch (Exception e) {

    }
}
```

```
void method2() throws Exception {
    method3();
}
```

```
void method3() throws Exception {
    method4();
}
```

```
void method4() throws Exception {
    throw new Exception();
}
```

Figure 12-2:
Throwing,
passing, and
catching an
exception.

If you call yourself a hero, you'd better catch the exception so that all the other code can get on with its regular business. Listing 12-2 shows the catching of an exception.

Listing 12-2:   A Hero Counts Boxes

```
import static java.lang.System.out;
import java.util.Scanner;
import java.text.NumberFormat;

class InventoryB {

    public static void main(String args[]) {
        final double boxPrice = 3.25;
        Scanner myScanner = new Scanner(System.in);
        NumberFormat currency =
            NumberFormat.getCurrencyInstance();

        out.print("How many boxes do we have? ");
        String numBoxesIn = myScanner.next();

        try {
            int numBoxes = Integer.parseInt(numBoxesIn);
            out.print("The value is ");
            out.println(currency.format(numBoxes *
            boxPrice));
        } catch (NumberFormatException e) {
            out.println("That's not a number.");
        }
    }
}
```

Figure 12-3 shows three runs of the code from Listing 12-2. When a misguided user types **three** instead of **3**, the program maintains its cool by displaying `That's not a number`. The trick is to enclose the call to `Integer.parseInt` inside a `try` clause. If you do this, the computer watches for exceptions when any statement inside the `try` clause is executed. If an exception is thrown, the computer jumps from inside the `try` clause to a `catch` clause below it. In Listing 12-2, the computer jumps directly to the `catch` (`NumberFormatException e`) clause. The computer executes the `println` statement inside the clause, and then marches on with normal processing. (If there were statements in Listing 12-2 after the end of the `catch` clause, the computer would go on and execute them.)

Figure 12-3: Catch that exception.

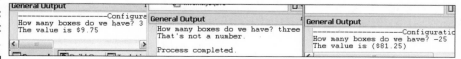

An entire `try-catch` assembly — complete with a `try` clause, `catch` clause, and what have you — is called a *try statement*. Sometimes, for emphasis, I call it a *try-catch statement*.

The parameter in a catch clause

Take a look at the `catch` clause in Listing 12-2 and pay particular attention to the words `(NumberFormatException e)`. This looks a lot like a method's parameter list, doesn't it? In fact, every `catch` clause is like a little mini-method with its own parameter list. The parameter list always has an exception type name and then a parameter.

In Listing 12-2, I don't do anything with the `catch` clause's e parameter, but I certainly could if I wanted to. Remember, the exception that's thrown is an object — an instance of the `NumberFormatException` class. When an exception is caught, the computer makes the `catch` clause's parameter refer to that exception object. In other words, the name *e* stores a bunch of information about the exception. To take advantage of this, you can call some of the exception object's methods.

```
} catch (NumberFormatException e) {
    out.println("That's not a number.");

    out.println("Message: " + e.getMessage());

    out.println("Here comes a stack trace: ");
    e.printStackTrace();
    out.println("Did you like the stack trace?");
}
```

With this enhanced `catch` clause, a run of the `inventory` program may look like the run shown in Figure 12-4. When you call `getMessage`, you fetch some detail about the exception. (In Figure 12-4, the detail is the fact that the user mistakenly typed the word *three*.) When you call `printStackTrace`, you get a display showing the methods that were running at the moment when the exception was thrown. (In Figure 12-4, the display includes `Integer.parseInt` and the `main` method.) Both `getMessage` and `printStackTrace` present information to help you find the source of the program's difficulties.

Figure 12-4:
Calling an
exception
object's
methods.

```
How many boxes do we have? three
That's not a number.
Message: For input string: "three"
Here comes a stack trace:
java.lang.NumberFormatException: For input string: "three"
        at java.lang.NumberFormatException.forInputString(NumberFormatException.java:48)
        at java.lang.Integer.parseInt(Integer.java:446)
        at java.lang.Integer.parseInt(Integer.java:496)
        at InventoryB.main(InventoryB.java:17)
Did you like the stack trace?

Process completed.
```

Exception types

So what else can go wrong today? Are there other kinds of exceptions — things that don't come from the `NumberFormatException` class? Sure, plenty of different exception types are out there. You can even create one of your own. You wanna try? If so, look at Listings 12-3 and 12-4.

Listing 12-3:   Making Your Own Kind of Exception

```
class OutOfRangeException extends Exception {
}
```

Listing 12-4:   Using Your Custom Made Exception

```
import static java.lang.System.out;
import java.util.Scanner;
import java.text.NumberFormat;

class InventoryC {

    public static void main(String args[]) {
        final double boxPrice = 3.25;
        Scanner myScanner = new Scanner(System.in);
        NumberFormat currency =
            NumberFormat.getCurrencyInstance();

        out.print("How many boxes do we have? ");
        String numBoxesIn = myScanner.next();

        try {
            int numBoxes = Integer.parseInt(numBoxesIn);

            if (numBoxes < 0) {
                throw new OutOfRangeException();
```

(continued)

Listing 12-4 (continued)

```
        }

        out.print("The value is ");
        out.println(currency.format(numBoxes *
        boxPrice));
    } catch (NumberFormatException e) {
        out.println("That's not a number.");
    } catch (OutOfRangeException e) {
        out.print(numBoxesIn);
        out.println("? That's impossible!");
    }

    }
}
```

Listings 12-3 and 12-4 remedy a problem that cropped up in Figure 12-3. Look at the last of the three runs in Figure 12-3. The user reports that the shelves have –25 boxes, and the computer takes this value without blinking an eye. The truth is that you would need a black hole (or some other exotic space-time warping phenomenon) to have a negative number of boxes on any shelf in your warehouse. So the program should get upset if the user enters a negative number of boxes, which is what the code in Listing 12-4 does. To see the upset code, look at Figure 12-5.

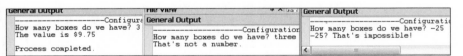

The code in Listing 12-3 declares a new kind of exception class — OutOfRangeException. In many situations, typing a negative number would be just fine, so OutOfRangeException isn't built into the Java API. However, in the inventory program, a negative number should be flagged as an anomaly.

The OutOfRangeException class in Listing 12-3 wins the award for the shortest self-contained piece of code in the book. The class's code is just a declaration line and an empty pair of braces. The code's operative phrase is extends Exception. Being a subclass of the Java API Exception class allows any instance of the OutOfRangeException class to be thrown.

Back in Listing 12-4, a new `OutOfRangeException` instance is thrown. When this happens, the `catch` clause (`OutOfRangeException e`) catches the instance. The clause echoes the user's input and displays the message `That's impossible!`

Who's going to catch the exception?

Take one more look at Listing 12-4. Notice that more than one `catch` clause can accompany a single `try` clause. When an exception is thrown inside a `try` clause, the computer starts going down the accompanying list of `catch` clauses. The computer starts at whatever `catch` clause comes immediately after the `try` clause and works its way down the program's text.

For each `catch` clause, the computer asks itself, "Is the exception that was just thrown an instance of the class in this clause's parameter list?"

- ✔ If not, the computer skips this `catch` clause and moves on to the next `catch` clause in line.

- ✔ If so, the computer executes this `catch` clause and then skips past all the other `catch` clauses that come with this `try` clause. The computer goes on and executes whatever statements come after the whole `try`-`catch` statement.

For some concrete examples, see Listings 12-5 and 12-6.

Listing 12-5:   Yet Another Exception

```
class NumberTooLargeException extends OutOfRangeException
        {
}
```

Listing 12-6:   Where Does the Buck Stop?

```
import static java.lang.System.out;
import java.util.Scanner;
import java.text.NumberFormat;

class InventoryD {

    public static void main(String args[]) {
        final double boxPrice = 3.25;
        Scanner myScanner = new Scanner(System.in);
        NumberFormat currency =
```

(continued)

Listing 12-6 (continued)

```
            NumberFormat.getCurrencyInstance();

        out.print("How many boxes do we have? ");
        String numBoxesIn = myScanner.next();

        try {
            int numBoxes = Integer.parseInt(numBoxesIn);

            if (numBoxes < 0) {
                throw new OutOfRangeException();
            }

            if (numBoxes > 1000) {
                throw new NumberTooLargeException();
            }

            out.print("The value is ");
            out.println(currency.format(numBoxes *
            boxPrice));
        }
        catch (NumberFormatException e) {
            out.println("That's not a number.");
        }

        catch (OutOfRangeException e) {
            out.print(numBoxesIn);
            out.println("? That's impossible!");
        }

        catch (Exception e) {
            out.print("Something went wrong, ");
            out.print("but I'm clueless about what ");
            out.println("it actually was.");
        }

        out.println("That's that.");
    }
}
```

To run the code in Listings 12-5 and 12-6, you need one additional Java program file. You need the OutOfRangeException class in Listing 12-3.

Listing 12-6 addresses the scenario in which you have limited shelf space. You don't have room for more than 1,000 boxes, but once in a while, the program asks how many boxes you have, and somebody enters the number *100000* by accident. In cases like this, Listing 12-6 does a quick reality check. Any number of boxes over 1,000 is tossed out as being unrealistic.

Listing 12-6 watches for a NumberTooLargeException, but to make life more interesting, Listing 12-6 doesn't have a catch clause for the

NumberTooLargeException. In spite of this, everything still works out just fine. It's fine because NumberTooLargeException is declared to be a subclass of OutOfRangeException, and Listing 12-6 has a catch clause for the OutOfRangeException.

You see, because NumberTooLargeException is a subclass of OutOfRangeException, any instance of NumberTooLargeException is just a special kind of OutOfRangeException. So in Listing 12-6, the computer may start looking for a clause to catch a NumberTooLargeException. When the computer stumbles upon the OutOfRangeException catch clause, the computer says, "Okay, I've found a match. I'll execute the statements in this catch clause."

To keep from having to write this whole story over and over again, I introduce some new terminology. I say that the catch clause with parameter OutOfRangeException *matches* the NumberTooLargeException that's been thrown. I call this catch clause a *matching catch clause*.

The following bullets describe different things that the user may do and how the computer responds. As you read through the bullets, you can follow along by looking at the runs shown in Figure 12-6.

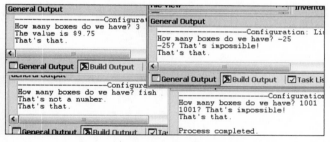

Figure 12-6:
Running the
code from
Listing 12-6.

✔ **The user enters an ordinary whole number, like the number *3*.**

All the statements in the try clause are executed. Then the computer skips past all the catch clauses and executes the code that comes immediately after all the catch clauses. (See Figure 12-7.)

✔ **The user enters something that's not a whole number, like the word *fish*.**

The code throws a NumberFormatException. The computer skips past the remaining statements in the try clause. The computer executes the statements inside the first catch clause — the clause whose parameter is of type NumberFormatException. Then the computer skips past the second and third catch clauses and executes the code that comes immediately after all the catch clauses. (See Figure 12-8.)

```
try {

        //Normal processing (throw no exception)

}

catch (NumberFormatException e) {
        out.println("That's not a number.");
}

catch (OutOfRangeException e) {
        out.print(numBoxesIn);
        out.println("? That's impossible!");
}

catch (Exception e) {
        out.print("Something went wrong, ");
        out.print("but I'm clueless about what ");
        out.println("it actually was.");
}

out.println("That's that.");
```

Figure 12-7:
No
exception is
thrown.

```
try {

        throw new NumberFormatException ();

}

catch (NumberFormatException e) {
        out.println("That's not a number.");
}

catch (OutOfRangeException e) {
        out.print(numBoxesIn);
        out.println("? That's impossible!");
}

catch (Exception e) {
        out.print("Something went wrong, ");
        out.print("but I'm clueless about what ");
        out.println("it actually was.");
}

out.println("That's that.");
```

Figure 12-8:
A Number-
Format-
Exception is
thrown.

✔ **The user enters a negative number, like the number –25.**

The code throws an OutOfRangeException. The computer skips past the remaining statements in the try clause. The computer even skips past the statements in the first catch clause. (After all, an OutOfRangeException isn't any kind of a NumberFormatException. The catch clause with parameter NumberFormatException isn't a match for this OutOfRangeException.) The computer executes the statements inside the second catch clause — the clause whose parameter is of type OutOfRangeException. Then the computer skips past the third catch clause and executes the code that comes immediately after all the catch clauses. (See Figure 12-9.)

✔ **The user enters an unrealistically large number, like the number 1001.**

The code throws a NumberTooLargeException. The computer skips past the remaining statements in the try clause. The computer even skips past the statements in the first catch clause. (After all, a NumberTooLargeException isn't any kind of NumberFormat Exception.)

```
try {

            throw new OutOfRangeException ();

    }

    catch (NumberFormatException e) {
            out.println("That's not a number.");
    }

    catch (OutOfRangeException e) {
            out.print(numBoxesIn);
            out.println("? That's impossible!");
    }

    catch (Exception e) {
            out.print("Something went wrong, ");
            out.print("but I'm clueless about what ");
            out.println("it actually was.");
    }

    out.println("That's that.");
```

Figure 12-9:
An
OutOfRange-
Exception is
thrown.

But, according to the code in Listing 12-5, NumberTooLargeException is a subclass of OutOfRangeException. When the computer reaches the second catch clause, the computer says, "Hmm! A NumberToo LargeException is a kind of OutOfRangeException. I'll execute the statements in this catch clause — the clause with parameter of type OutOfRangeException." In other words, it's a match.

So, the computer executes the statements inside the second catch clause. Then the computer skips the third catch clause and executes the code that comes immediately after all the catch clauses. (See Figure 12-10.)

✔ **Something else, something very unpredictable, happens (I don't know what).**

With my unending urge to experiment, I reached into the try clause of Listing 12-6 and added a statement that throws an IOException. No reason — I just wanted to see what would happen.

When the code threw an IOException, the computer skipped past the remaining statements in the try clause. Then the computer skipped past the statements in the first and second catch clauses. When the computer reached the third catch clause, I could hear the computer say, "Hmm! An IOException is a kind of Exception. I've found a matching catch clause — a clause with a parameter of type Exception. I'll execute the statements in this catch clause."

Figure 12-10:
A
NumberToo-
Large-
Exception is
thrown.

```java
try {

          throw new NumberTooLargeException ();

}

catch (NumberFormatException e) {
      out.println("That's not a number.");
}

catch (OutOfRangeException e) {
      out.print(numBoxesIn);
      out.println("? That's impossible!");
}

catch (Exception e) {
      out.print("Something went wrong, ");
      out.print("but I'm clueless about what ");
      out.println("it actually was.");
}

out.println("That's that.");
```

So, the computer executed the statements inside the third `catch` clause. Then the computer executed the code that comes immediately after all the `catch` clauses. (See Figure 12-11.)

```
try {

            throw new IOException ();

}

catch (NumberFormatException e) {
        out.println("That's not a number.");
}

catch (OutOfRangeException e) {
        out.print(numBoxesIn);
        out.println("? That's impossible!");
}

catch (Exception e) {
        out.print("Something went wrong, ");
        out.print("but I'm clueless about what ");
        out.println("it actually was.");
}

out.println("That's that.");
```

Figure 12-11:
An
IOException
is thrown.

When the computer looks for a matching `catch` clause, the computer latches on to the topmost clause that fits one of the following descriptions:

✔ The clause's parameter type is the same as the type of the exception that was thrown.

✔ The clause's parameter type is a superclass of the exception's type.

If a better match appears farther down the list of `catch` clauses, that's just too bad. For instance, imagine that you added a `catch` clause with a parameter of type `NumberTooLargeException` to the code in Listing 12-6. Imagine, also, that you put this new `catch` clause *after* the `catch` clause with parameter of type `OutOfRangeException`. Then, because `NumberTooLarge Exception` is a subclass of the `OutOfRangeException` class, the code in your new `NumberTooLargeException` clause would never be executed. That's just the way the cookie crumbles.

Throwing caution to the wind

Are you one of those obsessive-compulsive types? Do you like to catch every possible exception before the exception can possibly crash your program? Well, watch out. Java doesn't let you become paranoid. You can't catch an exception if the exception has no chance of being thrown.

Consider the following code. The code has a very innocent `i++` statement inside a `try` clause. That's fair enough. But then the code's `catch` clause is pretending to catch an `IOException`.

```
// Bad code!
try {
    i++;
} catch (IOException e) {
    e.printStackTrace();
}
```

Who is this `catch` clause trying to impress? A statement like `i++` doesn't do any input or output. The code inside the `try` clause can't possibly throw an `IOException`. So the compiler comes back and says, "Hey, `catch` clause. Get real. Get off your high horse." Well, to be a bit more precise, the compiler's reprimand reads as follows:

```
exception java.io.IOException is never thrown in body of
            corresponding try statement
```

Doing useful things

So far, each example in this chapter catches an exception, prints a "bad input" message, and then closes up shop. Wouldn't it be nice to see a program that actually carries on after an exception has been caught? Well, it's time for something nice. Listing 12-7 has a `try-catch` statement inside a loop. The loop keeps running until the user types something sensible.

Listing 12-7:   Keep Pluggin' Along

```
import static java.lang.System.out;
import java.util.Scanner;
import java.text.NumberFormat;

class InventoryLoop {

    public static void main(String args[]) {
```

```
        final double boxPrice = 3.25;
        boolean gotGoodInput = false;
        Scanner myScanner = new Scanner(System.in);
        NumberFormat currency =
            NumberFormat.getCurrencyInstance();

        do {
            out.print("How many boxes do we have? ");
            String numBoxesIn = myScanner.next();

            try {
                int numBoxes =
            Integer.parseInt(numBoxesIn);
                out.print("The value is ");
                out.println
                    (currency.format(numBoxes *
            boxPrice));
                gotGoodInput = true;
            } catch (NumberFormatException e) {
                out.println();
                out.println("That's not a number.");
            }
        } while (!gotGoodInput);

        out.println("That's that.");
    }
}
```

Figure 12-12 shows a run of the code from Listing 12-7. In the first three attempts, the user types just about everything except a valid whole number. At last, the fourth attempt is a success. The user types **3**, and the computer leaves the loop.

Figure 12-12:
A run of the
code in
Listing 12-7.

```
--------------------Configuration:
How many boxes do we have? 3.5

That's not a number.
How many boxes do we have? three

That's not a number.
How many boxes do we have? fish

That's not a number.
How many boxes do we have? 3
The value is $9.75
That's that.

Process completed.
```

Our friends, the good exceptions

A rumor is going around that Java exceptions always come from unwanted, erroneous situations. Although there's some truth to this rumor, the rumor isn't entirely accurate. Occasionally, an exception arises from a normal, expected occurrence. Take, for instance, the detection of the end of a file. The following code makes a copy of a file:

```
try {
    while (true) {
        dataOut.writeByte(dataIn.readByte());
    }
} catch (EOFException e) {
    numFilesCopied = 1;
}
```

To copy bytes from `dataIn` to `dataOut`, you just go into a `while` loop. With its `true` condition, the `while` loop is seemingly endless. But eventually, you reach the end of the `dataIn` file. When this happens, the `readByte` method throws an `EOFException` (an end-of-file exception). The throwing of this exception sends the computer out of the `try` clause and out of the `while` loop. From there, you do whatever you want to do in the `catch` clause, and then proceed with normal processing.

Handle an Exception or Pass the Buck

So you're getting to know Java, hey? What? You say you're all the way up to Chapter 12?

I'm impressed. You must be a hard worker. But remember, all work and no play. . . .

So, how about taking a break? A little nap could do you a world of good. Is ten seconds okay? Or is that too long? Better make it five seconds.

Listing 12-8 has a program that's supposed to pause its execution for five seconds. The problem is that the program in Listing 12-8 is incorrect. Take a look at Listing 12-8 for a minute, and then I'll tell you what's wrong with it.

Listing 12-8: An Incorrect Program

```
/*
 * This code does not compile.
 */

import static java.lang.System.out;

class NoSleepForTheWeary {

    public static void main(String args[]) {
        out.print("Excuse me while I nap ");
        out.println("for just five seconds...");

        takeANap();

        out.println("Ah, that was refreshing.");
    }

    static void takeANap() {
        Thread.sleep(5000);
    }
}
```

The strategy in Listing 12-8 isn't bad. The idea is to call the `sleep` method, which is defined in the Java API. This `sleep` method belongs to the API `Thread` class. When you call the `sleep` method, the number that you feed it is a number of milliseconds. So, `Thread.sleep(5000)` means pause for five seconds.

The problem is that the code inside the `sleep` method can throw an exception. This kind of exception is an instance of the `InterruptedException` class. When you try to compile the code in Listing 12-8, you get the following unwanted message:

```
unreported exception java.lang.InterruptedException; must
        be caught or declared to be thrown
```

For the purpose of understanding exceptions in general, you don't need to know exactly what an `InterruptedException` is. All you really have to know is that a call to `Thread.sleep` can throw one of these `Interrupted Exception` objects. But if you're really curious, an `InterruptedException` is thrown when some code interrupts some other code's sleep. Imagine that you have two pieces of code running at the same time. One piece of code calls the `Thread.sleep` method. At the same time, another piece of code calls the `interrupt` method. By calling the `interrupt` method, the second piece of code brings the first code's `Thread.sleep` method to a screeching halt. The `Thread.sleep` method responds by spitting out an `Interrupted Exception`.

Now, the Java programming language has two different kinds of exceptions. They're called *checked* and *unchecked* exceptions:

 ✔ The potential throwing of a checked exception must be acknowledged in the code.

 ✔ The potential throwing of an unchecked exception doesn't need to be acknowledged in the code.

An InterruptedException is one of Java's checked exception types. When you call a method that has the potential to throw an InterruptedException, you need to acknowledge that exception in the code.

Now, when I say that an exception is *acknowledged in the code,* what do I really mean?

```
// The author wishes to thank that InterruptedException,
// without which this code could not have been written.
```

No, that's not what it means to be acknowledged in the code. Acknowledging an exception in the code means one of two things:

 ✔ The statements (including method calls) that can throw the exception are inside a try clause. That try clause has a catch clause with a matching exception type in its parameter list.

 ✔ The statements (including method calls) that can throw the exception are inside a method that has a throws clause in its header. The throws clause contains a matching exception type.

If you're confused by the wording of these two bullets, don't worry. The next two listings illustrate the points made in the bullets.

In Listing 12-9, the method call that can throw an InterruptedException is inside a try clause. That try clause has a catch clause with exception type InterruptedException.

Listing 12-9:   Acknowledging with a try-catch Statement

```java
import static java.lang.System.out;

class GoodNightsSleepA {

    public static void main(String args[]) {
        out.print("Excuse me while I nap ");
```

```
        out.println("for just five seconds...");

        takeANap();

        out.println("Ah, that was refreshing.");
    }

    static void takeANap() {
        try {
            Thread.sleep(5000);
        } catch (InterruptedException e) {
            out.println("Hey, who woke me up?");
        }
    }
}
```

It's my custom, at this point in a section, to remind you that a run of Listing Such-and-Such is shown in Figure So-and-So. But the problem here is that Figure 12-13 doesn't do justice to the code in Listing 12-9. When you run the program in Listing 12-9, the computer displays Excuse me while I nap for just five seconds, pauses for five seconds, and then displays Ah, that was refreshing. The code works because the call to the sleep method, which can throw an InterruptedException, is inside a try clause. That try clause has a catch clause whose exception is of type InterruptedException.

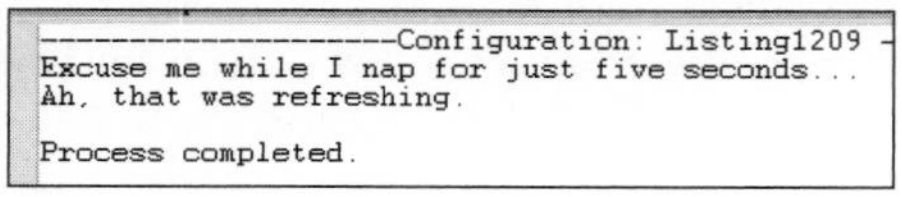

Figure 12-13:
There's a
five-second
pause
before the
"Ah" line.

```
------------------------Configuration: Listing1209 -
Excuse me while I nap for just five seconds...
Ah, that was refreshing.

Process completed.
```

So much for acknowledging an exception with a try-catch statement. You can acknowledge an exception another way, shown in Listing 12-10.

Listing 12-10:   Acknowledging with throws

```
import static java.lang.System.out;

class GoodNightsSleepB {

    public static void main(String args[]) {
```

(continued)

Listing 12-10 (continued)

```
        out.print("Excuse me while I nap ");
        out.println("for just five seconds...");

        try {
            takeANap();
        } catch (InterruptedException e) {
            out.println("Hey, who woke me up?");
        }

        out.println("Ah, that was refreshing.");
    }

    static void takeANap() throws InterruptedException {
        Thread.sleep(5000);
    }
}
```

To see a run of the code in Listing 12-10, refer to Figure 12-13. Once again, Figure 12-13 fails to capture the true essence of the run, but that's okay. Just remember that in Figure 12-13, the computer pauses for five seconds before it displays Ah, that was refreshing.

The important part of Listing 12-10 is in the takeANap method's header. That header ends with throws InterruptedException. By announcing that it throws an InterruptedException, method takeANap passes the buck. What this throws clause really says is, "I realize that a statement inside this method has the potential to throw an InterruptedException, but I'm not acknowledging the exception in a try-catch statement. Java compiler, please don't bug me about this. Instead of having a try-catch statement, I'm passing the responsibility for acknowledging the exception to the main method (the method that called the takeANap method)."

Indeed, in the main method, the call to takeANap is inside a try clause. That try clause has a catch clause with a parameter of type InterruptedException. So everything is okay. Method takeANap passes the responsibility to the main method, and the main method accepts the responsibility with an appropriate try-catch statement. Everybody's happy. Even the Java compiler is happy.

To better understand the throws clause, imagine a volleyball game in which the volleyball is an exception. When a player on the other team serves, that player is throwing the exception. The ball crosses the net and comes right to you. If you pound the ball back across the net, you're catching the exception. But if you pass the ball to another player, you're using the throws clause. In essence, you're saying, "Here, other player. You deal with this exception."

A statement in a method can throw an exception that's not matched by a `catch` clause. This includes situations in which the statement throwing the exception isn't even inside a `try` block. When this happens, execution of the program jumps out of the method that contains the offending statement. Execution jumps back to whatever code called the method in the first place.

A method can name more than one exception type in its `throws` clause. Just use commas to separate the names of the exception types, as in the following example:

```
throws InterruptedException, IOException,
       ArithmeticException
```

The Java API has hundreds of exception types. Several of them are sub-classes of the `RuntimeException` class. Anything that's a subclass of `RuntimeException` (or a sub-subclass, sub-sub-subclass, and so on) is unchecked. Any exception that's not a descendent of `RuntimeException` is checked. The unchecked exceptions include things that would be hard for the computer to predict. Such things include the `NumberFormatException` (of Listings 12-2, 12-4, and others), the `ArithmeticException`, the `IndexOutOfBoundsException`, the infamous `NullPointerException`, and many others. When you write Java code, much of your code is suscepti-ble to these exceptions, but enclosing the code in `try` clauses (or passing the buck with `throws` clauses) is completely optional.

The Java API also has its share of checked exceptions. The computer can readily detect exceptions of this kind. So Java insists that, for an exception of this kind, any potential exception-throwing statement is acknowledged with either a `try` statement or a `throws` clause. Java's checked exceptions include the `InterruptedException` (Listings 12-9 and 12-10), the `IOException`, the `SQLException`, and a gang of other interesting exceptions.

Finishing the Job with a finally Clause

Once upon a time, I was a young fellow, living with my parents in Philadelphia, just starting to drive a car. I was heading toward a friend's house and thinking about who knows what when another car came from nowhere and bashed my car's passenger door. This kind of thing is called a *RunARedLightException*.

Anyway, both cars were still drivable, and we were right in the middle of a busy intersection. To avoid causing a traffic jam, we both pulled over to the nearest curb. I fumbled for my driver's license (which had a very young pic-ture of me on it), and opened the door to get out of my car.

And that's when the second accident happened. As I was getting out of my car, a city bus was coming by. The bus hit me and rolled me against my car a few times. This kind of thing is called a *DealWithLawyersException*.

The truth is that everything came out just fine. I was bruised but not battered. My parents paid for the damage to the car, so I never suffered any financial consequences. (I managed to pass on the financial burden by putting the `RunARedLightException` into my `throws` clause.)

This incident helps to explain why I think the way I do about exception handling. In particular, I wonder, "What happens if, while the computer is recovering from one exception, a second exception is thrown?" After all, the statements inside a `catch` clause aren't immune to calamities.

Well, the answer to this question is anything but simple. For starters, you can put a `try` statement inside a `catch` clause. This protects you against unexpected, potentially embarrassing incidents that can crop up during the execution of the `catch` clause. But when you start worrying about cascading exceptions, you open up a very slimy can of worms. The number of scenarios is large, and things can become complicated very quickly.

One not-too-complicated thing that you can do is to create a `finally` clause. Like a `catch` clause, a `finally` clause comes after a `try` clause. The big difference is that the statements in a `finally` clause are executed whether or not an exception is thrown. The idea is, "No matter what happens, good or bad, execute the statements inside this `finally` clause." Listing 12-11 has an example.

Listing 12-11:   Jumping Around

```
import static java.lang.System.out;

class DemoFinally {

    public static void main(String args[]) {
        try {
            doSomething();
        } catch (Exception e) {
            out.println("Exception caught in main.");
        }
    }

    static void doSomething() {
        try {
            out.println(0 / 0);
        } catch (Exception e) {
```

```
            out.println("Exception caught in
       doSomething.");
            out.println(0 / 0);
    } finally {
        out.println("I'll get printed.");
    }

    out.println("I won't get printed.");
}
}
```

Normally, when I think about a `try` statement, I think about the computer recovering from an unpleasant situation. The recovery takes place inside a `catch` clause, and then the computer marches on to whatever statements come after the `try` statement. Well, if something goes wrong during execution of a `catch` clause, this picture can start looking different.

Listing 12-11 gets a workout in Figure 12-14. First, the `main` method calls `doSomething`. Then, the stupid `doSomething` method goes out of its way to cause trouble. The `doSomething` method divides 0 by 0, which is illegal and undoable in anyone's programming language. This foolish action by the `doSomething` method throws an `ArithmeticException`, which is caught by the `try` statement's one and only `catch` clause.

nside the `catch` clause, that lowlife `doSomething` method divides 0 by 0 again. This time, the statement that does the division isn't inside a protective `try` clause. That's okay, because an `ArithmeticException` isn't checked. (It's one of those `RuntimeException` subclasses. It's an exception that doesn't have to be acknowledged in a `try` or a `throws` clause. For details, see the previous section.)

Well, checked or not, the throwing of another `ArithmeticException` causes control to jump out of the `doSomething` method. But, before leaving the `doSomething` method, the computer executes the `try` statement's last will and testament — namely, the statements inside the `finally` clause. That's why, in Figure 12-14, you see the words `I'll get printed`.

Figure 12-14:
Running the
code from
Listing 12-11.

```
General Output
-----------------------Configuration
Exception caught in doSomething.
I'll get printed.
Exception caught in main.

Process completed.
```

IInterestingly enough, you don't see the words `I won't get printed` in Figure 12-14. Because the `catch` clause's execution throws its own uncaught exception, the computer never makes it down past the `try-catch-finally` statement.

So, the computer goes back to where it left off in the `main` method. Back in the `main` method, word of the `doSomething` method's `ArithmeticException` mishaps causes execution to jump into a `catch` clause. The computer prints `Exception caught in main`, and then this terrible nightmare of a run is finished.

Part V
The Part of Tens

The 5th Wave   By Rich Tennant

"I'm sure there will be a good job market when I graduate. I created a virus that will go off that year."

In this part . . .

You're near the end of the book, and the time has come to sum it all up. This part of the book is your slam-bam, two-thousand-words-or-less resource for Java. What? You didn't read every word in the chapters before this one? That's okay. You can pick up a lot of useful information in this Part of Tens.

Chapter 13

Ten Ways to Avoid Mistakes

● ●

In This Chapter

▶ Checking your capitalization and value comparisons

▶ Watching out for fall-through

▶ Putting methods, listeners, and constructors where they belong

▶ Using static and nonstatic references

▶ Avoiding other heinous errors

● ●

"**T**he only people who never make mistakes are the people who never do anything at all." One of my college professors said that. I don't remember the professor's name, so I can't give him proper credit. I guess that's my mistake.

Putting Capital Letters Where They Belong

Java is a case-sensitive language, so you really have to mind your *P*s and *Q*s — along with every other letter of the alphabet. Here are some things to keep in mind as you create Java programs:

✔ Java's keywords are all completely lowercase. For instance, in a Java `if` statement, the word *if* can't be *If* or *IF*.

✔ When you use names from the Java API (Application Programming Interface), the case of the names has to match what appears in the API.

✔ You also need to make sure that the names you make up yourself are capitalized the same way throughout your entire program. If you declare a `myAccount` variable, you can't refer to it as `MyAccount`, `myaccount`, or `Myaccount`. If you capitalize the variable name two different ways, Java thinks you're referring to two completely different variables.

For more info on Java's case-sensitivity, see Chapter 3.

Breaking Out of a switch Statement

If you don't break out of a switch statement, you get fall-through. For instance, if the value of verse is 3, the following code prints all three lines — Last refrain, He's a pain, and Has no brain.

```
switch (verse) {
case 3:
    out.print("Last refrain, ");
    out.println("last refrain,");
case 2:
    out.print("He's a pain, ");
    out.println("he's a pain,");
case 1:
    out.print("Has no brain, ");
    out.println("has no brain,");
}
```

For the full story, see Chapter 5.

Comparing Values with a Double Equal Sign

When you compare two values with one another, you use a double equal sign. The line

```
if (inputNumber == randomNumber)
```

is correct, but the line

```
if (inputNumber = randomNumber)
```

is not correct. For a full report, see Chapter 5.

Adding Components to a GUI

Here's a constructor for a Java frame:

```
public SimpleFrame() {
    JButton button = new JButton("Thank you...");
    setTitle("...Katie Feltman and Heidi Unger");
    setLayout(new FlowLayout());
    add(button);
    button.addActionListener(this);
    setSize(300, 100);
    setVisible(true);
}
```

Whatever you do, don't forget the call to the add method. Without this call, you go to all the work of creating a button, but the button doesn't show up on your frame. For an introduction to such issues, see Chapter 9.

Adding Listeners to Handle Events

Look again at the previous section's code to construct a SimpleFrame. If you forget the call to addActionListener, nothing happens when you click the button. Clicking the button harder a second time doesn't help. For the run-down on listeners, see Chapter 16, which is on the CD-ROM.

Defining the Required Constructors

When you define a constructor with parameters, as in

```
public Temperature(double number)
```

then the computer no longer creates a default parameterless constructor for you. In other words, you can no longer call

```
Temperature roomTemp = new Temperature();
```

unless you explicitly define your own parameterless Temperature constructor. For all the gory details on constructors, see Chapter 9.

Fixing Non-Static References

If you try to compile the following code, you get an error message:

```
class WillNotWork {
    String greeting = "Hello";

    public static void main(String args[]) {
        System.out.println(greeting);
    }
}
```

You get an error message because main is static, but greeting isn't static. For the complete guide to finding and fixing this problem, see Chapter 10.

Staying within Bounds in an Array

When you declare an array with ten components, the components have indices 0 through 9. In other words, if you declare

```
int guests[] = new int[10];
```

then you can refer to the guests array's components by writing guests[0], guests[1], and so on, all the way up to guests[9]. You can't write guests[10], because the guests array has no component with index 10.

For the latest gossip on arrays, see Chapter 11.

Anticipating Null Pointers

This book's examples aren't prone to throwing the NullPointerException, but in real-life Java programming, you see that exception all the time. A NullPointerException comes about when you call a method that's supposed to return an object, but instead the method returns nothing. Here's a cheap example:

```
import static java.lang.System.out;
import java.io.File;

class ListMyFiles {

    public static void main(String args[]) {
        File myFile = new File("\\windows");

        String dir[] = myFile.list();

        for (String fileName : dir) {
```

```
                    out.println(fileName);
            }
        }
    }
```

This program displays a list of all the files in the `windows` directory. (For clarification on the use of the double backslash in `"\\windows"`, see Chapter 8.)

But what happens if you change `\\windows` to something else — something that doesn't represent the name of a directory?

```
File myFile = new File("&*%$!!");
```

Then the `new File` call returns `null` (a special Java word meaning *nothing*), so the variable `myFile` has nothing in it. Later in the code, the variable `dir` refers to nothing, and the attempt to loop through all the `dir` values fails miserably. You get a big `NullPointerException`, and the program comes crashing down around you.

To avoid this kind of calamity, check Java's API documentation. If you're calling a method that can return `null`, add exception-handling code to your program.

For the story on handling exceptions, see Chapter 12. For some advice on reading the API documentation, see Chapter 3 and this book's Web site.

Helping Java Find Its Files

You're compiling Java code, minding your own business, when the computer gives you a `NoClassDefFoundError`. All kinds of things can be going wrong, but chances are that the computer can't find a particular Java file. To fix this, you must align all the planets correctly.

✔ Your project directory has to contain all the Java files whose names are used in your code.

✔ If you use named packages, your project directory has to have appropriately named subdirectories.

✔ Your CLASSPATH must be set properly.

For specific guidelines, see Chapter 15 (on the CD-ROM) and this book's Web site.

Chapter 14

Ten Sets of Web Resources for Java

*N*o wonder the Web is so popular. It's both useful and fun. This chapter has ten bundles of resources. Each bundle has Web sites for you to visit. Each Web site has resources to help you use Java more effectively. And as far as I know, none of these sites uses adware, pop-ups, or other grotesque things.

The Horse's Mouth

Sun's official Web site for Java is `java.sun.com`. This site has all the latest development kits, and many of them are free. In addition, Sun has two special-purpose Java Web sites. Consumers of Java technology should visit `www.java.com`. Programmers and developers interested in sharing Java technology can go to `www.java.net`.

And be sure to visit `www.jcp.org`, home of the Java Community Process. At this site, you can read the latest proposals for improving Java. Who knows? You may even want to contribute.

Finding News, Reviews, and Sample Code

The Web has plenty of sites devoted exclusively to Java. Many of these sites feature reviews, links to other sites, and best of all, oodles of sample Java code. Some also offer free mailing lists that keep you informed of the latest Java developments. Here's a brief list of such sites:

- **Java Boutique:** `javaboutique.internet.com`
- **JavaRanch:** `www.javaranch.com`
- **Javalobby:** `www.javalobby.org`
- **Gamelan:** `www.developer.com/java`

Improving Your Code with Tutorials

To find out more about Java, you can visit Sun's online training pages. The Web address is `java.sun.com/developer/onlineTraining`. Some other nice tutorials are available at the following Web sites:

- **Richard Baldwin's Web site:** `www.dickbaldwin.com`
- **IBM developerWorks:** `www-106.ibm.com/developerworks/training`
- **ProgrammingTutorials.com:** `www.programmingtutorials.com`

Finding Help on Newsgroups

Have a roadblock that you just can't get past? Try posting your question on an Internet newsgroup. Almost always, some friendly expert posts just the right reply.

With or without Java, you should definitely start exploring newsgroups. You can find thousands of newsgroups — groups on just about every conceivable topic. (Yes, there are more newsgroups than *For Dummies* titles!) To get started with newsgroups, visit `groups.google.com`. For postings specific to Java, look for the groups whose names begin with `comp.lang.java`. For a novice, the following three groups are probably the most useful:

✔ `comp.lang.java.programmer`

✔ `comp.lang.java.help`

✔ `comp.lang.java.gui`

Checking the FAQs for Useful Info

Has the acronym FAQ made it to the Oxford English Dictionary yet? Everybody seems to be using FAQ as an ordinary English word. In case you don't already know, FAQ stands for *frequently asked questions.* In reality, an FAQ should be called ATQTWTOSPOTN. This acronym stands for *Answers to Questions That We're Tired of Seeing Posted on This Newsgroup.*

You can find several FAQs at the official Sun Web site. You can also check `www.www-net.com/java/faq` — a page that links to several Java FAQs.

Reading Documentation with Additional Commentary

When programmers write documentation, they ask themselves questions and then answer those questions as best they can. But sometimes, they don't ask themselves all the important questions. And often, they assume that the reader already knows certain things. If you're a reader who doesn't already know these things, you may be plain out of luck.

One way or another, all documentation omits some details. That's why other peoples' comments about the documentation can be so helpful. At `www.jdocs.com` experienced Java programmers annotate existing Java documentation with their own comments. The comments include tips and tricks, but they also add useful pieces of information — pieces that the documentation's original authors omitted. If you need help with an aspect of the Java API, this is a great Web site to visit.

Opinions and Advocacy

Blogs are hot stuff these days. Business people, politicians, and others write blogs to draw attention to their ideas. And many people write blogs just for fun.

When it comes to reading about Java, I have a few favorite blogs. I list them here in alphabetical order:

- **Simon Phipps's blog** — `www.webmink.net/minkblog.htm`

  Simon is Chief Technology Evangelist at Sun Microsystems. No matter what subject he chooses, Simon always speaks his mind.

- **Jonathan Schwartz's blog** — `blogs.sun.com/jonathan`

  Jonathan is Chief Operating Officer at Sun Microsystems. When Jonathan speaks, people listen. And when Jonathan writes, people read.

- **Mary Smaragdis's blog** — `blogs.sun.com/mary`

  Mary is Marketing Manager at Sun Microsystems. When you read Mary's blog, her enthusiasm gushes from the computer screen. And I've met her at several conferences. She's even livelier in person.

Looking for Java Jobs

Are you looking for work? Would you like to have an exciting, lucrative career as a Java programmer? Then try visiting a Web site that's specially designed for people like you. Point your Web browser to `www.javajobs.com` or `java.computerwork.com`.

Becoming Certified in Java

These days, everybody is anxious to become certified. If you're one of these people, you can find plenty of resources about Java certification on the Web. Just start by visiting `www.javaprepare.com` and `www.javaranch.com/ring.jsp`. Both of these sites link to other interesting sites, including sites with practice certification exams.

Everyone's Favorite Sites

It's true — these two sites aren't devoted exclusively to Java. However, no geek-worthy list of resources would be complete without Slashdot and SourceForge.

Slashdot's slogan, "News for nerds, stuff that matters," says it all. At `slashdot.org` you find news, reviews, and commentary on almost anything related to computing. There's even a new word to describe a Web site that's reviewed or discussed on the Slashdot site. When a site becomes overwhelmed with hits from Slashdot referrals, one says that the site has been *slashdotted*.

Although it's not quite as high-profile, sourceforge.net is the place to look for open source software of any kind. The SourceForge repository contains over 80,000 projects. At the SourceForge site, you can download software, read about works in process, contribute to existing projects, and even start a project of your own. SourceForge is a great site for programmers and developers at all levels of experience.

Appendix A

Using the CD-ROM

Sure, you can read, read, read until your eyes bug out. But you won't get to know Java until you write and run some code. Besides, it's no fun to just read about programming. You've got to experiment, try things, make some mistakes, and discover some things on your own.

So this book's CD-ROM has everything you need to get going interactively. First, read the little warning about all the legal consequences of your breaking the seal on this book's disc pack. Then, throw caution to the wind and rip that pack open. Put the CD-ROM in the drive, and you're ready to go.

What You Can Expect to Find on the CD-ROM

This CD-ROM has four kinds of files on it:

✔ **Files that I, the author, created:** For the most part, these files contain all the listings in this book (Listing 3-1 in Chapter 3, for instance). Most of these listings are Java program files.

✔ **The JCreator integrated development environment:** A free copy of the software, specially customized for this book.

✔ **Extra chapters in PDF format:** When I start writing, I can't stop. Eventually, the folks at Wiley Publishing ran out of paper, so they put additional chapters on the CD-ROM.

✔ **Various pieces of freeware, shareware, and whateverware:** I generally lapse into laziness and call all these things by the name *shareware,* but the legal department tells me that I should be more careful.

System Requirements

Your system requirements depend on the kind of computer that you have and the kind of operating system that you use. To run the Java 1.5 Software Development Kit on a typical Windows computer, you need at least the following resources:

✔ A Pentium II processor. (A processor that's older and clunkier than a Pentium II may be okay, but I make no guarantees.)

✔ Microsoft Windows (98, Me, 2000, XP, Server 2003, or Vista).

✔ Enough RAM, whatever that means. The official word from Sun Microsystems isn't specific about this, but I suspect that 128MB is the bare minimum.

✔ You'd better have a CD-ROM drive. Otherwise, you'll have difficulty grabbing software off this book's CD-ROM.

✔ For the basic tools to write and run your own Java programs, you need about 140MB of disk space. (If you want to store Sun's documentation, the source files, demos, and other goodies, you need over 400MB.)

If your computer doesn't match up to most of these requirements, you may have problems getting your Java programs to run. But remember, "may have problems" doesn't mean that Java won't work. For more information on Windows configurations, visit `java.sun.com/j2se/1.5.0/install-windows.html`. (And be prepared to change `1.5.0` in the Web address to `1.6.`*something-else*. These version numbers are moving targets.)

If you're not a fan of Microsoft Windows, visit `java.sun.com/j2se/1.5.0/system-configurations.html` for a list of supported system configurations. (Once again, be prepared to change `1.5.0` to `1.6.`*something-else*.)

Additional Java compiler versions (versions for computers not officially supported by the folks at Sun Microsystems) appear frequently on the Web. So if your computer runs Macintosh OS, OpenVMS, or FLKOS (Fred's Little Known Operating System), search the Web for the compiler that you need. Who knows? You may just find it.

Of course, if you can't find the correct Web address, and you don't enjoy guessing games, you have another alternative. Pay a visit to this book's Web site. At that site, I (try to) keep a fairly up-to-date list of useful Java links.

Finally, if you need more information on basic hardware and software issues, check out these books published by Wiley Publishing, Inc.: *PCs For Dummies*, 10th Edition, by Dan Gookin; *Macs For Dummies*, 9th Edition, by Edward C. Baig; *Windows 2000 Professional For Dummies*, by Andy Rathbone and Sharon Crawford; *Windows XP All-in-One Desk Reference For Dummies*, 2nd Edition, by Woody Leonhard, *Windows 98 For Dummies*, *Microsoft Windows ME Millennium Edition For Dummies*, and *Windows Vista For Dummies*, all by Andy Rathbone.

Using the CD with Microsoft Windows

To install items from the CD to your hard drive (with the Autorun feature enabled), follow these steps:

1. **Insert the CD into your computer's CD-ROM drive.**

   A window appears with the following options: HTML Interface, Browse CD, and Exit.

2. **Select one of the options, as follows:**

   - **HTML Interface:** Click this button to view the contents of the CD in standard *For Dummies* presentation. It looks like a Web page. Here you can also find a list of useful Web links from the book.

   - **Browse CD:** Click this button to skip the fancy presentation and simply view the CD contents from the directory structure. This means that you see just a list of folders — plain and simple.

   - **Exit:** Well, what can I say? Click this button to quit.

If you don't have the Autorun feature enabled, or if the Autorun window doesn't appear, follow these steps to access the CD:

1. **Insert the CD into your computer's CD-ROM drive.**

2. **Click the Start button and choose Run from the menu.**

3. **In the dialog box that appears, type** d:\start.htm.

   Replace *d* with the proper drive letter for your CD-ROM if it uses a different letter. (If you don't know the letter, double-click the My Computer icon on your desktop and see what letter is listed for your CD-ROM drive.)

Your browser opens, and the license agreement appears. If you don't have a browser, Microsoft Internet Explorer is included on the CD.

4. **Read through the license agreement, nod your head, and click the Agree button if you want to use the CD.**

   After you click Agree, you're taken to the Main menu, where you can browse through the contents of the CD.

5. **To navigate within the interface, click a topic of interest to take you to an explanation of the files on the CD and how to use or install them.**

6. **To install software from the CD, simply click the software name.**

   You see two options: to run or open the file from the current location or to save the file to your hard drive. Choose to run or open the file from its current location, and the installation procedure continues. When you finish using the interface, close your browser as usual.

Note: I've included an "easy install" in these HTML pages. If your browser supports installations from within it, go ahead and click the links of the program names you see. You see two options: Run the File from the Current Location and Save the File to Your Hard Drive. Select the Run the File from the Current Location option and the installation procedure continues. A Security Warning dialog box appears. Click Yes to continue the installation.

Using the CD with Mac OS X

To install items from the CD to your hard drive, follow these steps:

1. **Insert the CD into your computer's CD-ROM drive.**

   In a moment, an icon representing the CD that you just inserted appears on your Mac desktop. Chances are that the icon looks like a CD-ROM.

2. **Double-click the CD icon to show the CD's contents.**

3. **Double-click** `start.htm` **to open your browser and display the license agreement.**

   If your browser doesn't open automatically, open it as you normally would by choosing File⇨Open File (in Internet Explorer) or File⇨Open⇨Location in Netscape and select Java 2 For Dummies. The license agreement appears.

4. **Read through the license agreement, nod your head, and click the Accept button if you want to use the CD.**

   After you click Accept, you're taken to the Main menu. This is where you can browse through the contents of the CD.

5. **To navigate within the interface, click any topic of interest, and you're taken you to an explanation of the files on the CD and how to use or install them.**

6. **To install software from the CD, simply click the software name.**

Running the Java Code That's in This Book

The CD-ROM has all the code from the listings in this book. It also has some helper files (data files and other things) that you need to make the most of all the listings.

If you install JCreator from the CD-ROM, all the code from the book's listings gets installed automatically. The code is installed in JCreator's `MyProjects` directory on your computer's hard drive. For details, see Chapter 2.

If you don't install JCreator from the CD-ROM, you can still copy this book's code to your computer's hard drive. Just navigate to the folder named Author on the CD-ROM. Copy everything in that Author folder to your hard drive.

I've tried to organize the book's listings in a simple, yet sensible way. I thought a long time and came up with a grand plan. The plan is pretty intuitive, so you can either read about the plan or just follow your nose. Personally I like noses, but you may like the security of having neatly printed rules. If you want rules, I present them right here:

✔ If you use JCreator, all the code is in subdirectories of the `MyProjects` directory. (See Chapter 2.)

✔ Each example has its own subdirectory, and each subdirectory constitutes a single project. For instance, the code from Listing 3-1 is in its own little directory named `Listing0301`. The tree in JCreator's File View pane has a branch labeled `Listing0301`.

✔ In some cases, several of the book's listings combine to make one big example. In such cases, that example's subdirectory has a big combined name. For instance, in Chapter 7, you get the first full example when you compile and run Listings 7-1 and 7-2. So the directory for this example is named `Listings0701-02`. The tree in JCreator's File View pane has a branch labeled `Listings0701-02`.

✔ As a rule of thumb, when a listing's code begins with `class` *SomeName*, the code is in a file called *SomeName*`.java`.

✔ Examples are grouped by chapter, and each chapter has its own JCreator workspace.

For instance, JCreator's MyProjects directory has subdirectories named Listing0501, Listing0502, Listing0601, and so on. The MyProjects directory also has files named Chapter05.jcw, Chapter06.jcw, and so on.

If you choose File⇨Open Workspace, and select Chapter05.jcw (or just plain Chapter05), you open the Chapter 5 workspace. After doing this, you don't see Listing0601 in JCreator's File View pane. You see only the projects named Listing0501, Listing0502, Listing0503, and so on.

Freeware, Shareware, and Just Plain Ware

The following sections provide a summary of the software and other goodies that you can find on the CD. If you need help with installing the items provided on the CD, refer to the installation instructions in the preceding section.

Shareware programs are fully functional, free, trial versions of copyrighted programs. If you like particular programs, register with their authors for a nominal fee and receive licenses, enhanced versions, and technical support. *Freeware programs* are free, copyrighted games, applications, and utilities. You can copy them to as many computers as you like — for free — but they offer no technical support. *GNU software* is governed by its own license, which is included inside the folder of the GNU software. The distribution of GNU software is not restricted. See the GNU license at the root of the CD for more details. *Trial, demo,* or *evaluation* versions of software are usually limited either by time or functionality (such as not letting you save a project after you create it).

JCreator

Special edition

For Windows. Back when I started working on this book's *second* edition, I went looking for the right Java development environment. I needed something that would satisfy all your needs:

- ✔ **Easy to use:** You want to use Java. You don't want to memorize thousands of ways to point and click.

- ✔ **Powerful:** You want a scalable tool. As you write bigger and better programs, you want an environment that can support your growing, complex requirements.

- ✔ **Efficient:** Memory hogs and CPU hogs need not apply.

- ✔ **Inexpensive:** Hey, how about free?

I found all these qualities in only one product: JCreator from Xinox Software.

As if this list of demands wasn't enough, I needed a company that could work with me to customize its tool. Based on the examples found in this book's second edition, I had certain specialized needs. I wanted to change this default here and change that option there. I wanted to install my book's code along with the development environment. Once again, the people at Xinox Software came through for me then — and came through for me again when I updated my examples for the present edition.

JCreator was a wonderful product for this book's second edition and is equally wonderful for the fourth edition of *Java For Dummies.* I hope that you enjoy using it.

For more information and a free trial of JCreator PRO, visit www.jcreator.com.

Adobe Acrobat Reader

Commercial version

For Windows and Mac. Talk about added value! This book has several extra chapters on its CD-ROM. To view these chapters, you need a program called Adobe Acrobat Reader. That's no problem, because a free copy of Reader is on the CD-ROM.

For more information, visit www.adobe.com/acrobat.

If you're on the road, and you need some light reading, just pull into a nearby cybercafe. You can find the extra chapters on this book's Web site.

Jindent

Trial version

Platform independent. When it comes to writing code, beauty is more than skin deep. An ugly program is hard to read. If anything goes wrong, no one, not even the program's author, can wade through lines and lines of cryptic, poorly formatted classes and methods.

To make code look good, you can follow some clear, uniform style guidelines. Always indent by a certain number of spaces, always arrange curly braces a certain way, always do this, never do that. You can memorize lots of rules, or you can have software do it for you.

So write code any way that you want. Then hand your code over to Jindent. The Jindent program beautifies your code, making it easier to read, easier to understand, and (yes!) cheaper to maintain.

For more information, visit `www.jindent.com`.

NetCaptor

Freeware version

For Windows. NetCaptor uses tabs to keep track of several open Web pages. These tabs replace the need to open several browser windows. Sure, lots of Web browsers use tabs, but NetCaptor is my favorite. When I visit a search engine, I keep the results page open while I investigate some of the page's entries. When I do Java development, I keep the API documentation open while I visit one or more of my own documents.

For more information, visit `www.netcaptor.com`.

WinOne

Evaluation

For Windows. If you use Windows, and you're a real geek, you know how clumsy MS-DOS can be. The years I've wasted retyping commands is dwarfed only by the time that I've spent drilling for items in deeply-nested menus and Explorer trees. To make your life simpler, try WinOne. The WinOne shell is like the built-in Windows command prompt. But WinOne has multicolored text, smart filename completion, a scroll bar, command grouping, smart delete, macros, command history, extended batch commands, and (best of all) delightfully easy access to directories.

For more information on WinOne, visit `www.winone.com.au`.

And, If You Run into Any Trouble . . .

I tried my best to find shareware programs that work on most computers with the minimum system requirements. Alas, your computer may differ, and some programs may not work properly for some reason.

If you have problems with the shareware on this CD-ROM, the two likeliest problems are that you don't have enough memory (RAM) or that you have other programs running that are affecting installation or running of a program. If you get an error message such as `Not enough memory` or `Setup cannot continue`, try one or more of the following suggestions and then try using the software again:

- ✔ **Turn off any antivirus software running on your computer.** Installation programs sometimes mimic virus activity and may make your computer incorrectly believe that a virus is infecting it.

- ✔ **Close all running programs.** The more programs that you have running, the less memory is available to other programs. Installation programs typically update files and programs. So if you keep other programs running, installation may not work properly.

- ✔ **Have your local computer store add more RAM to your computer.** This is, admittedly, a drastic and somewhat expensive step. However, adding more memory can really help the speed of your computer and allow more programs to run at the same time.

If you still have trouble installing the items from the CD, please call the Wiley Publishing, Inc. Customer Service phone number at 800-762-2974 (outside the U.S.: 317-572-3993) or send an e-mail to the address of your choice: `JavaForDummies@BurdBrain.com` or `techsupdum@wiley.com`.

Index

• T •

Wiley Publishing, Inc.
End-User License Agreement

READ THIS. You should carefully read these terms and conditions before opening the software packet(s) included with this book "Book". This is a license agreement "Agreement" between you and Wiley Publishing, Inc. "WPI". By opening the accompanying software packet(s), you acknowledge that you have read and accept the following terms and conditions. If you do not agree and do not want to be bound by such terms and conditions, promptly return the Book and the unopened software packet(s) to the place you obtained them for a full refund.

1. **License Grant.** WPI grants to you (either an individual or entity) a nonexclusive license to use one copy of the enclosed software program(s) (collectively, the "Software") solely for your own personal or business purposes on a single computer (whether a standard computer or a workstation component of a multi-user network). The Software is in use on a computer when it is loaded into temporary memory (RAM) or installed into permanent memory (hard disk, CD-ROM, or other storage device). WPI reserves all rights not expressly granted herein.

2. **Ownership..** WPI is the owner of all right, title, and interest, including copyright, in and to the compilation of the Software recorded on the physical packet included with this Book "Software Media". Copyright to the individual programs recorded on the Software Media is owned by the author or other authorized copyright owner of each program. Ownership of the Software and all proprietary rights relating thereto remain with WPI and its licensers.

3. **Restrictions on Use and Transfer.**

    (a) You may only (i) make one copy of the Software for backup or archival purposes, or (ii) transfer the Software to a single hard disk, provided that you keep the original for backup or archival purposes. You may not (i) rent or lease the Software, (ii) copy or reproduce the Software through a LAN or other network system or through any computer subscriber system or bulletin-board system, or (iii) modify, adapt, or create derivative works based on the Software.

    (b) You may not reverse engineer, decompile, or disassemble the Software. You may transfer the Software and user documentation on a permanent basis, provided that the transferee agrees to accept the terms and conditions of this Agreement and you retain no copies. If the Software is an update or has been updated, any transfer must include the most recent update and all prior versions.

4. **Restrictions on Use of Individual Programs.** You must follow the individual requirements and restrictions detailed for each individual program in the "Using the CD-ROM" appendix of this Book or on the Software Media. These limitations are also contained in the individual license agreements recorded on the Software Media. These limitations may include a requirement that after using the program for a specified period of time, the user must pay a registration fee or discontinue use. By opening the Software packet(s), you agree to abide by the licenses and restrictions for these individual programs that are detailed in the "Using the CD-ROM" appendix and/or on the Software Media. None of the material on this Software Media or listed in this Book may ever be redistributed, in original or modified form, for commercial purposes.

BUSINESS, CAREERS & PERSONAL FINANCE

0-7645-9847-3

0-7645-2431-3

Also available:
- Business Plans Kit For Dummies
  0-7645-9794-9
- Economics For Dummies
  0-7645-5726-2
- Grant Writing For Dummies
  0-7645-8416-2
- Home Buying For Dummies
  0-7645-5331-3
- Managing For Dummies
  0-7645-1771-6
- Marketing For Dummies
  0-7645-5600-2

- Personal Finance For Dummies
  0-7645-2590-5*
- Resumes For Dummies
  0-7645-5471-9
- Selling For Dummies
  0-7645-5363-1
- Six Sigma For Dummies
  0-7645-6798-5
- Small Business Kit For Dummies
  0-7645-5984-2
- Starting an eBay Business For Dummies
  0-7645-6924-4
- Your Dream Career For Dummies
  0-7645-9795-7

HOME & BUSINESS COMPUTER BASICS

0-470-05432-8

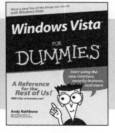

0-471-75421-8

Also available:
- Cleaning Windows Vista For Dummies
  0-471-78293-9
- Excel 2007 For Dummies
  0-470-03737-7
- Mac OS X Tiger For Dummies
  0-7645-7675-5
- MacBook For Dummies
  0-470-04859-X
- Macs For Dummies
  0-470-04849-2
- Office 2007 For Dummies
  0-470-00923-3

- Outlook 2007 For Dummies
  0-470-03830-6
- PCs For Dummies
  0-7645-8958-X
- Salesforce.com For Dummies
  0-470-04893-X
- Upgrading & Fixing Laptops For Dummies
  0-7645-8959-8
- Word 2007 For Dummies
  0-470-03658-3
- Quicken 2007 For Dummies
  0-470-04600-7

FOOD, HOME, GARDEN, HOBBIES, MUSIC & PETS

0-7645-8404-9

0-7645-9904-6

Also available:
- Candy Making For Dummies
  0-7645-9734-5
- Card Games For Dummies
  0-7645-9910-0
- Crocheting For Dummies
  0-7645-4151-X
- Dog Training For Dummies
  0-7645-8418-9
- Healthy Carb Cookbook For Dummies
  0-7645-8476-6
- Home Maintenance For Dummies
  0-7645-5215-5

- Horses For Dummies
  0-7645-9797-3
- Jewelry Making & Beading For Dummies
  0-7645-2571-9
- Orchids For Dummies
  0-7645-6759-4
- Puppies For Dummies
  0-7645-5255-4
- Rock Guitar For Dummies
  0-7645-5356-9
- Sewing For Dummies
  0-7645-6847-7
- Singing For Dummies
  0-7645-2475-5

INTERNET & DIGITAL MEDIA

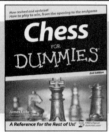

0-470-04529-9

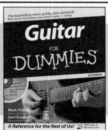

0-470-04894-8

Also available:
- Blogging For Dummies
  0-471-77084-1
- Digital Photography For Dummies
  0-7645-9802-3
- Digital Photography All-in-One Desk Reference For Dummies
  0-470-03743-1
- Digital SLR Cameras and Photography For Dummies
  0-7645-9803-1
- eBay Business All-in-One Desk Reference For Dummies
  0-7645-8438-3
- HDTV For Dummies
  0-470-09673-X

- Home Entertainment PCs For Dummies
  0-470-05523-5
- MySpace For Dummies
  0-470-09529-6
- Search Engine Optimization For Dummies
  0-471-97998-8
- Skype For Dummies
  0-470-04891-3
- The Internet For Dummies
  0-7645-8996-2
- Wiring Your Digital Home For Dummies
  0-471-91830-X

SPORTS, FITNESS, PARENTING, RELIGION & SPIRITUALITY

0-471-76871-5

0-7645-7841-3

Also available:
- Catholicism For Dummies
  0-7645-5391-7
- Exercise Balls For Dummies
  0-7645-5623-1
- Fitness For Dummies
  0-7645-7851-0
- Football For Dummies
  0-7645-3936-1
- Judaism For Dummies
  0-7645-5299-6
- Potty Training For Dummies
  0-7645-5417-4
- Buddhism For Dummies
  0-7645-5359-3

- Pregnancy For Dummies
  0-7645-4483-7 †
- Ten Minute Tone-Ups For Dummies
  0-7645-7207-5
- NASCAR For Dummies
  0-7645-7681-X
- Religion For Dummies
  0-7645-5264-3
- Soccer For Dummies
  0-7645-5229-5
- Women in the Bible For Dummies
  0-7645-8475-8

TRAVEL

0-7645-7749-2

0-7645-6945-7

Also available:
- Alaska For Dummies
  0-7645-7746-8
- Cruise Vacations For Dummies
  0-7645-6941-4
- England For Dummies
  0-7645-4276-1
- Europe For Dummies
  0-7645-7529-5
- Germany For Dummies
  0-7645-7823-5
- Hawaii For Dummies
  0-7645-7402-7

- Italy For Dummies
  0-7645-7386-1
- Las Vegas For Dummies
  0-7645-7382-9
- London For Dummies
  0-7645-4277-X
- Paris For Dummies
  0-7645-7630-5
- RV Vacations For Dummies
  0-7645-4442-X
- Walt Disney World & Orlando
  For Dummies
  0-7645-9660-8

GRAPHICS, DESIGN & WEB DEVELOPMENT

0-7645-8815-X

0-7645-9571-7

Also available:
- 3D Game Animation For Dummies
  0-7645-8789-7
- AutoCAD 2006 For Dummies
  0-7645-8925-3
- Building a Web Site For Dummies
  0-7645-7144-3
- Creating Web Pages For Dummies
  0-470-08030-2
- Creating Web Pages All-in-One Desk
  Reference For Dummies
  0-7645-4345-8
- Dreamweaver 8 For Dummies
  0-7645-9649-7

- InDesign CS2 For Dummies
  0-7645-9572-5
- Macromedia Flash 8 For Dummies
  0-7645-9691-8
- Photoshop CS2 and Digital
  Photography For Dummies
  0-7645-9580-6
- Photoshop Elements 4 For Dummies
  0-471-77483-9
- Syndicating Web Sites with RSS Feeds
  For Dummies
  0-7645-8848-6
- Yahoo! SiteBuilder For Dummies
  0-7645-9800-7

NETWORKING, SECURITY, PROGRAMMING & DATABASES

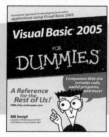

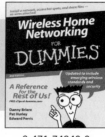

0-7645-7728-X

0-471-74940-0

Also available:
- Access 2007 For Dummies
  0-470-04612-0
- ASP.NET 2 For Dummies
  0-7645-7907-X
- C# 2005 For Dummies
  0-7645-9704-3
- Hacking For Dummies
  0-470-05235-X
- Hacking Wireless Networks
  For Dummies
  0-7645-9730-2
- Java For Dummies
  0-470-08716-1

- Microsoft SQL Server 2005 For Dummies
  0-7645-7755-7
- Networking All-in-One Desk Reference
  For Dummies
  0-7645-9939-9
- Preventing Identity Theft For Dummies
  0-7645-7336-5
- Telecom For Dummies
  0-471-77085-X
- Visual Studio 2005 All-in-One Desk
  Reference For Dummies
  0-7645-9775-2
- XML For Dummies
  0-7645-8845-1

HEALTH & SELF-HELP

0-7645-8450-2

0-7645-4149-8

Also available:
- Bipolar Disorder For Dummies
  0-7645-8451-0
- Chemotherapy and Radiation
  For Dummies
  0-7645-7832-4
- Controlling Cholesterol For Dummies
  0-7645-5440-9
- Diabetes For Dummies
  0-7645-6820-5* †
- Divorce For Dummies
  0-7645-8417-0 †

- Fibromyalgia For Dummies
  0-7645-5441-7
- Low-Calorie Dieting For Dummies
  0-7645-9905-4
- Meditation For Dummies
  0-471-77774-9
- Osteoporosis For Dummies
  0-7645-7621-6
- Overcoming Anxiety For Dummies
  0-7645-5447-6
- Reiki For Dummies
  0-7645-9907-0
- Stress Management For Dummies
  0-7645-5144-2

EDUCATION, HISTORY, REFERENCE & TEST PREPARATION

0-7645-8381-6

0-7645-9554-7

Also available:
- The ACT For Dummies
  0-7645-9652-7
- Algebra For Dummies
  0-7645-5325-9
- Algebra Workbook For Dummies
  0-7645-8467-7
- Astronomy For Dummies
  0-7645-8465-0
- Calculus For Dummies
  0-7645-2498-4
- Chemistry For Dummies
  0-7645-5430-1
- Forensics For Dummies
  0-7645-5580-4

- Freemasons For Dummies
  0-7645-9796-5
- French For Dummies
  0-7645-5193-0
- Geometry For Dummies
  0-7645-5324-0
- Organic Chemistry I For Dummies
  0-7645-6902-3
- The SAT I For Dummies
  0-7645-7193-1
- Spanish For Dummies
  0-7645-5194-9
- Statistics For Dummies
  0-7645-5423-9

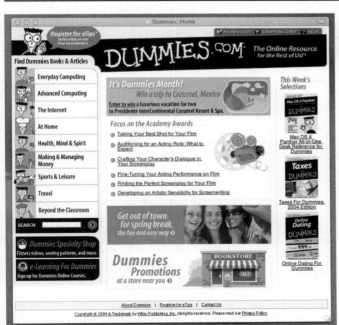

Get smart @ dummies.com®

- **Find a full list of Dummies titles**
- **Look into loads of FREE on-site articles**
- **Sign up for FREE eTips e-mailed to you weekly**
- **See what other products carry the Dummies name**
- **Shop directly from the Dummies bookstore**
- **Enter to win new prizes every month!**

* Separate Canadian edition also available
† Separate U.K. edition also available

Available wherever books are sold. For more information or to order direct: U.S. customers visit www.dummies.com or call 1-877-762-2974.
U.K. customers visit www.wileyeurope.com or call 0800 243407. Canadian customers visit www.wiley.ca or call 1-800-567-4797.